SEATTLE FAMILY ADVENTURES

Seattle Family ADVENTURES

City Escapades, Day Trips,
Weekend Getaways, and Itineraries
for Fun-Loving Families

KATE CALAMUSA

SASQUATCH BOOKS
SEATTLE

Published by Sasquatch Books

21 20 19 18 17   9 8 7 6 5 4 3 2 1

Editor: SUSAN ROXBOROUGH
Production editor: EMMA REH
Cover design: ANDREW BROZYNA
Interior design: TONY ONG
Maps: Copyright © 2017 DIGITAL VECTOR MAPS
Copyeditor: ELIZABETH JOHNSON

Library of Congress Cataloging-in-Publication Data is available.

ISBN: 978-1-63217-097-2

Sasquatch Books
1904 Third Avenue, Suite 710
Seattle, WA 98101
(206) 467-4300
www.sasquatchbooks.com
custserv@sasquatchbooks.com

CONTENTS

INTRODUCTION

Perched on the edge of Puget Sound, Seattle is an adventurer's playground, with forested parks for frolicking, nearby mountains for hiking, and sandy beaches for sunny-day play, plus all the landmark attractions of a bustling big city. Among the attractions of this Northwest destination are many curiosities that are seemingly made for curious kiddos. What other town boasts a "living computer museum" and a (supposedly haunted) historic market within a few miles of each other? Whether you're visiting for a quick sojourn or you're a local rediscovering the city with your own children, this guide introduces you to the Emerald City with a kid's viewpoint in mind—and what a wild, wacky, and whimsical perspective that is. Meet the troll under the Aurora Bridge, explore beneath the city sidewalks, and even be awestruck anew by the futuristic Space Needle.

This field guide is broken up into four easy-to-plan sections to pick and choose from, depending on your mood and brood. Part 1 explores the city by activity (perfect for spontaneous afternoons of fun) and themed itinerary (for when you have an entire day to gallivant about). Part 2 delves into Seattle's diverse set of neighborhoods and suburbs, with step-by-step guides to exploring each one. Part 3 satisfies the food cravings of you and your kids, with recommendations on restaurants. And Part 4 takes the show on the road, with family-ready day trips and weekend getaways that tour Washington State.

So pile on the layers for that oft-mercurial Seattle weather, pile in the car, and let the adventuring begin. And may the nap schedules, backseat quibbles, and traffic lights ever be in your favor.

HOW TO USE THIS GUIDE

Take this guide along for the ride. Pop it into the diaper bag or glove box so it's handy the next time you want to plan a grand day out or are in need of a we've-got-two-hours-to-kill type of activity. Star it, bookmark it, and keep the following pointers in mind.

Each listing contains information on the neighborhood or suburb where the business is located, as well as nitty-gritty contact details. And while every effort has been made to ensure that listed business hours, programming details, admission rates, and potential discount opportunities were accurate as of press time, these details are subject to change (often on a whim), so best to check the website or give a ring before sallying forth.

In general, activities within Part 1 have been kept to the Seattle metro area unless it seemed they were worth the extra trek; activities farther afield can be found in Part 4, the day trips and weekend getaway section. Omitted are classes or organized activities that require registration beyond a few days in advance; instead, the fun-filled destinations in this book are ones you can do with little or no notice. (Spontaneity can be fun, after all!)

Listings have been evaluated with value in mind, but locals would also do well to keep an eye on discount sites such as Groupon and Living Social, which often offer coupons to local hot spots. Out-of-towners planning a whirlwind tour of our fair city may want to consider snapping up a CityPass (www.citypass.com /seattle), which offers admission to several of Seattle's most popular attractions—the Space Needle (page 105), the Seattle Aquarium (page 11), and an Argosy Cruises harbor tour (page 114), plus a choice of the MoPOP (page 57) or the Woodland Park Zoo (page 12), and Chihuly Garden and Glass (page 121) or Pacific Science Center (page 84)—at a steeply discounted package rate.

And finally, as one of Seattle's main mantras is to "go local" (don't ask a Seattleite for recommendations on the best independent coffee shop unless you have more than a few minutes to spare), you won't find many chains listed in this guide. Instead, the focus is on the locally owned restaurants and businesses that help make Seattle the nature-loving, tech-savvy, escapade-filled city that it is.

KEY

This guidebook is broken up into four main sections. In addition to listing full contact information for every business, restaurant, and attraction mentioned, several sections also include the following **icons to help guide your travels**, indicating **general pricing information** and **suggested age ranges** for each activity, as well as insights on great **rainy-day spots**, **birthday-party places**, and **nearby playgrounds**, should little ones get a case of the wiggles while you're out and about.

PRICING INFORMATION

FREE!   Free

$ Under $10 per person

$$ Under $20 per person

$$$ $20 and up per person

RECOMMENDED AGE RANGE

ALL AGES   Fit for everyone, from babes in arms to budding teenagers

AGES 0–2   Great for babies and toddlers

AGES 3–5   Well suited to the preschool crowd

AGES 6–9   Perfect for elementary-age kids

AGES 10–14   Tops for tweens or teens

OTHER HANDY NOTES

Stroller-friendly

Just right for rainy days

Near a playground

Near a restaurant

Good for parties

PART 1:

OUT & ABOUT

Buckle those seat belts and pack up the sippy cups—it's time to get out and about! This section explores the Emerald City in kid-friendly fashion, culling down the myriad options in the metropolis to the **best family outings by activity**.

Got a petite pirate on your hands? Hop aboard one of the boat rides listed in **Tour de Seattle** (page 112), or take a ferry trip as outlined in **All Aboard** (page 4). Do the tykes go wild for animals? Check out the zoos, aquariums, and other creature features in **Animal Attractions** (page 8). From **sports** to **science museums**, from **rainy-day romps** to **fountains and water parks**, there are ideas for just about everyone, putting you on the road to adventure in no time.

If you've got an entire day to while away, follow one of the suggested **itineraries** (page 124), which range from a step-by-step exploration of **the great outdoors** (page 131) to an entirely **free day** (page 132) of no-pay fun.

Because traversing the busy city can be a travail (especially with tots in tow), each listing is also packed with **insider tips** on discounts and admission rates, plus the best seasons, days, and times to explore with as much ease as possible when lugging around strollers, snacks, and all those other pint-size accoutrements.

CITY HIGHLIGHTS
The Ultimate Seattle Bucket List

Featuring such iconic landmarks as the Space Needle, Pike Place Market, and the newly added Seattle Great Wheel, the city is primed for near-countless family outings. Here are Seattle's top fifteen must-see sights for families.

CITY CENTER

The high-tech city center boasts both towering skyscrapers—which play host to such high-profile tenants as Amazon and Nordstrom—and historical curiosities that recall the city's origins as a pit stop for prospectors heading for Alaskan gold.

First constructed for the 1962 World's Fair, the **(1) Space Needle** (page 105), in the heart of Seattle Center, offers stunning 360-degree views of Downtown Seattle, Queen Anne Hill, South Lake Union, and Puget Sound from its observatory deck, while the **(2) Museum of Pop Culture (MoPOP)** (page 57), formerly known as EMP Museum and, before that, Experience Music Project, at the Needle's base, is devoted to all things science fiction, pop culture, and rock 'n' roll. Seattle Center is also home to the **(3) Seattle Children's Museum** (page 79) and the expansive **(4) Pacific Science Center** (page 84), an exploratory museum featuring touring exhibits plus immersive experiences for kiddos, including two IMAX theaters.

The extremely walkable downtown core stretches from the glass-encased Washington State Convention Center to the 110-year-old **(5) Pike Place Market** (page 104). Home to the famous "flying fish," which are chucked to and fro by energetic fishmongers, this local treasure also offers colorful flowers and locally grown produce. Down the winding Pike Street Hill Climb from the Market is the Elliott Bay waterfront, where you can watch the **(6) Washington State Ferries** (page 4) go by, then brave the line at one of the city's newest attractions: **(7) the Seattle Great Wheel** (page 95). This 175-foot-tall Ferris wheel is perched on the Pier 57 dock, lending itself to spectacular city and water views.

The city's origins as a frontier town are still apparent in many popular attractions, like the **(8) Underground Tour** (page 106), where kids can catch a glimpse of a bygone era hidden underneath the city streets, and in the educational and engaging exhibits at the **(9) Museum of History & Industry**, a.k.a. MOHAI (page 107).

PARKS & REC

The bustling metropolis is flanked by the majestic Olympic Mountains to the west and the wooded foothills of the Cascades to the east, a picturesque setting further complemented by Seattle's 465 parks. In the neighborhood of Magnolia, **(10) Discovery Park** (page 88), the city's largest, boasts easy-access walking trails, picnic areas, and a swath of beach fronting the Sound. In the south end of the city, the 300-acre **(11) Seward Park** (page 88) offers a gorgeous old-growth forest, plus an eagle's nest or two.

Farther north, in Ballard, lies an engineering marvel: the **(12) Hiram M. Chittenden Locks** (page 104), which link Puget Sound with Lake Union and Lake Washington. Little scientists will be fascinated by the engineered set of locks that manage the boat traffic traveling between the bodies of water, which are at different elevations. Beach lovers should drive 2 miles north to **(13) Golden Gardens Park** (page 62), a sandy spit on the Sound, replete with tide pools, bonfire pits, and sailboat sightings.

Seattle's other favorite beach lies across Elliott Bay from Downtown, in West Seattle. **(14) Alki Beach** (page 61) is reminiscent of classic Nantucket, with white sandy stretches, fish-fry stands, and even the occasional seal or sea-turtle sighting. From there, you can drink in views of the paddleboarders and kayakers, plus the downtown skyline, including the Space Needle. And if you just can't get enough of the Needle, check out pocket-size **(15) Kerry Park** (page 178) on Queen Anne Hill. This park makes for a great family photo op, with the famous landmark peeking up in the background.

For more on all these attractions, including further details and contact information, see full listings within the **Activities** section; specific page numbers are noted for each must-see stop.

ACTIVITIES

ALL ABOARD

From boats to buses, and trains to trolleys, these cool commuter rides are sure to rev your tyke's engine.

BY BOAT

King County Water Taxi

WEST SEATTLE OR VASHON ISLAND TO DOWNTOWN SEATTLE

206-296-0100

www.kingcounty.gov/transportation/kcdot/watertaxi.aspx

$ ALL AGES

This commuter fleet of boats makes for a fun ride for families too, as it carries riders to and fro between Pier 50 on the Seattle waterfront and the Seacrest Dock in West Seattle, and between the same pier and bucolic Vashon Island. The quick ten-minute voyage from West Seattle to Seattle, aboard either the *Spirit of Kingston* catamaran or the new 104-foot MV *Doc Maynard*, is particularly swell, with a broad, sweeping view of the city skyline, including the Space Needle and the stadiums.

Washington State Ferries

VARIOUS PORTS TO BAINBRIDGE, VASHON, AND WHIDBEY ISLANDS, PLUS POINTS BEYOND

206-464-6400

www.wsdot.wa.gov/ferries

$ ALL AGES

Almost as iconic to the city as the Space Needle or the Market, the state ferries are a fantastic (and inexpensive!) way to joyride across the water. Routes run to Bainbridge Island and Bremerton from the Downtown Seattle dock, to Vashon Island from Fauntleroy in West Seattle, and to Whidbey Island from the Mukilteo dock. A cruise on one of the white-and-green behemoths will float everyone's boat. Tykes can explore every nook and cranny of the ferry during your crossing, tasting the salt spray from the open-air front balcony or catching some rays from the top-tier sundeck.

Insider tip: Park on the mainland and walk onto the boat for both the cheapest fares and the shortest wait times, which can grow very, very long during the busy summer months.

BY BUS

King County Metro Transit
VARIOUS ROUTES THROUGHOUT THE CITY AND BEYOND
206-553-3000
metro.kingcounty.gov/tops/bus
$ ALL AGES

Whether you have a "Wheels on the Bus" fan on your hands or you're in need of an easy ride around town, it's worth noting that King County maintains an extensive bus line that traverses Seattle and its suburbs. Use Metro's user-friendly website to plan whatever trip you have in mind.

BY RAIL

Link Light Rail
WESTLAKE CENTER TO SEATTLE-TACOMA INTERNATIONAL AIRPORT, UNIVERSITY OF WASHINGTON, AND CAPITOL HILL
www.soundtransit.org/link
$ ALL AGES

In addition to new routes connecting Downtown to the University of Washington and Capitol Hill, Link light rail runs north-south from the airport to Downtown Seattle and back, making it a convenient hop-on, hop-off mode of transportation. Call dibs on a window seat; kids will get a kick out of the sleek ride as it slides along the tunnel stations and city streets. Automated stations are available at each platform for paying your fare. Adult one-way fares range from $2.25–$3.25; youth ages 6–18 are a flat $1.50; kids age 5 and under are free.

Insider tip: If you're taking in a Seahawks, Sounders, or Mariners game, the light rail also proves to be a hassle-free way to get to the stadiums.

Seattle Center Monorail
SEATTLE CENTER TO WESTLAKE CENTER
206-905-2620
www.seattlemonorail.com
$ ALL AGES ✕ 🚼

A carryover from the 1962 World's Fair that also helped build the Space Needle and surrounding Seattle Center, the monorail continues to make speedy little trips between there and the Westlake Center shopping mall downtown. Departing approximately every ten minutes, the trip is quick, at two minutes, but long on sights—fork over $1 for kids ($2.25 for adults), and you'll spot the MoPOP, the Space Needle, and myriad skyscrapers as you cruise by.

BY TRAIN

Sounder Trains
TACOMA TO SEATTLE AND SEATTLE TO EVERETT
888-889-6368
www.soundtransit.org/sounder
$ ALL AGES

These double-decker trains are sure to delight; with routes running both north and south (primarily during commute hours, but with occasional weekend runs too), the Sounder makes for an inexpensive day trip. One-way fares vary depending on your destination: adults range from $3.25–$5.75, youth ages 6–18 from $2.50–$4.25, and kids age 5 and under are free; pay at the automated pay stations before boarding. One favorite is the incredibly beautiful route from Seattle's International District up north to the seaside town of Edmonds; the tracks wind along the rocky coastline, dropping visitors off near a sandy beach. See the Edmonds suburb guide (page 197) for tips on what to do once there.

BY TROLLEY

Issaquah Valley Trolley
ISSAQUAH
78 1st Ave. NE
425-392-3500
www.issaquahhistory.org
$ AGES 3-5 AGES 6-9 ✗

Boasting an adorable cherry-red 1925 electric streetcar and a classically clad conductor, the Issaquah Valley Trolley traverses a half-mile track along the tree-lined streets of this Eastside suburb. Though the trolley runs infrequently—only from 11 a.m. to 3 p.m. on weekends, May to September—the price is well worth the wait, at $5 for adults and free for kids age 5 and under.

Seattle Streetcar
SOUTH LAKE UNION AND FIRST HILL
206-553-3000
www.seattlestreetcar.org
$ ALL AGES 🛒

The Seattle Streetcar system canvases the city streets with its colorful cars, which operate in the glossy South Lake Union and First Hill hoods, with an extension route along Broadway, in Capitol Hill, in the years to come. Though built for commuters, these cheery streetcars are beloved by children for the happy little "ding-ding!" they emit at each and every stop. Kids age 5 and under ride free; youth fare for ages 6-18 is $1.50 and adults hop aboard for $2.25—just don't forget to fork over your fare at the platform pay stations before hitching a ride.

For transportation tours, such as on **Argosy Cruises** or the **Emerald City Trolley**, see listings in **Tour de Seattle** (page 112).

ANIMAL ATTRACTIONS

The kids will go critter-crazy for these petting zoos, pony rides, and wildlife parks.

ANIMAL FARMS

Farrel-McWhirter Farm Park

REDMOND

19545 NE Redmond Rd.

425-556-2300

www.redmond.gov/parksrecreation/farrel-mcwhirterfarmpark

$-$$ ALL AGES

Nestled within a larger 68-acre park, the multifaceted Farrel-McWhirter Farm Park offers fun at every turn for little animal lovers, offering a year-round horseback riding school, pony and trail rides, and a birthday-party facility, plus an educational program that lets kids as young as age 2 learn about farming in its All About Animals classes. The weekly farm tours ($100 flat rate for up to twenty participants) are especially popular here, allowing curious kids to get up close to the resident chickens, pigs, cows, and sheep; call or e-mail ahead of time to reserve a spot.

Forest Park Animal Farm

EVERETT

802 E. Mukilteo Blvd.

425-257-8300

www.everettwa.gov/773/animal-farm

$ AGES 0-2 AGES 3-5

Open during the summer months, this free petting zoo is perfect for toddlers and preschoolers. The silly gaggle of goats is always a draw, as are the ducks, hens, rabbits, and muddy pigs. The farm also offers $3 pony rides Thursdays through Sundays, as well as birthday-party packages, complete with a take-home picture snapped of children with their favorite "barnyard buddy."

Kelsey Creek Farm
BELLEVUE
410 130th Pl. SE
425-452-7688
www.farmerjayne.com
$-$$ AGES 0-2 AGES 3-5 AGES 6-9 🏃 🎁

Quiet and secluded, despite being located in the heart of Bellevue, Kelsey Creek Farm is home to ponies, sheep, goats, chickens, pigs, rabbits, and waterfowl, all of which are on view (for free!) daily on scenic pastureland from dawn to dusk. To get a closer peek at the animals, gather up some friends and schedule a farm tour ($85 total for up to fifteen participants), led by Farmer Jayne, with a seasonal focus in mind. Springtime allows kids to visit the farm's newest baby animals, while in winter, kiddos can learn to grind wheat or pump water in the 1890s-era farmhouse.

MORE FARM FUN!
For more ideas on farms to visit, plus seasonal activities, such as u-cut Christmas trees, summer berry picking, or autumn corn mazes, see the agendas for **winter** (page 134), **summer** (page 138), and **fall** (page 140) in **Itineraries**.

Cougar Mountain Zoo
ISSAQUAH
19525 SE 54th St.
425-391-5508
www.cougarmountainzoo.org
$$ AGES 0-2 AGES 3-5 🚼

Nestled in the Cascade foothills, the Cougar Mountain Zoo focuses primarily on endangered species, with an eclectic animal collection that ranges from lemurs and wallabies to wolves and, naturally, cougars. Easily accomplished in an afternoon with little kids (who will be more enthralled than older ones here because of its smaller size), this zoo allows for up-close viewing of those playful white Bengal tigers.

Northwest Trek Wildlife Park
EATONVILLE
11610 Trek Dr. E
360-832-6117
www.nwtrek.org
$$ AGES 3-5 AGES 6-9 AGES 10-14 🏃

Though admittedly a trek from Seattle, at an hour and fifteen minutes away, this impressive wildlife preserve is well worth it. Sprawling across 435 acres, this wooded paradise is home to such native North American species as grizzly bears, moose, elk, and bison, and offers myriad ways to meet these creatures—with a tram tour, walking trails, and even trailside encounters to get up close to the likes of opossum, skunks, and beavers. Well suited to older kids too, thanks to the thrilling zip-line course (more on page 95), the park also recently opened a half-acre nature-inspired play area, which features a 20-foot-high hollow tree structure for climbing, kid-size log cabins for playing pretend, and a construction zone with sand and shovels for full-on giddy fun.

Point Defiance Zoo & Aquarium
TACOMA
5400 N. Pearl St.
253-591-5337
www.pdza.org
$$ ALL AGES ⛐ ⚐

Another destination worth the extra drive time, Point Defiance in Tacoma is the only combined zoo and aquarium in the state, packing seahorses and sharks, polar bears and peacocks, and walruses and wolves all in the same locale. The zoo features numerous interactive exhibits. Take the kids to Budgie Buddies, and fork over $1.50 for a seed stick to feed the colorful Australian birds, then stroll over to Kids' Zone, a bright and lively spot that includes both a play area and the Contact Junction, a spot where kids can feed Nigerian dwarf goats. The Animal Avenue exhibit next door features snakes, tortoises, and frogs, sure to please your little reptile-and-amphibian enthusiast.

Seattle Aquarium
WATERFRONT
1483 Alaskan Way
206-386-4300
www.seattleaquarium.org
$$ ALL AGES ⛐ ☂ ✕

One of the keystones of the bustling waterfront, the Seattle Aquarium is a feast for the senses. Kiddos will experience all the sights and sounds of the Pacific Ocean—from chatty seals and sea otters to majestic and luminous moon jellyfish. They can also get touchy-feely with the likes of sea anemones and starfish at the interactive tide-pool exhibit. Little ones will especially enjoy the underwater viewing dome ("Is that a shark?") and the dress-up area, where they can don a scuba suit for a silly selfie.

Insider tip: Be sure to schedule your visit during one of the twice-daily not-to-be-missed octopus feedings.

Woodland Park Zoo
PHINNEY RIDGE
5500 Phinney Ave. N
206-548-2500
www.zoo.org
$$ ALL AGES 🛒 🏃

Home to more than a thousand animals in exhibits sprawling across 92 acres, the Woodland Park Zoo may be located in the heart of the city, but it feels worlds away, with its extensive walking trails and exotic habitats that house the likes of lions, tigers, and bears. Fit for whiling away an entire day, the zoo features animals from the African savanna, the Australian wilds, and the temperate rain forest, in addition to an antique carousel, picnic shelters, and an interactive education center. Don't miss the family favorite Zoomazium, an indoor play area replete with wooden blocks for building, snare drums for banging, and blaring tunes for dancing.

Insider tip: The zoo offers 50 percent off admission on certain rainy days, so if it's drippy, be sure to check www.zoo.org /rainyday to score the discount.

OTHER CREATURE FEATURES

Outback Kangaroo Farm
ARLINGTON
10030 SR 530 NE
360-403-7474
www.outbackkangaroofarm.com
$ AGES 3-5 AGES 6-9 AGES 10-14

Open March through October, this delightful farm an hour-ish outside the city is home to a menagerie of animals hailing from the Australian outback and beyond, from lemurs to llamas, wallabies to wallaroos, and of course, kangaroos. The forty-minute farm tour is offered four times daily, with kids getting an up-close look at the hop-happy marsupials during a feeding or petting session; tickets are $9 for kids ages 2-12; $10 for adults.

Insider tip: The tour is outdoors, so pack rain boots for your puddle-jumper if it's wet.

The Reptile Zoo
MONROE

22715 SR 2

360-805-5300

www.thereptilezoo.org

$ AGES 3-5 AGES 6-9 AGES 10-14

If your explorer loves things that slither, croak, or hop, this one is for you. Located in the small town of Monroe, about an hour outside of Seattle, this unique zoo boasts the most extensive collection of reptiles and amphibians in the Pacific Northwest, including tortoises and lizards, as well as such rare sights as a two-headed turtle, an albino alligator, and the world's deadliest snake, the black mamba. For enthusiasts who want to get real up close and personal, many of the snakes and turtles are available to hold and pet.

Seattle Meowtropolitan
WALLINGFORD

1225 N. 45th St.

www.seattlemeowtropolitan.com

$ AGES 10-14 ✕

Time for petting and purring! The city's first cat café, Seattle Meowtropolitan, allows your older kids (age 8 and up) to cuddle shelter cats while enjoying a tasty drink. Home to seven resident cats as well as a revolving cast of adoptable cats from the Regional Animal Services of King County, the posh little shop requires reservations in advance for each one-hour session; but at just $10, it makes for a memorable (and very heartwarming) experience for cat lovers.

PONY EXPRESS

Cougar Mountain Stables
RENTON
15019 SE May Valley Rd.
www.cougarmountainstables.com
$$-$$$ AGES 6-9 AGES 10-14 🎁

In addition to private riding lessons for children beginning at age 5, this picturesque farm offers birthday parties, with packages that include such features as pony decorating (where the littles can help braid manes and further bedazzle their four-legged friends) and access to the farm's petting zoo.

Equine Escapes
ISSAQUAH
4368 257th Pl. SE
425-242-4774
www.equineescapes.com
$$-$$$ AGES 6-9 AGES 10-14

This trail-riding operation offers one- to two-hour rides in the Cascade foothills. Suited to beginners and experienced riders alike, starting from age 6, Equine Escapes provides a relaxed environment for little riders to get used to the horses before setting out on a woodland adventure.

Fall City Pony & Horse Farm
FALL CITY
2411 316th Ave. SE
425-765-0558
www.kidsandponies.com
$$-$$$ AGES 6-9 AGES 10-14 🎁

A one-stop stable for all things horsey—including riding lessons for children as young as 5 years old, summer camps, and toddler-friendly birthday parties—this operation even takes the show on the road, bringing ponies and petting zoo animals (including an adorable donkey) to your preferred location as part of its extensive party services.

BE A SPORT

Take a few swings in the cage, knock down pins at the local bowling alley, or clamber up an indoor rock wall. You may even encounter a new pastime or two—like indoor bubble soccer!

BATTING CAGES

Double Play Sports Complex
REDMOND
15046 NE 95th St.
425-449-9456
www.doubleplaysportscomplex.com
$-$$ AGES 3-5 AGES 6-9 AGES 10-14 ☂

This 9,600-square-foot facility in Redmond has "family-friendly" written all over it. In addition to six retractable batting cages outfitted with baseball or softball pitching machines, tee stations, or pitching mounds (for sluggers who are eager to smack a fastball from mom or dad), Double Play has a play area with a crawl-through tunnel, bowling sets, and mini T-ball stations to entertain the preschool crowd while their older sibs are busy at the plate. For those who are inclined, this sweet facility also offers bubble soccer (for more on this wacky sport, see page 20).

Family Fun Center
EDMONDS
7212 220th St. SW
425-774-4263
www.fun-center.com

TUKWILA
7300 Fun Center Way
425-228-7300

$ AGES 3-5 AGES 6-9 AGES 10-14 ☂ ✗

Batter up! Take a few swings in the cage at either the Tukwila or Edmonds outpost of this indoor/outdoor amusement center. Helmets and bats are available on site, and a session in the cage ranges from $3 to $3.50 per session (twenty-five to thirty pitches, clocking in at anywhere between 40 and 70 miles an hour); cages are outdoors and do close during inclement weather, so give 'em a jingle before heading out.

Stods Baseball

BELLEVUE

5606 119th Ave. SE

425-643-8384

www.stods.com

$-$$ AGES 10-14 👕

Located in a tucked-away warehouse in Bellevue, Stods is tailor-made for little sluggers—with baseball and softball pitching machines, plus a budget-friendly rate of fifty cents a minute in the cage.

BOWLING ALLEYS

Acme Bowl

TUKWILA

100 Andover Park W

206-340-2263

www.acmebowl.com

$ AGES 3-5 AGES 6-9 AGES 10-14 👕 ✕ 🎁

Adults and tykes alike love Acme Bowl. Located across the street from the Westfield Southcenter mall, the thirty-lane alley is just $3.75–$6.75 a player to bowl depending on the day, and the Break Room restaurant churns out such gourmet comfort food as candied-bacon BLTs and key-lime-pie milkshakes. Chow down in between games while the kids amuse themselves at the nearby shuffleboard tables. Also, get your glow on for just $10 per person during the 3–5 p.m. Monday-afternoon family cosmic bowling sessions.

Lynnwood Bowl & Skate

LYNNWOOD

6210 200th St. SW

425-778-3133

www.bowlandskate.com

$-$$ AGES 3-5 AGES 6-9 AGES 10-14 👕 ✕ 🎁

A twenty-four-lane wooden bowling alley and roller rink wrapped up into one, this old-school-style spot is extremely family-friendly. Families bowl for just $8 per person on Saturdays and Sundays from 12 to 2 p.m. (that rate applies

Monday through Thursday too). Plus, if junior gets bored bowling, you can lace up some skates and hit the rink—see page 98 for more information.

Round 1 Bowling & Amusement
TUKWILA
2351 Southcenter Mall
206-243-2787
www.round1usa.com/location/south-center-mall
$-$$ AGES 3-5 AGES 6-9 AGES 10-14 ☂ ✕ 🎁

Offering billiards, karaoke, and arcade games in addition to fourteen lanes of bowling outfitted with electronic bumpers, dinosaur ball ramps, and child-size bowling balls, the massive 40,000-square-foot Round 1 is a one-stop shop for fun. Kids will get a kick out of the Moon Light Strike Game as well; once an hour, the lights are dimmed and all up-to-bowl players roll at once for the chance to win prizes. For more on the arcade, see page 78.

TechCity Bowl
KIRKLAND
13033 NE 70th Pl.
425-827-0785
www.techcitybowl.com
$$ AGES 10-14 ☂ 🎁

TechCity offers up a live DJ and laser lights for its glow-in-the-dark X-Bowl sessions on Friday and Saturday evenings. Jump online to reserve your spot (designed for those budding tweens and teens—loud blaring music and all); $20 per person.

West Seattle Bowl
WEST SEATTLE
4505 39th Ave. SW
206-932-3731
www.westseattlebowl.com
$-$$ AGES 6-9 AGES 10-14 ☂ 🎁

Established in 1948, this beloved bowling alley boasts classic charm along with some awesome modern amenities, including electronic bumpers that pop out just for the half-pints so the adults can still bowl their own gutter balls. Check out the

Breakfast & Bowl special on Sundays from 9 a.m. to 2 p.m.; order up a piping hot breakfast at the in-house Highstrike Grill and receive two free games of bowling.

GYMNASTICS & TUMBLING

School of Acrobatics and New Circus Arts (SANCA)
Single Serving Classes
GEORGETOWN
674 S. Orcas St.
206-652-4433
www.sancaseattle.org
$$$ AGES 6–9 AGES 10–14 ☂ ✗

Kids will (literally) flip for SANCA, a high-energy circus arts school that offers one-time Intro to Circus classes for $30 per person. During each two-hour Saturday session, kids and any willing adults will get the 411 on tumbling, trampolining, juggling, and balancing acts. Participants must be age 6 and up; be sure to reserve a spot online ahead of time.

Seattle Gymnastics Academy Indoor Playground

BALLARD	COLUMBIA CITY	LAKE CITY
1415 NW 52nd St.	*5034 37th Ave. S,*	*12535 26th Ave. NE*
206-782-1496	*Suite 200*	*206-362-7447*
	206-708-7497	

www.seattlegymnastics.com
$ AGES 0–2 AGES 3–5 ☂

For an hour each day, Seattle Gymnastics Academy opens up to drop-in play for tiny tumblers (12 months on up to age 5; $6 per child). Available at all three of the gym's locations, this playground contains classic gymnastic equipment, such as balance beams and bars, as well as trampolines, a tumbling track, and the ever-popular foam pit, for tiny gymnasts to flip, tumble, and roll those wiggles out on a rainy day.

MINIATURE GOLF & DRIVING RANGES

Discovery Trail at Willows Run
REDMOND

10402 Willows Rd. NE

425-885-5476

www.willowsrun.com/course/discovery-trail

$ AGES 6–9 AGES 10–14 ✕ 🎒

Complemented by a beautiful forested backdrop and views of the Sammamish Plateau, the eighteen-hole putting course at Willows Run takes golfers through wacky obstacles, footbridges, and more (beware of a sound effect or two!). Kids 12 and under play for $6; adults for $9; play before 11 a.m. and receive $1 off each person's fee. Check ahead on the website during rainy spring months as the course is often open Wednesday to Sunday only. Golfers looking to go long should seek out the on-site driving range, which offers a great weekday Lunch Bucket deal: $10 for a medium bucket of balls, plus a sandwich, chips, and soda. Fore!

Family Fun Center
EDMONDS AND TUKWILA

Contact information on page 15

$ AGES 3–5 AGES 6–9 AGES 10–14 ⚲ ✕

With three courses to choose from across two locations, Family Fun Center offers up sweet spots to get your mini golf on. The Tukwila location's eighteen-hole outdoor Arctic Adventure course is always a crowd-pleaser, with a Pacific Northwest theme that includes rugged, woodsy obstacles.

Green Lake Pitch & Putt
GREEN LAKE

5701 W. Green Lake Way N

206-632-2280

www.seattle.gov/parks/athletics/golfcrse.htm

$ AGES 6–9 AGES 10–14 ✕

This little pitch-and-putt course is great for future PGA and LPGA stars just getting into the swing of things. For just $7 a round, the course offers up nine holes of par-3 fun—the longest hole is 115 yards, so leave your long irons in the car—in a gorgeous setting just steps from Green Lake.

Interbay Golf Center
INTERBAY
2501 15th Ave. W
206-285-2200
www.premiergc.com/interbay
$ AGES 3-5 AGES 6-9 AGES 10-14 ✗

Interbay packs in a trio of treats for the golf lover: a heated and covered two-story driving range, a sweet mini golf course, and nine holes of par-3 golf. The classic mini course is just $6.50 for kids (14 and under) and $9 for adults, which means there should be plenty of moolah leftover for a postgolf treat at Red Mill Burgers nearby (page 220).

OFF-THE-WALL SPORTS

Northshore Sports Complex Indoor Bubble Soccer
WOODINVILLE
14220 NE 193rd Pl.
425-485-3238
www.nshoresports.weebly.com/bubble-soccer.html
$$$ AGES 6-9 AGES 10-14 ⚐

Combining the best of indoor soccer with inflatable bouncy fun, bubble soccer is the newest sport to take over Seattle. Players slip into inflatable see-through bubble orbs (which sit from the waist up, enveloping precious heads) and then hit the field for the giggliest game of soccer ever, bouncing off, into, and around the opposing players. At Northshore—which is also home to some sweet batting cages—kids can party it up for two hours with up to fourteen participants. For $250, the facility provides equipment, a referee, and an indoor playing field.

Seattle Bubble Soccer

FREMONT

3518 Fremont Ave. N, Suite 285
425-647-8088
www.bubblesoccerseattle.us

$$$ AGES 6-9 AGES 10-14 🎁

This organization brings the party to you: you supply the park and they supply six adult- or kid-size bubbles and a ref to guide your game. Minimum age is 7 years old, and it's available for groups of four to ten; $275 flat fee for one-hour event.

Snohomish Sports Institute Indoor Bubble Soccer

SNOHOMISH

1820 Bickford Ave.
360-863-2375
www.snohomishsportsinstitute.com

$$$ AGES 6-9 AGES 10-14 🎁

This 13,000-square-foot facility allows for even more pals to get in on the fun. With room for up to thirty participants, all games are played on a full-size indoor soccer court; $350 for ninety minutes, referee also provided.

WhirlyBall

EDMONDS

23401 SR 99
425-672-3332
www.whirlyballseattle.com

$$$ AGES 10-14 ☂

Dubbed "the world's only mechanized team sport," WhirlyBall is best described as a combination of basketball, hockey, and pelota. Players ride in go-cart-esque "WhirlyBugs" and, in teams, try to score goals by picking up and flinging a ball with their handheld plastic scoops. Fast, furious, and way too much fun, WhirlyBall lets kids age 8 and up get in on the fun; the 4,000-square-foot courts are available for $198 an hour for up to twenty-five players, so gather a group to give it a (less expensive) whirl.

ROCK-CLIMBING GYMS

Seattle Bouldering Project

SoDo/Rainier Valley

900 Poplar Pl. S

206-299-2300

www.seattlebouldaringproject.com

$$ AGES 6-9 AGES 10-14 🛒 ☂

This modern, airy two-story gym specializes in "bouldering" (climbing sans ropes or harnesses) and boasts an impressive number of climbing walls, as well as a thriving youth program. After snagging a youth day pass for your climber ($12), head down to the basement level for the easiest climbing and the dedicated kids' area, which also contains a spot for birthday parties.

Stone Gardens

Ballard

2839 NW Market St.

206-781-9828

www.stonegardens.com

Bellevue

15600 NE 8th St., Suite C-1

425-644-2445

$$ AGES 6-9 AGES 10-14 ☂

This gym is a mecca for Seattle climbers and their kids. With options for both bouldering and traditional top-rope climbing, the two Stone Gardens locations offer over 28,000 square feet of combined space to explore. The location in Bellevue boasts a darling kids' climbing area with a towering boat and a skybridge. Pick up a day pass ($14–$16 for youth under 14), or hire a belayer for kiddos itching to climb way up ($70 per hour for up to four kids); adult supervision from a belayer or experienced climber is required, so plan ahead accordingly.

Vertical World

Interbay

2330 W. Commodore Way

206-283-4497

www.verticalworld.com

Lynnwood

12300 Beverly Park Rd.

425-366-8041

Redmond

15036 NE 95th St.

425-881-8826

$$ AGES 6-9 AGES 10-14 ☂

Restless kids practically climbing the walls on a wet day? Take 'em to Vertical World, where that kind of behavior is actually encouraged. With bouldering walls that reach as high as 14 feet for kiddos, all of Vertical World's three outposts gladly welcome little climbers for programs or drop-in adventuring ($14 for youth age 13 and under).

SKATEBOARDING

All Together Skatepark
FREMONT
3500 Stone Way N
206-632-7090
www.alltogetherskatepark.com
$ AGES 6-9 AGES 10-14 ☂ ✗

Seattle's only indoor skateboard park, this kickin' 7,000-square-foot park features everything from ledges and banks to stairs, rails, and a vertical wall. A popular stop during the wet months, the park offers daily open sessions ($10 per person) as well as a designated Saturday time slot for boarders age 11 and under.

Bellevue Skatepark
BELLEVUE
14224 Bel-Red Rd.
425-452-2722
www.ci.bellevue.wa.us/highland_skate_parks.htm
$ AGES 3-5 AGES 6-9 AGES 10-14 ☂

This skating oasis encompasses both a newly remodeled indoor facility—boasting 3- and 4-foot mini ramps, wall rides, and a launch box—plus a 13,000-square-foot plaza outside, which is chock-full of street-skating favorites, such as benches and stairs. Indoor sessions are $4 for Bellevue residents, $5 for nonresidents; check the website for special youth-only times for kids 12 and under; half-hour lessons are recommended for skaters under age 6.

Seattle City Skateparks
VARIOUS LOCATIONS THROUGHOUT THE CITY
www.seattle.gov/parks/skateparks/default.htm
FREE! AGES 3-5 AGES 6-9 AGES 10-14

Check out the plethora of city-maintained skateparks in Seattle, starting with three favorites for ripping it up. Ballard Commons Park (5701 22nd Ave. NW), complete with a water feature and lawn seating to accompany the skating bowl, is fantastic for baby boarders. Delridge Playfield in West Seattle (4458 Delridge Way SW) is an ideal family spot, located right next to playing fields and sports activities. And Lower Woodland Park (5201 Green Lake Way N) sprawls 17,000 square feet and features multiple bowls for catching major hang time.

Skate Like a Girl
VARIOUS LOCATIONS
888-401-0195, ext. 701
www.skatelikeagirl.com
$ AGES 3-5 AGES 6-9 AGES 10-14

The Skate Like a Girl organization encourages girls to get boarding too, through its awesomely supportive clinics, classes, and camps. Often held at All Together Skatepark (page 23) during the wetter fall, winter, and spring months, weekend group classes are open to kids age 12 and under (half-hour lessons are recommended for skaters under age 6); $20 per class for walk-ins. Also be on the lookout for free summer clinics, held at various Seattle-area parks.

Looking for skating or snow sports? Never fear. Read up on **roller and ice rinks,** plus get all the deets to **tubing, skiing, and snowboarding** down the mountains in **Thrills & Chills** (page 93).

BEST BIG SCREENS

From the epic (say, the six-story-tall Boeing IMAX Theater) to the obliging (those outfitted with crying rooms for babes in arms), these theaters are made for mini moviegoers.

BUDGET THEATERS

Admiral Theater
WEST SEATTLE
2343 California Ave. SW
206-938-3456
www.farawayentertainment.com/location/admiral-theater
$ AGES 6–9 AGES 10–14 ☂ ✕

With $8.50 admission for kids all day and the same for adults during matinees, this neighborhood theater is a charming spot to take in a first-run flick. Originally built in the 1940s, the Admiral has preserved much of its original nautical decor, such as the art murals festooning the walls and the quirky seahorse-etched chandeliers.

Crest Cinema Center
SHORELINE
16505 5th Ave. NE
206-363-6339
www.landmarktheatres.com/seattle/crest-cinema-center
$ AGES 3–5 AGES 6–9 AGES 10–14 ☂

At this four-screen North End cinema, $4 will get you into any movie, at any time and for any age, making it a wallet-friendly spot to get caught up on the movies you just missed. (The Crest shows a variety of second-run flicks—including 3-D options, which are still only $5.50.)

The Edmonds Theater
EDMONDS
415 Main St.
425-778-4554
www.theedmondstheater.com
$ AGES 3-5 AGES 6-9 AGES 10-14 🍴 ✗

Family-run for over 30 years, this one-screen theater is tucked inside a 1925 building in Edmonds and offers up first-run flicks at $6 for kids and $8 for adults. Adult tickets are also $6 each at matinees, before 5 p.m.

CRY IT OUT, BABY

It's easy to bring baby along to theaters with designated on-site "crying rooms," should the little one get fussy during the movie. Try these two: **Guild 45th Theatre** in Wallingford (2115 N. 45th St.; 206-547-2127; www .landmarktheatres.com/seattle/guild-45th-theatre) and the **Varsity Theatre** in the University District (4329 University Way NE; 206-632-2267; www .farawayentertainment.com/location/varsity-theatre).

EPIC EXPERIENCES

Pacific Science Center Boeing IMAX Theater
SEATTLE CENTER
200 2nd Ave. N
206-443-4629
www.pacificsciencecenter.org/imax
$$ AGES 6-9 AGES 10-14 🍴 ✗

There are IMAX movie theaters, and then there is *this* IMAX theater, which boasts a 60-foot-high-by-80-foot-wide curved screen, 12,000-watt surround sound, and a special 373-seat tiered auditorium so each and every spectator is close to the action. Showing both current movie releases as well as award-winning 3-D documentaries on the theater's other IMAX screen, the PACCAR, ranging in subject from space travel to our national parks, this spot is a must for little movie buffs.

LOCAL FAVORITES

Cinerama
BELLTOWN
2100 4th Ave.
206-448-6688
www.cinerama.com
$$ AGES 10-14 ☂ ✗

Originally built in 1963, the Cinerama is a Seattle institution. Now owned by tech billionaire Paul Allen, it emerged from an extensive 2014 renovation with a state-of-the-art digital laser projector system, epic surround sound, and seats with more legroom. In keeping with its Seattle-centric focus, the concession stand is fully stocked with locally crafted treats, such as Full Tilt ice cream and Brave Horse Tavern's warm soft pretzels.

Majestic Bay Theatres
BALLARD
2044 NW Market St.
206-781-2229
www.majesticbay.com
$-$$ AGES 6-9 AGES 10-14 ☂ ✗

This locally owned triplex was rescued from ruin in 1998 and has since been known for classically warm decor and the nautical accents that pay homage to its seaside home. Stop by for a first-run film and then make a day of it, by strolling the shops and restaurants along NW Market Street. (See Ballard guide for suggested stops, page 152.)

SIFF Cinema Uptown
LOWER QUEEN ANNE
511 Queen Anne Ave. N
206-324-9996
www.siff.net/cinema
$-$$ AGES 6-9 AGES 10-14 ☂ ✗

One of three theaters operated by the Seattle International Film Festival, SIFF Cinema Uptown offers an eclectic mix of independent and studio pictures on its three screens, while also being conveniently located next to beloved burger joint Dick's Drive-In (page 219). SIFF also offers an annual holiday showing of *Willy Wonka and the Chocolate Factory* in "Smell-O-Vision" (kids are gifted a bag of goodies to sniff or taste at certain points in the film), which is a real treat.

MOMMY & ME AT THE MOVIES

Cooped up with a bouncing baby or wriggly tot? The swank **Lincoln Square Cinemas** in downtown Bellevue (700 Bellevue Way NE; 425-450-9100; www.cinemark .com/theatre-detail.aspx?node_id=84007) offers once-weekly morning Mommy & Me showings for new parents who want to take in a current flick without having to worry about disturbing fellow moviegoers; check the website for current dates and times.

OFFBEAT OPTIONS

McMenamins Anderson School Theater
BOTHELL
18607 Bothell Way NE
425-398-0122
www.andersonschooltheater.com
$-$$ AGES 6-9 AGES 10-14 ☂ ✕

Housed inside a recently revitalized hotel in the burgeoning suburb of Bothell (see more, page 194), this quirky theater not only offers up first-run movies at a reasonable rate ($7 for kids age 12 and under; $7-$9 for adults, depending on the time of day), but will bring dinner to your seat too. Order up a few of McMenamins' pub-style favorites—such as burgers, fries, or pizza—then munch away while the film plays.

Medgar Evers Pool Dive-In Movie Nights
CENTRAL DISTRICT
500 23rd Ave.
206-684-4766
www.seattle.gov/parks/aquatics/pools/evers/schedule.htm
$ AGES 3-5 AGES 6-9 ☂

A movie is great and all, but catching that same movie while swimming in a pool? Pure awesome. Once a month, this public Central District facility offers Dive-In Movie Night from 6:30 to 8 p.m., which allows moviegoers to splish-splash or cannonball away in between scenes of a kid-friendly flick.

OUTDOOR MOVIES!

Bellevue Movies in the Park
VARIOUS LOCATIONS THROUGHOUT BELLEVUE
www.bellevuewa.gov/outdoor-movies.htm
FREE! AGES 3-5 AGES 6-9 AGES 10-14 ✗

The summer sun has finally set in Seattle—time to snag a blanket, pop some corn, and take in a film under the stars. Traditionally held at the sprawling Bellevue Downtown Park and Crossroads Park, these (free!) city-sponsored showings also feature kids activities such as crafts and games before the 7:30 p.m. start time. (As with all outdoor movie spots, lineups and dates vary each year, so be sure to check the website for up-to-date details.)

Movies at Marymoor Park
REDMOND
6046 W. Lake Sammamish Pkwy.
www.epiceap.com/movies-at-marymoor
FREE! AGES 3-5 AGES 6-9 AGES 10-14 ✗

Kiddos age 5 and under get in for free at this popular outdoor showing on the Eastside, which often features live music before the revolving set of movies that start at dusk. (Other fam members get in for $5 each, plus a $5 parking fee per car; gates open at 6:30 p.m.) There is also an incentive to get there early as the first two hundred attendees receive glow-in-the-dark necklaces to wear all magical evening long.

Outdoor Movies at Magnuson Park
SAND POINT
7400 Sand Point Way
www.epiceap.com/seattle-outdoor-movies
FREE! AGES 3–5 AGES 6–9 AGES 10–14 ✗

Take the kids to dinner and a movie at Magnuson Park, where some of the city's most popular food trucks park on movie nights. Snag some chow and then kick back for the flick—seating opens at 6:30 p.m., with contests and games before the shows start at dusk. ($5 per person; no parking fee; children age 5 and under are free.)

Seattle Center Movies at the Mural
SEATTLE CENTER
305 Harrison St.
www.seattlecenter.com/moviesatthemural
FREE! AGES 3–5 AGES 6–9 AGES 10–14 ✗

It's hard to beat the truly spectacular setting here as this outdoor movie screen is nestled at the base of Space Needle. (Free admission is yet another bonus; movies start at dusk or around 9 p.m.)

West Seattle Outdoor Movies
WEST SEATTLE
4410 California Ave. SW
www.wsmovies.org
FREE! AGES 3–5 AGES 6–9 AGES 10–14 ✗

West Seattleites flock to this free outdoor series held at the Junction on balmy summer nights—seating opens at 6:30 p.m. and shows start at dusk.

CRAFTY KIDS

Make some room on the fridge. These drop-in art studios are the perfect canvases for your mini Michelangelos to create their next masterpieces.

CERAMICS & POTTERY

Emerald City Fired Arts

MOUNT BAKER

3333 Rainier Ave. S

206-721-0450

www.emeraldcityfiredarts.com

$-$$ AGES 3-5 AGES 6-9 AGES 10-14 ☂ ⛏

In addition to classic paint-your-own-pottery options, Emerald City Fired Arts offers clay for kids to craft their own pinch pots. The welcoming studio is always up for drop-ins, with painted pieces ranging in price from $5 to $55; it also hosts a wide range of weekend workshops and its once-weekly Mommy & Me Pottery class for kiddos under age 8. (Dads are welcome too!)

Mudhouse Pottery Painting

ISSAQUAH

317 NW Gilman Blvd.

425-677-7334

www.mudhousepottery.com

$-$$ AGES 3-5 AGES 6-9 AGES 10-14 ☂ ✕ ⛏

This relaxed paint-your-own spot in the charming Gilman Village is well suited to families, with a plethora of restaurants and stores, including a toy store, nearby to explore post–art session. Paint-ready pieces range from mugs ($12) to platters ($45), and kids are helped along by the superattentive staffers.

Paint Away

REDMOND

7345 164th Ave. NE, Suite I-130

425-861-8388

www.paintawaynow.com

$-$$ AGES 3-5 AGES 6-9 AGES 10-14 ☂ ⛏

In addition to a wide range of kid-centric ceramics for painting—think funny figurines, piggy banks, frames, and magnets—this charming Redmond Town Center studio also offers glass fusion (the art of stacking two or more glass layers together to make a design). Its special "kiddie glass" has fewer pointy-jabby ends, so it's safe for littles to try their hand at the unique medium.

Paint the Town
UNIVERSITY VILLAGE
4611 Village Ct. NE
206-527-8554
www.ceramics-painting.com
$-$$ AGES 3-5 AGES 6-9 AGES 10-14 ⛱ ✗ 🎁

This sweet studio opens its doors to little painters daily for stop-in sessions, providing all the paint and materials they need to craft a creation. The shop has over 250 ceramic pieces to choose from (ranging in price from $6 to $60), as well as a design center stocked with stamps, stencils, and more.

CRAFTS OF ALL KINDS

Curious Kidstuff
WEST SEATTLE
4740 California Ave. SW
206-937-8788
www.curiouskidstuff.com
$$ AGES 3-5 AGES 6-9 ⛱ ✗ 🎁

This 3,000-square-foot toy store recently added a dedicated arts space in order to offer classes for toddlers and elementary-school-aged children. Currently offered on Mondays and Fridays, the one-hour all-ages class is $12 per child and features a revolving set of hands-on projects. Older children will love the WordPlay class, which explores storytelling through games, writing, and crafts (available for grades 2–5; preregistration suggested).

Insider tip: If your kids tire of doodling, the store is chock-full of toy stations to explore.

Lakeshore Learning

11027 NE 4th St.

425-462-8076

www.lakeshorelearning.com

FREE! AGES 3-5 AGES 6-9 ☂

Flush with educational toys, games, books, and art projects, Lakeshore Learning offers free, seasonally inspired crafts for kids age 3 and up every Saturday from 11 a.m. to 3 p.m.

Roaring Mouse Creative Arts Studio

RAVENNA

7526 20th Ave. NE

206-522-1187

www.roaringmouse.org

$$ AGES 3-5 AGES 6-9 ☂ ⚑

This cheerful spot is well-known for its popular summer art camps (hint, hint), but there are sometimes drop-in options too, for kids ages 4–7. Petite Picassos can experiment with a variety of mediums during the ninety-minute session—drawing, collage, painting, even sculpture—which is $14 per child. The staff recommends bringing a box to take still-wet projects home.

Seattle ReCreative

GREENWOOD

8408 Greenwood Ave. N

206-297-1528

www.seattlerecreative.org

$ AGES 0-2 AGES 3-5 AGES 6-9 ☂

This lovely art collective offers several drop-in options in addition to a wide array of set classes, which include the STEM-based Maker Mania class (where kids make everything from stomp rockets to veggie pianos). This wildly creative attitude extends to the Paint Playground, which is outfitted with pint-size acrylic panels for painting and interactive stations for kids ages 1–5. Pop by Monday through Saturday, from 10 a.m. to 12 p.m.;

$10 per child, and siblings are half off. The center also offers Friday Crafternoons, with a new craft each week for kids age 4 and up (also $10 per child).

West Seattle Art Nest
WEST SEATTLE
4138 California Ave. SW
206-466-6028
www.westseattleartnest.com
$-$$ AGES 3-5 AGES 6-9 AGES 10-14 🌂 ✗ 🎁

A beacon for families on gray, drippy days, West Seattle Art Nest boasts the goods for just about any craft you can imagine. Beads, stamps, paints, crayons, even a bevy of recycled items, are all itching to be transformed into some zany creation. The studio charges one flat rate ($10 per hour for kids under 6, $15 per hour for older children) for little ones to create as many pieces as they can muster. Artists with more avant-garde leanings will especially enjoy the "splatter room," where they can use trucks, Koosh balls, and other tools to literally paint the room (walls, floor, and ceiling included!).

CROSS-CULTURAL EXPLORATIONS
Trot the globe all in one city; devour a Swedish pancake, tour the International District, and discover the Duwamish Tribe.

CULTURAL CENTERS & MUSEUMS

Daybreak Star Cultural Center
MAGNOLIA
5011 Bernie Whitebear Way
206-285-4425
www.unitedindians.org/daybreak-star-center
FREE! AGES 6-9 AGES 10-14

Tucked inside Discovery Park, the Daybreak Star Cultural Center is worth a stop. Free of charge to visit, this airy museum, open Monday through Friday, plays host to myriad paintings from Native American artists, as well as a snap-worthy totem pole and a huge wall mural featuring Northwest animals. The museum is unstaffed, so pick up a visitor's guide from the in-house gift shop for full explanations on each piece. (Because the kids are sure to ask, right?)

Duwamish Longhouse & Cultural Center
WEST SEATTLE
4705 W. Marginal Way SW
206-431-1582
www.duwamishtribe.org/longhouse.html
FREE! AGES 6-9 AGES 10-14 ☂

At the mouth of the Duwamish River, the traditional-style cedar-and-beam longhouse (which is free to visit) celebrates Seattle's first residents, the Duwamish Tribe, through a small but engaging selection of art and storytelling devices. Don't miss the video presentation of children speaking the Lushootseed language and then invite your own kiddos to try out a few words.

Nordic Heritage Museum
BALLARD
3014 NW 67th St.
206-789-5707
www.nordicmuseum.org
$ AGES 3-5 AGES 6-9 AGES 10-14 ☂ ✕

Fittingly located in Ballard (the original settling spot for many Swedish and Norwegian immigrants), the Nordic Heritage Museum contains a wealth of curiosities gathered from families, dating back to the 1840s, from a Viking-style rowboat to colorful Swedish garb in the textiles exhibit. Little ones are welcomed here. The museum offers a free story time the first Thursday of every month, with adventure tales geared toward preschoolers; folk dancing classes for kids age 4 and up; and the extremely popular Viking Days festival every summer.

Northwest African American Museum

CENTRAL DISTRICT

2300 S. Massachusetts St.

206-518-6000

www.naamnw.org

$ AGES 6-9 AGES 10-14 ☂ 🏃

Housed in the historic brick Colman School, NAAM features local art and interactive exhibits that explore the history of African Americans in the Northwest. Once the kids get their fill of the museum, head outside to neighboring Jimi Hendrix Park, which sprawls across 2.3 acres and includes a "wave wall" art installation, plus rain and butterfly gardens.

Swedish Cultural Center Pancake Breakfast

WESTLAKE

1920 Dexter Ave. N

206-283-1090

www.swedishclubnw.org

$ ALL AGES ☂

A great introduction to the Swedish culture for the littlest of kids, Seattle's Swedish Club hosts an extremely popular, extremely delicious pancake breakfast on the first Sunday of the month (though there is no breakfast in July) from 8 a.m. to 1 p.m. Featuring traditional Swedish pancakes topped with your choice of berries and cream or syrup, as well as music and traditional folk dancing, the event is absolutely charming. (Plus, children ages 5–12 are just $5, and kids under age 5 eat for free, so feel free to bring the whole crew.)

Wing Luke Museum of the Asian Pacific American Experience
719 S. King St.
206-623-5124
www.wingluke.org
$-$$ AGES 6-9 AGES 10-14 ☂ ✕

Dedicated to honoring the culture of Asian Pacific American citizens, the Wing celebrates its home in the International District too, with a fascinating permanent exhibit outlining the history of the neighborhood. On the first Thursday of every month, the museum is free for families; the day kicks off with an 11 a.m. story time for the tykes. Also be sure to check out KidPlace, the museum's dedicated gallery for families. The Wing also occasionally offers Family Fun Day, a free-of-charge daylong celebration that includes such kid favorites as face painting, movie screenings, and crafts.

TOURS

Chinatown Discovery Tours
719 S. King St.
206-623-5124
www.seattlechinatowntour.com; www.wingluke.org/tours
$$-$$$ AGES 6-9 AGES 10-14

For an in-depth look at the Chinatown area within the bustling International District neighborhood, the Wing Luke Museum (above) offers a wealth of tours. And there is an option for just about everyone, from a ninety-minute walking tour to the three-hour Not Just Tofu culinary tour, where participants can eat their way through the hood. Spots go quickly, so be sure to book ahead online.

37 PART 1: OUT & ABOUT

Tillicum Village Cruises
WATERFRONT
1101 Alaskan Way
206-623-1445
www.argosycruises.com/tillicum-village
$$$ AGES 6-9 AGES 10-14

This classic boat tour by Argosy Cruises invites kids to walk in the steps of Chief Seattle as they learn about Northwest Native American history at this longhouse and cultural center on Blake Island. The four-hour excursion takes guests back in time to the birthplace of Chief Seattle. You'll enjoy a buffet feast (starring traditional alderwood-smoked salmon), followed by a performance highlighting the myth, magic, and dances of the native Coast Salish tribes.

CURTAIN TIME
From modern dance and ballet to plays and puppet shows, these productions will receive a standing O from the littlest of audience members.

DANCE THEATER

City Opera Ballet
BELLEVUE
Most performances held at the Theatre at Meydenbauer Center,
  11100 NE 6th St.
425-455-1345
www.cityoperaballet.org/balletbellevue
$$$ AGES 10-14

Presenting classic works such as *Romeo and Juliet* as well as new works by Northwest artists, this captivating ballet company, often accompanied by students from Ballet Bellevue School, makes for a lovely date with your tiny dancer.

Kaleidoscope Dance Company

HALLER LAKE

12577 Densmore Ave. N

206-363-7281

www.creativedance.org/kaleidoscope

$-$$ AGES 6-9 AGES 10-14 ☂

Composed entirely of boys and girls ages 7–16, Kaleidoscope Dance Company bills itself as the longest-running modern dance company in the city, hosting several performances a year, including its annual spring anniversary extravaganza. Tickets for the wildly creative and awe-inspiring shows are just $8 for kids.

Pacific Northwest Ballet

SEATTLE CENTER

321 Mercer St.

206-441-2424

www.pnb.org

$$-$$$ AGES 3-5 AGES 6-9 AGES 10-14 ☂

Though many of Pacific Northwest Ballet's expertly crafted productions will interest dance aficionados, its annual showcase of *The Nutcracker* is what draws families from near and far to McCaw Hall during the holiday season. The bright colors; beautiful costumes; and appearances of sugar plum fairies, toy soldiers, and more will truly entrance all viewers and provide a fantastic introduction to ballet for little tykes.

KIDS' SHOWS & STORYTELLING

Northwest Puppet Center

MAPLE LEAF

9123 15th Ave. NE

205-523-2579

www.nwpuppet.org

$-$$ AGES 3-5 AGES 6-9 ☂ 🏃

It's puppets galore at the Northwest Puppet Center, which not only produces weekend shows for the public that pull in guest puppeteers from all over the Northwest, but also offers a puppet museum to poke through after the show. Built with kids in mind, the cute converted church also has a playground out front for kids to clamber on before the show starts. Tickets are $9 for kids and $11 for adults.

Seattle Children's Theatre
SEATTLE CENTER
201 Thomas St.
206-441-3322
www.sct.org
$$$ AGES 3-5 AGES 6-9 ⚟ ✗

Seattle Children's Theatre projects run the gamut from tried-and-true classics like *The Cat in the Hat* to imaginative new works like *Fire Station 7*, a rollicking musical about fire safety, all held in a sweet performance hall at Seattle Center. Kids as young as age 3 can enjoy many of the performances. Special performances are offered for kids with sensory issues or other special needs.

Seattle Public Theater at the Bathhouse Youth Performances
GREEN LAKE
7312 W. Green Lake Dr. N
206-524-1300
www.seattlepublictheater.org
FREE! AGES 6-9 AGES 10-14 ⚟ ⭐

This lovely theater nestled along the shore of Green Lake runs a vibrant youth program for kid actors from elementary school on up to the high school level. The finished plays are performed for free to the public; tickets are available on a walk-up basis starting an hour before each show, giving you just enough time to let the kids burn off some energy on the lakeside path before settling in for a sure-to-be imaginative performance.

StoryBook Theater
PERFORMANCES HELD AT VARIOUS LOCATIONS
Box office at 11730 118th Ave. NE, Kirkland
425-820-1800
www.storybooktheater.org
$$ AGES 3-5 AGES 6-9 ⚟

StoryBook Theater's charming fifty-five-minute musicals based on classic fairy tales are always a rollicking good time, complete with catchy songs, clever stories, and even a life lesson or two snuck in. Kids are sure to recognize such characters as Sleeping Beauty and Red Riding Hood in each play. Shows are designed to please kids ages 3–10, and ticket prices can't be beat ($11–$15). Productions are held throughout the Puget Sound area, so check the website for the show nearest you.

Youth Theatre Northwest
MERCER ISLAND
4400 86th Ave. SE
206-232-4145
www.youththeatre.org
$-$$ AGES 6-9 AGES 10-14 ☂

With twelve productions per year, there is bound to be a little something for everyone at Youth Theatre Northwest, as the company offers whimsical plays led by all-kid casts. Ticket prices range from $10 to $15 per person.

MAINSTREAM THEATERS

The 5th Avenue Theatre
DOWNTOWN
1308 5th Ave.
206-625-1900
www.5thavenue.org
$$$ AGES 6-9 AGES 10-14 ☂ ✗

Housed in a historic building in the heart of Seattle, this theater company often brings the house down with rousing performances of Broadway's best musicals, such as recent favorites *The Little Mermaid* and *The Secret Garden*. Some shows are more family-friendly than others, so check the parental guidelines listed on the theater's website. Kids under age 4 are not admitted.

Seattle Theatre Group

DOWNTOWN

Paramount Theatre: 911 Pine St.
Moore Theatre: 1932 2nd Ave.
Phone number for all: 206-682-1414
www.stgpresents.org

$$$ AGES 6-9 AGES 10-14 🌂 ✘

UNIVERSITY DISTRICT

Neptune Theatre: 1303 NE 45th St.

Check STG's website for the current lineup of traveling shows to hit town, from the touring Broadway plays hosted by the historic Paramount Theatre to musical acts and bands that rock out at the Moore.

Village Theatre & Kidstage

EVERETT

2710 Wetmore Ave.
425-257-8600
www.villagetheatre.org

$$$ AGES 6-9 AGES 10-14 🌂 ✘

ISSAQUAH

303 Front St. N
425-392-2202

While the Village Theatre's mainstage puts on such family-friendly shows as *Billy Elliot* and *Singin' in the Rain* and even has a special family section where kids won't disturb older theatergoers, it's Kidstage that is truly enrapturing, where youth actors put on their own (often stellar) shows. Tickets for these performances start at $16 for youth.

GATHER IN THE GARDEN

Roll up your shirt sleeves and dig into the Puget Sound area's growing array of gardens and patches.

BOTANICAL GARDENS

Bellevue Botanical Garden
BELLEVUE
12001 Main St.
425-452-2750
www.bellevuebotanical.org
FREE! ALL AGES ✖

You wouldn't know it by the peaceful setting and lush greenery, but the Bellevue Botanical Garden is mere steps from the downtown corridor. Free to all, and open dawn to dusk, the lovely garden features a rhododendron glen, a fuchsia section, and a Japanese garden to explore. During the holiday season, the garden also hosts a superpopular light display, which is free on certain nights (see Winter Wonderland itinerary, page 134).

Center for Urban Horticulture & Washington Park Arboretum
LAURELHURST
3501 NE 41st St.
206-543-8616

MONTLAKE/MADISON PARK
2300 Arboretum Dr. E
206-543-8800

www.depts.washington.edu/uwbg/gardens/wpa.shtml
FREE!-$ ALL AGES

At 230 acres in size, the Arboretum boasts over ten thousand different kinds of plants. For families, there is lots of open space to roam, with shelters, lookout gazebos, and even kayak landings along the way. The Center for Urban Horticulture is a destination all its own, with 16 acres of beautiful tour-able courtyards and a smell-tastic fragrance garden. Both parks are free, though the Japanese Garden (at the south end of the Arboretum) has an entrance fee of $6 for adults and $4 for kids ages 6–17.

Kruckeberg Botanic Garden
SHORELINE
20312 15th Ave. NW
206-546-1281
www.kruckeberg.org
FREE! ALL AGES

Once a private estate, this beautiful 4-acre garden just north of Seattle is a real gem, overflowing with bright blooms, natural ferns, and fantastic trees. Drop in on summer Fridays with tots ages 2–6 for the Garden Tots program, which runs from 10 a.m. to 1 p.m. and features a themed garden exploration, a simple plant activity, and a craft ($7 per family).

Kubota Garden
RAINIER BEACH
9817 55th Ave. S
206-684-4075
www.seattle.gov/parks/find/parks/kubota-garden
FREE! ALL AGES

Interlaced with streams, ponds, woods, and waterfalls, as well as picturesque pergolas, gazebos, and red footbridges, this 20-acre Japanese-style garden is a registered historic landmark. It is well worth stopping into the visitor center for a self-guided-tour map, also available on the Kubota Garden Foundation's website.

Volunteer Park Conservatory
CAPITOL HILL
1400 E. Galer St.
206-684-4743
www.seattle.gov/parks/parkspaces/volunteerpark
   /conservatory.htm
$ ALL AGES ☂

A hidden oasis on Capitol Hill, the glass-encased collection of plants is a true haven during the drippy winter months, flush with exotic succulents, cacti, and vivid orchids all kept at a balmy 70 to 80 degrees. Take a tropical tour from one of the friendly docents (free with admission, which is $4 for adults, $2 for budding botanists ages 13–17, and free under age 13) and then poke about the ever-changing seasonal display. The Friends of the Conservatory also frequently offers workshops, including the popular terrarium- and holiday-wreath-making classes, which are open to all ages ($20 per person). Keep an eye on www.volunteerparkconservatory.org for upcoming events.

COMMUNITY PATCHES & HANDS-ON GARDENING

P-Patch Community Gardening Program
OVER EIGHTY LOCATIONS THROUGHOUT THE CITY
206-684-0264
www.seattle.gov/neighborhoods/programs-and-services
   /p-patch-community-gardening
$ ALL AGES

Vegetable gardens are springing up in unused plots and empty lots throughout Seattle, thanks to the city's innovative P-Patch Community Gardening Program, which allows budding and master gardeners alike to plant in designated plots near their homes. Some patches have a 1 - to 2-year waiting list, but all are open to the public for roaming, so plan a visit to see what's poking up out of the soil. And if you can stand the wait, annual fees are $26 per plot, plus $12 per 100 square feet.

Seattle Farm School
VARIOUS LOCATIONS THROUGHOUT WEST SEATTLE
206-218-4948
www.seattlefarmschool.com
FREE! AGES 3–5 AGES 6–9

This innovative center provides hands-on instruction in crafts and cooking as well as urban farming, and recently planted a children's learning garden at the Episcopal Church of Saint

John the Baptist. All hands are invited to dig in and help out with the communal space. Events occur frequently throughout the growing cycle of the gardens, from spring planting parties to a summer picnic and finally a grand harvest fest. Fruits and veggies not gobbled up by little gardeners are donated to the West Seattle Food Bank.

Tilth Alliance
WALLINGFORD
4649 Sunnyside Ave. N, Suite 100
206-633-0451
www.tilthalliance.org
$-$$$ ALL AGES

Tilth Alliance, formerly Seattle Tilth, is the mecca for all things urban gardening, with sites around the city, including its main garden space in Wallingford. The organization allows pre-K kids to taste herbs and forage for compost critters during its very popular garden tours ($6.50 per child with $100 minimum; available for up to thirty students, so rustle up the entire preschool). Kids can also join in at a volunteer garden party alongside their parents. Tilth Alliance also offers fantastic summer camps and how-to workshops for kids as young as 12 months old; book the $25 parent-and-child Fun with Flowers class for a sweet time together.

GET LOST IN A BOOK
The city's vast collection of bookshops and libraries offers a plethora of programs and unique story times for tots (like tales on a tugboat!).

BOOKSTORES

Alphabet Soup
WALLINGFORD
1406 N. 46th St.
206-547-4555
www.alphabetsoupchildrensbooks.blogspot.com
AGES 0-2 AGES 3-5 AGES 6-9 ☂

Conveniently located near a Molly Moon's ice-cream shop (that's definitely a hint; see page 249), this beloved bookshop sells new, used, and vintage children's books. Cozy, with little rockers to sit in while perusing the goods, Alphabet also does trade-ins on select Saturdays, so gather up a neglected stack of books before heading over.

Elliott Bay Book Company
CAPITOL HILL
1521 10th Ave.
206-624-6600
www.elliottbaybook.com
FREE! ALL AGES ☂

This shop has been serving Seattle's readers since 1973 and is well-known for its extensive collection of books. The friendly staffers, who seem to have a near-encyclopedic knowledge of that collection, are great at making recommendations. Join other families for the free weekly story time at 11 a.m. on Saturdays (designed for age 2 and up), or send older kiddos to the YA book group (more info below).

YAY FOR YA

Have a teen who hankers for more Hunger Games? A tween who would pledge allegiance to *Allegiant*? Then get that avid reader to a meeting of Elliott Bay's YA teen book group, The Elliott Bay Underground. Designed for 6th to 12th graders, this lively group picks their own books (no assigned reading here) and then meets the 2nd Thursday of each month at the Capitol Hill shop to discuss their finds. Members also receive exclusive access to advanced copies of buzzy new YA titles. The Underground is free to join and there's no need for advanced registration; more info available at www.elliottbaybook .com/bookgroups/underground.

Third Place Books

LAKE FOREST PARK	RAVENNA	SEWARD PARK
17171 Bothell Way NE	*6504 20th Ave. NE*	*5041 Wilson Ave. S*
206-366-3333	*206-525-2347*	*206-474-2200*

www.thirdplacebooks.com

FREE! ALL AGES ☂ ✕

This lovely local chain sells new and used books; its stores are built for burrowing into a good one or meeting up with friends, with accompanying cafés in each. The unofficial gathering place in each of its respective hoods, Third Place also offers free story times; check the events calendar on the website for upcoming dates.

University Book Store
Six locations, with two offering kids' sections

MILL CREEK	UNIVERSITY DISTRICT
15311 Main St.	*4326 University*
425-385-3530	*Way NE*
	206-634-3400

www.bookstore.washington.edu

FREE! ALL AGES ☂

These UW-run bookstores are great for stocking up on Husky gear, but they're also go-to stops for stellar children's books, ranging from classics to the latest-and-greatest offerings. The stores listed above, which include the primary main campus location, both hold a weekday story time at 11 a.m., with tales quite often followed by a craft activity.

LIBRARIES

King County Library System
VARIOUS LOCATIONS THROUGHOUT KING COUNTY
425-369-3200
www.kcls.org

FREE! ALL AGES ☂

The county-run library system—with locations from Kent, to the south; Bellevue, to the east; and Bothell, to the north—offers a wide range of programs for babies on to up to teenagers. Highlights include bilingual story times and evening story sessions for the whole fam, in addition to weekday tales for toddlers to attend while the older ones are in school; check the website for times and locations.

The Seattle Public Library
VARIOUS LOCATIONS THROUGHOUT THE CITY
206-386-4636
www.spl.org
FREE! ALL AGES ☂

The Seattle Public Library is known for its extensive programming and its many beautiful buildings (the ultramodern downtown Central Library, designed by famous architect Rem Koolhaas, is well worth a gander). With twenty-seven locations throughout the city, there is bound to be a free story time happening nearby; check the website for the one nearest you.

Beyond Seattle and the Eastside, both **Pierce** (www .piercecountylibraries.org) and **Snohomish Counties** (www.sno-isle.org) also run stellar library systems.

ONE-OF-A-KIND STORY TIMES

Chocolate Story Time
FREMONT
3400 Phinney Ave. N
206-632-5100
www.theochocolate.com/factory-tours
$ AGES 3-5 AGES 6-9 ☂

The minute your kids hear the words "chocolate factory," they'll be bounding for the door. Offered once a week at Theo

Chocolate's Fremont factory, the imaginative $8 per person story-time sessions explore the world of chocolate through a kid-friendly tour with samples (yes, please) and a reading of "Molly and the Chocolate Tree," written by a Theo tour guide for kids ages 4–7. Don't worry, the factory also has tours for families with older kids—see page 114.

PJ Storytime
MERCER ISLAND
3014 78th Ave. SE
206-232-6920
www.mercerislandbooks.com
FREE! AGES 0–2 AGES 3–5 AGES 6–9 ☂

Held the first Saturday of every month at 6:30 p.m. in the charming storybook corner of Island Books, PJ Storytime often features acts from the Seattle Storytellers Guild (www .seattlestorytellers.org) and is fun for the whole crew. Little ones can come clad in—you guessed it—pajamas so they can drift off to slumberland on the way home.

Tugboat
SOUTH LAKE UNION
1010 Valley St.
206-382-2628
www.cwb.org
FREE! AGES 0–2 AGES 3–5 AGES 6–9 ☂

This delightful story time aboard a historic tugboat moored at the Center for Wooden Boats fittingly features seafaring stories and magical maritime tales; it's held every second and fourth Thursday of every month from 11 a.m. to 12 p.m. For more on the museum, which offers a wide range of family-friendly activities, see the full listing on page 63.

GO, TEAM

Get in the grandstands and root, root, root for the home team. From professional sports to college athletics, these events are champs of family fun.

BASEBALL

Everett AquaSox

EVERETT

3900 Broadway

425-258-3673

www.aquasox.com

$-$$ AGES 3-5 AGES 6-9 AGES 10-14

The Class A farm team for the nearby Seattle Mariners, the Everett AquaSox play ball from June to September in the classic open-air Everett Memorial Stadium. The laid-back atmosphere and close proximity to the action make this a good time for the whole fam, from teeny fans just getting introduced to the game to true aficionados hankering for autographs. The most expensive ticket in the place is $18, plus there's free parking on the grounds, so it's a home run for the budget too.

Seattle Mariners

SoDo

1250 1st Ave. S

206-346-4001

seattle.mariners.mlb.com

$$-$$$ ALL AGES ✕

Play ball! Seattle's resident Major League Baseball team calls beautiful Safeco Field home. This stadium offers great people-watching and local eats, like Ivar's fish 'n' chips and Kidd Valley burgers, in addition to any given day's ball game. In action April through October, the Mariners take on such American League rivals as the Yanks and the Red Sox in a setting made for families. Check out the popular area called the 'Pen, where kids can get an up-close look at the pitchers in the bullpen. For little ones who can't quite sit still the full nine innings, head to the center field play area, replete with slides and tunnels. Bringing *le bébé* is also a cinch, thanks to the air-conditioned nursing lounge, near the guest service center at section 128.

Tacoma Rainiers
TACOMA
2502 S. Tyler St.
253-752-7707
www.tacomarainiers.com
$-$$ ALL AGES

Take the troop to Tacoma for a Rainiers game at historic Cheney Stadium—there's almost no better place to be on a hot summer's eve. The Triple A affiliate of the Mariners, the Rainiers slug ball April to September, and there's a fireworks show after every Friday home game. Pack up a picnic blanket and head out to the grass open-seating area down the first-base line near the outfield ($7.50 per ticket; kids age 3 and under are free), where the kids can cheer, shout, and roam to their hearts' content.

BASKETBALL

Seattle Storm
SEATTLE CENTER
305 Harrison St.
206-217-9622
storm.wnba.com
$$$ AGES 3-5 AGES 6-9 AGES 10-14 ☂ ✘

The two-time WNBA champs take it to the hoop May to October at Key Arena, led by such electrifying stars as Sue Bird, Abby Bishop, and Alysha Clarke. There are multiple discount and theme nights on Storm games throughout the season; families would do well to check the website before heading to the game.

COLLEGIATE SPORTS

Seattle Pacific University Athletics
QUEEN ANNE
Ticket office at Royal Brougham Pavilion, 3414 3rd Ave. W
206-281-2085
www.spufalcons.com
$ AGES 3-5 AGES 6-9 AGES 10-14

This private NCAA Division II university, located on the edge of Queen Anne near Fremont, offers plenty of teams to cheer—basketball, soccer, volleyball, and the ever-popular gymnastics team—all $3 each for kids; free for age 2 and under. If you plan on frequenting the campus, enroll your fans (8th grade and under) in the Junior Falcon program; for a flat $25 fee, they can then get into any Falcon sporting event sans additional charge all season long.

Seattle University Athletics

CAPITOL HILL

Ticket office at 1218 E. Cherry St.

206-398-4678

www.goseattleu.com

$ AGES 3-5 AGES 6-9 AGES 10-14 ✗

Give the tykes a taste of the college experience by taking in a Seattle U Redhawks game. If you preregister for the BECU Rudy's Kids Club on the website, your grade-school children (through 6th grade) get into every SU ticketed home game for free—from women's volleyball to the men's basketball games, held at Key Arena.

University of Washington Athletics

UNIVERSITY DISTRICT

Ticket office at 3910 Montlake Blvd., Graves Building, Room 101

206-543-2200

www.gohuskies.com

$-$$$ AGES 3-5 AGES 6-9 AGES 10-14 ✗

One of the powerhouses of the Pac-12 Conference, the University of Washington's thriving athletic program encompasses twenty teams, with sports ranging from volleyball and softball to track and field, basketball, and, of course, football. Tickets vary, with football games being the most expensive, but UW offers two programs that give families more bang for the buck. Get in some bonding time with the $35 Dads & Daughters program—good for one adult and one youth admission to six Husky sporting events throughout the season. Or join Dubs' Club, a free program for kids age 13 and under; join up and get one free ticket to all regular-season matches (excluding football and men's basketball), plus enjoy discount tickets for the rest of the fam too.

FOOTBALL

Seattle Seahawks
SoDo
800 Occidental Ave. S
888-635-4295
www.seahawks.com
$$$ AGES 6-9 AGES 10-14 ✗

One of the most electrifying teams in the National Football League, the Seahawks also boast one of the most electrifying fan experiences in the country. The extremely loud, extremely proud 12th Man fan base fills CenturyLink Field for every home game, often breaking sound records (so, sensitive little ears should probably be left with a sitter for this one). Ticket prices are steep—available for as little as $62, but averaging around $200—so for a less expensive way to watch, consider checking out the preseason camp held at the team's lakeside training facility in Renton. Plan (way) ahead and preregister at trainingcamp .seahawks.com to attend practice for just $8 per person.

HOCKEY

Everett Silvertips
Everett
2000 Hewitt Ave.
425-252-5100
www.everettsilvertips.com
$$-$$$ AGES 3-5 AGES 6-9 AGES 10-14 ☂

If it's September through March at Xfinity Arena, it's time for the puck drop. Take the tykes to see the Everett Silvertips, a semiprofessional hockey team that provides fast and furious action on the ice, as well as a great loud crowd, raffle prizes (toss a puck for a chance to win!), and of course, every kid's favorite, a Zamboni sighting in between each period.

Seattle Thunderbirds
KENT
625 W. James St.
253-239-7825
www.seattlethunderbirds.com
$$-$$$ AGES 3-5 AGES 6-9 AGES 10-14 ☂

The area's other semipro team—and, naturally, the archrivals of the Silvertips—the Seattle Thunderbirds call the south-side suburb of Kent home. Families and fans flock to ShoWare Center for high-octane hockey during the winter months. Tickets start at $16, but the team offers quite a few discounts and family packages (hot dogs and popcorn included), so check the website beforehand.

HORSE RACING

Emerald Downs
AUBURN
2300 Emerald Downs Dr.
253-288-7000
www.emeralddowns.com
$ AGES 3-5 AGES 6-9 AGES 10-14 🛒

The Emerald Downs horse track, located about forty-five minutes south of Seattle, is extremely family-friendly, with sprawling grounds where kids can run, an on-site bounce house, and frequent free pony rides, in addition to the day's racing schedule. Open April through September with general admission $7 for adults and free for kids under age 18, the track is a relaxing spot on a sunny day. Horse lovers can get an up-close look at the pedigreed Thoroughbreds in the paddock before the race, then thrill in watching those same animals go pounding by the finish line.

SOCCER

Seattle Reign FC

SEATTLE CENTER

401 5th Ave.

855-734-4632

www.reignfc.com

$$-$$$ AGES 6-9 AGES 10-14

You goal, girls! The women's Seattle Reign FC team hosts a dozen home matches a year, taking to the pitch at the historic Memorial Stadium during the spring and summer months to do battle against such foes as the Portland Thorns, Chicago Red Stars, and Orlando Pride. This fiery club is sure to inspire your own future soccer star. Kids age 3 and under are admitted for free; tickets for adults and other youth begin at $18.

Seattle Sounders FC

SoDo

800 Occidental Ave. S

877-657-4625

www.soundersfc.com

$$$ AGES 6-9 AGES 10-14

Rivaled only by the 12th Man in their rabid and raucous devotion to their team, Sounders fans help make the Major League Soccer team's games a truly entertaining experience, often standing the full ninety minutes of the match. The kids will love cheering with this crew as the Sounders take the field for *fútbol* at CenturyLink Field. Don't forget to dress in bright blue and green!

HITTING THE HIGH NOTES

Rock out to those totally cool kindie bands, or pluck, bang, or blow on some instruments yourself with these musically inclined ideas.

MUSIC VENUES & ACTIVITIES

Bellevue Youth Symphony Orchestra

BELLEVUE

Performances usually held at
   Renton IKEA Performing Arts Center
400 S. 2nd St.
425-467-5604
www.byso.org

$$ AGES 6–9 AGES 10–14 ☂

Young musicians will be in awe of this all-youth symphony, which performs classic and contemporary favorites throughout the year at the performance hall in downtown Renton. Tickets are $12 for youth (through high school) and $15 for adults (kids under age 4 are free). Any envious kids can try out for the orchestra themselves; auditions are held in the fall.

Kindiependent

VARIOUS LOCATIONS THROUGHOUT SEATTLE

www.kindiependent.com

$ AGES 0–2 AGES 3–5 AGES 6–9

This local consortium of kiddie rock bands includes such popular acts as Recess Monkey, the Not-Its, and Caspar Babypants—who is Chris Ballew of the Presidents of the United States of America fame—all of whom play cheap (or free!) concerts around the city, including the awesome ten-part Kids Rock concert series held at Mount Baker Community Club every year.

Museum of Pop Culture (MoPOP)

SEATTLE CENTER

325 5th Ave. N
206-770-2700
www.mopop.org

$$-$$$ AGES 3–5 AGES 6–9 AGES 10–14 ☂ ✗

Housed in a funk-tastic building that resembles a smashed guitar, MoPOP (formerly known as the EMP Museum) almost defies classification. It's one part music museum, another part homage to science fiction, and all parts ode to pop culture. In addition to exhibits dedicated to such music legends as Nirvana and Jimi Hendrix, and to props and memorabilia from science fiction's most iconic films, kids will especially love the interactive Sound Lab, where they can rock out with a variety of instruments in (thankfully) soundproof rooms. Adults can save $3 off the usual $25 ticket price by buying admission online ahead of time; kids 5–17 are $16 and children 4 and under are free.

Soundbridge Seattle Symphony Music Discovery Center & Family Programs
Downtown
200 University St.
866-833-4747
www.seattlesymphony.org/families-learning
$-$$ ALL AGES 🌂 🎒

The Seattle Symphony goes above and beyond to welcome families, offering free tickets to kids ages 8–18 for many of its symphony performances at Benaroya Hall, and through the fantastic interactive-learning center, Soundbridge, a music-filled space where tykes can have jam sessions and attend music events. The popular Tiny Tots program allows the youngest music lovers (birth to age 5) to attend a five-week concert series ($49 per child-and-parent duo) featuring varying musical styles and instruments. Soundbridge is open for public browsing and banging Fridays from 10 a.m. to 2 p.m., when the suggested donation is $10 (but also runs on a pay-as-you-can basis); tiny tykes are treated to a musical story time at 10:30 a.m.

OUTDOOR CONCERT SERIES

Concerts at the Mural
SEATTLE CENTER
305 Harrison St.
206-684-7200
www.seattlecenter.com/concertsatthemural
FREE! AGES 3–5 AGES 6–9 AGES 10–14 ✖

The setting for this free all-ages series–which takes place Fridays in August–cannot be beat with local bands rocking out in front of the colorful mural at the base of the Space Needle.

Eastside Summer Concerts
VARIOUS EASTSIDE CITIES
Website information listed below
FREE! AGES 3–5 AGES 6–9 AGES 10–14

Warble your way all across the Eastside with an awesome array of concerts: Rocking Kirkland since 1977, the kids' portion of the free summer series there takes place at Juanita Beach Park on Tuesday mornings during July and August, with the little ones bebopping to kiddie tunes along the shores of Juanita Bay (www.kirklandsummerconcerts.weebly.com). Other Eastside burbs, such as Redmond (www.redmondtowncenter.com), Issaquah (www.ci.issaquah.wa.us), and Sammamish (www.sammamish.us), also host free outdoor shows.

Library Concerts
LIBRARIES THROUGHOUT SEATTLE,
    PLUS KING AND SNOHOMISH COUNTIES
Website information listed below
FREE! AGES 3–5 AGES 6–9 AGES 10–14

The Seattle Public Library (www.spl.org), the King County Library System (www.kcls.org), and Sno-Isle Libraries (www.sno-isle.org) all offer a stellar lineup of free concerts during the summer months. A favorite site is the shaded lawn at Mill Creek Library, which is oh-so-conveniently located near a Frost doughnut shop (page 246). Check each website for details.

Out to Lunch Concert Series
DOWNTOWN
206-623-0340
www.downtownseattle.com/summer/otl
FREE! AGES 3–5 AGES 6–9 AGES 10–14

July through early September, Seattleites are treated to free
weekday lunchtime concerts by Northwest artists in parks across
the downtown corridor, a perfect excuse for office dwellers to
meet the kiddos for a lunch break.

University Village Sounds of Summer
UNIVERSITY VILLAGE
2623 NE University Village St.
206-523-0622
www.uvillage.com
FREE! AGES 3–5 AGES 6–9 AGES 10–14 ✖

Little concert-goers will surely appreciate the kid's activity
zone (complete with activities!) at this free Wednesday-evening
series held during July and August, while the 'rents are sure to
dig the beer garden and bites from nearby restaurants like Blue
C Sushi (page 232), Din Tai Fung (page 184), or Elemental Wood
Fired Pizza.

Woodland Park Zoo Tunes
PHINNEY RIDGE
5500 Phinney Ave. N
206-548-2500
www.zoo.org/zootunes
$$$ AGES 3–5 AGES 6–9 AGES 10–14

Buy your tickets early for this extremely popular summer concert
series, which draws in big names like Ziggy Marley, Brandi
Carlile, and the B-52s. Shows are held on the zoo's expansive
rolling lawn so wriggly tots will have lots of room to twirl and
whirl to the music.

Youngershoot
SEATTLE CENTER
305 Harrison St.
www.bumbershoot.com/what_is_youngershoot
$$-$$$ AGES 3-5 AGES 6-9 AGES 10-14

Run as an accompaniment to the ever-popular annual
Bumbershoot music festival on Labor Day weekend,
Youngershoot targets the smallest music fans, with crafts and
interactive activities, in addition to kid-friendly entertainment;
free to kids age 8 and under with a paying adult.

MAKING WAVES

Don't sweat it. Combat the next heat wave by joining other
sun-deprived Seattleites at these supersoaker fountains, sandy
beaches, and cool pools.

BEACHES

Alki Beach
WEST SEATTLE
1702 Alki Ave. SW
206-684-4075
www.seattle.gov/parks/find/parks/alki-beach-park
FREE! ALL AGES 🚶 ✕

With white sandy shores, fish-fry stands, and colorfully clad
beachgoers, Alki is reminiscent of Nantucket with all the charm
of that region, plus an absolutely killer view of the downtown
skyline. While away a day along Elliott Bay, by biking along the
paved Alki Trail (page 75) to poke about the lighthouse, or by
swimming, building sand castles, and digging into shave ice at
Marination Ma Kai (page 233).

Golden Gardens Park

BALLARD

8498 Seaview Pl. NW

206-684-4075

www.seattle.gov/parks/find/parks/golden-gardens-park

FREE! ALL AGES 🏃

Get here early to claim one of the public bonfire pits, then sit back and enjoy the stellar view from the Ballard-area beach. Sailboats float by on Puget Sound in front of the snowcapped Olympic Mountains. Kids will be well entertained by the playground and the loop trail that explores the wetlands in the north end of the park. There's also a pier that's open for fishing.

Juanita Beach Park

KIRKLAND

9073 NE Juanita Dr.

425-587-3000

www.kirklandwa.gov/depart/parks

FREE! ALL AGES 🏃 ✕

With over 1,000 sandy feet of Lake Washington waterfront, there is plenty of room to spread out at this park about a half hour northeast of Seattle. Offering a playground, sand volleyball courts, and a fishing area, the park also has an enclosed lifeguarded area during the summer so little swimmers can safely get in some strokes.

Lake Sammamish State Park

ISSAQUAH

2000 NW Sammamish Rd.

425-649-4275

www.parks.state.wa.us/533/lake-sammamish

FREE! ALL AGES

This state park about thirty minutes outside Seattle is blessed with almost 7,000 feet of waterfront and two beaches for swimming and splashing. Lake Sammamish is a true Northwest beauty, nestled among towering pines that provide blissful shade on hot summer days. In the very off chance the kiddos should tire of the sand, there are miles upon miles of hiking trails to explore.

Insider tip: Parking fees apply, as for any other state-run park.

Newcastle Beach
BELLEVUE
4400 Lake Washington Blvd. SE
425-452-6914
www.ci.bellevue.wa.us/newcastle_beach.htm
FREE! ALL AGES 🏃

The largest beach in Bellevue is one of the swankiest in the burbs, outfitted with picnic shelters, a colorful children's area, and a nature trail. The pristine beach is monitored by lifeguards in the summer; adventurous kiddos can swim out to the floating dock to practice their cannonballing skills.

BOATING

Agua Verde Paddle Club
UNIVERSITY DISTRICT
1307 NE Boat St.
206-545-8570
www.aguaverde.com/paddleclub
$-$$ AGES 3-5 AGES 6-9 AGES 10-14 🍴

This popular Mexican eatery (see page 221) quite famously rents kayaks and stand-up paddleboards from its spot on Portage Bay, which sits at the intersection of Lake Union and Lake Washington. Explore either lake, cruising by Gas Works Park on the former, or the Arboretum on the latter. Kids must be accompanied by an adult paddler, and while double kayaks usually rent for $24 per hour, the club offers weekday discounts that save up to $6 per hour.

The Center for Wooden Boats
SOUTH LAKE UNION
1010 Valley St.
206-382-2628
www.cwb.org
$ AGES 3-5 AGES 6-9 AGES 10-14

Always free to visit and always fit for boating fanatics, the Center for Wooden Boats encourages visitors to first explore the beautiful selection of fishing schooners, sailboats, and sloops on view at its museum, then get on the water too. Boat rentals and boatbuilding classes are offered, and even free first-come-first-served sailboat rides every Sunday (sign-ups begin at 10 a.m.). The center also offers up model sailboats to race around a picturesque pond (available Saturdays, Sundays, and the first Thursday of the month, May through October; $5 suggested donation) and toy boat–building workshops the first Thursday of every month ($2 suggested donation, designed for kids ages 3–9).

The Electric Boat Company
WESTLAKE
2046 Westlake Ave. N, Suite 102
206-223-7476
www.theelectricboatco.com
$$–$$$ ALL AGES

The charming electric vessels offered by this company are a wonderful way to explore every nook and cranny of Lake Union. Available to rent for $99 per hour (two hours minimum), the boats hold up to ten passengers, so gather up a few families for a less expensive tour. No previous experience is required to rent, but kids can captain in name only; it's best to leave the actual steering to Mom or Pop.

Greenlake Boathouse
GREEN LAKE
7351 E. Green Lake Dr. N
206-527-0171
www.greenlakeboatrentals.net
$ AGES 3–5 AGES 6–9 AGES 10–14 🛶 ✗

Canoe, kayak, pedal boat, or even water bike around quaint Green Lake aboard a rental from Greenlake Boathouse, which has been helping Seattleites play on the lake since 1974. Most vessels are $20 per hour and can fit multiple adults and kids, so pile on in; life vests are provided, should any boater inadvertently answer the call of the water.

University of Washington Waterfront Activities Center

UNIVERSITY DISTRICT

3710 Montlake Blvd. NE

206-543-9433

www.washington.edu/ima/waterfront

$-$$ AGES 3-5 AGES 6-9 AGES 10-14

Located directly behind Husky Stadium on the Montlake Cut, the Waterfront Activities Center rents canoes and rowboats to the public for $9-$12 per hour per vessel. The primo location makes exploring easy. Just paddle toward the 520 Bridge for a beautiful tour through the waters near Marsh Island and the Arboretum, which are populated by lily pads, frogs, blue herons, and duckies.

FOUNTAINS, SPRAY PARKS & WADING POOLS

Cal Anderson Park

CAPITOL HILL

1635 11th Ave.

206-684-4075

www.seattle.gov/parks/find/parks/cal-anderson-park

FREE! ALL AGES 🛒 👪

From a fire-truck play structure to the oversize chessboards that dot the park, there's plenty to gawk and gape at here in addition to the main attraction: the volcano-esque fountain that gurgles up and over into the nearby wading area. The busy spot makes for great people-watching and picnicking for grown-ups as the kids cool off.

Bellevue Downtown Park

BELLEVUE

10201 NE 4th St.

425-452-6855

www.ci.bellevue.wa.us/downtown_park_and_rose_garden.htm

FREE! ALL AGES 🛒 👪

With a 240-foot-wide waterfall that cascades into a reflecting pond, plus a classic bowl-style fountain fit for dipping toes into, the water displays are the cornerstone of this lovely park, which also contains a walking trail and sprawling lawns for picnicking.

Do take note: there will be intermittent closures of the fountain and other areas of the park during 2017 as construction is underway on several projects, including the expansion of the current playground.

International Fountain
SEATTLE CENTER
305 Harrison St.
206-684-7200
www.seattlecenter.com/locations/detail.aspx?id=8
FREE! ALL AGES 👶

Just follow the shrieks of delight to find this one. First constructed for the 1962 World's Fair, the International Fountain makes a splash like no other, with a 220-foot-diameter bowl for kids to run around in as the 10-foot-high, 27-foot-wide center dome shoots water as far as 120 feet. Cool enough for even the tweens, this is one multitasking fountain, also offering synchronized water and light shows set to the scores of Duke Ellington, Beethoven, and Northwest rockers.

Other Seattle Wading Pools & Spray Parks
VARIOUS LOCATIONS
206-684-7796
www.seattle.gov/parks/wadingpools.asp
FREE! AGES 0–2 AGES 3–5 AGES 6–9

There's bound to be a quick cooldown in your future, thanks to the sweet wading pools and splash-happy spray parks at Seattle Parks and Recreation's thirty-plus locations around the city, open from late May to mid-September. For perfect pools to dip your toes, try Green Lake Park (7201 E. Green Lake Dr. N), Lincoln Park in West Seattle (page 145), and Warren G. Magnuson Park (page 89). For sweet spray-park options, head for Highland Park Playground in West Seattle (1100 SW Cloverdale St.), Lake Union Park (page 181), Northacres Park in North Seattle's Haller Lake hood (12718 1st Ave. NE), and Georgetown Playfield (750 S. Homer St.) The spray park in Georgetown is one of the newest in the city, filled with pop-up fountains and abundant shade just off the splash pad.

SWIMMING POOLS & WATER PARKS

Bellevue Aquatic Center
BELLEVUE
601 143rd Ave. NE
425-452-4444
www.ci.bellevue.wa.us/aquatic_center.htm
$ ALL AGES ⚐ ♞

Swim out the wiggles on a rainy day at this indoor city pool. The facility offers two different pools to choose from, the larger Blue Lagoon, outfitted with a curly tunnel slide and a diving board, and the smaller Warm Springs pool, which is kept at higher temps for therapy purposes and makes for a great place to introduce babies and toddlers to the water.

Seattle City Pools
VARIOUS LOCATIONS
206-684-7796
www.seattle.gov/parks/pools.asp
$ ALL AGES ✕ ♞

With eight indoor pools, plus two seasonal outdoor options, Seattle Parks and Recreation provides cheap and easy entertainment for kids. Admission rates for open swims average $3-$5. Indoor highlights include Ballard Pool, complete with rope swing (1471 NW 67th St.); Meadowbrook Pool in Wedgwood (10515 35th Ave. NE), which boasts two diving boards; and Medgar Evers Pool in the Central District, which offers monthly Dive-In Movie Nights (page 29). En plein air, Colman Pool in West Seattle (8603 Fauntleroy Way SW) builds on a 75-year tradition; this pool is filled with heated saltwater and offers breathtaking Sound views.

Weyerhaeuser King County Aquatic Center
FEDERAL WAY
650 SW Campus Dr.
206-447-4444
www.kingcounty.gov/services/parks-recreation/parks/activities
    /aquatics.aspx
$ AGES 3-5 AGES 6-9 AGES 10-14 ⚐ ♞

This absolutely huge aquatic center hosts competitive swimming events like the Olympic trials and, as such, seats 2,500 people in its impressive grandstand. (Don't miss the chance to stand on the edge of the Olympic-size pool and pretend to accept your gold medal.) Its recreational pool is open to the public, with a pirate-cove theme that kids will love; open swim rates are $3.25–$5 per person.

Wild Waves Water Park
FEDERAL WAY
Contact information on page 96
$-$$$ ALL AGES 🏕 ✕ 🎪

For details on this outdoor water park, see the amusement park listing on page 96.

TIDE POOLS

Lighthouse Park
MUKILTEO
609 Front St.
425-263-8180
www.mukilteowa.gov/departments/recreation/parks-open
   -spaces-trails/lighthouse-park/
FREE! ALL AGES 🧍

This picturesque point is next to the Mukilteo ferry dock, with crustaceans and seashells aplenty hanging about the private boat launch area.

Richmond Beach Saltwater Park
SHORELINE
2021 NW 190th St.
206-801-2700
www.cityofshoreline.com/government/departments/parks
   -recreation-cultural-services
FREE! ALL AGES 🧍

The old pier pilings can be spotted here at low tide, dotted with crabs, sea anemones, and other creatures from the deep.

Saltwater State Park
DES MOINES
25205 8th Pl. S
253-661-4956
www.parks.state.wa.us/578/saltwater
FREE! ALL AGES 🏃

Perhaps it's the artificial underwater reef just offshore, but many varieties of marine life flock to this South End beach, which is also home to sandy stretches for digging.

PARKS & PLAYGROUNDS

With 465 in Seattle proper alone, there are parks aplenty in the region; these standouts boast epic slides and cool climbs, plus unforgettable digs *and* digging.

BUILD!

Adventure Playground at Deane's Children's Park
MERCER ISLAND
5500 Island Crest Way
206-275-7862
www.mercergov.org/page.asp?navid=2768
FREE! AGES 3–5   AGES 6–9   AGES 10–14

Tucked into the forest at this Mercer Island park, the summertime Adventure Playground allows little builders to go wild. Kids are supplied with toolboxes and supplies to construct their own wildly creative play zones (tree fort time!). The play area is open Tuesday through Thursday, and Sunday afternoons from July through August, and then Sundays only in September; parents must sign a one-time waiver and kids must wear closed-toe shoes.

CLIMB!

Bayview-Kinnear Park
QUEEN ANNE
3rd Ave. W and W. Prospect St.
206-684-4075
www.seattle.gov/parks/park_detail.asp?id=1000342
FREE! AGES 3-5 AGES 6-9 AGES 10-14

Nestled down a flight of stairs from Kerry Park (and thus boasting one of the city's best views of the Space Needle), Bayview-Kinnear is also a fantastic climbing spot, with footholds covering the entirety of the long cement wall that anchors the park. After doing a little bouldering, kiddos can also enjoy the dual slides built into the hillside.

Roxhill Park
WEST SEATTLE
2850 SW Roxbury St.
206-684-4075
www.seattle.gov/parks/find/parks/roxhill-park
FREE! ALL AGES

This bustling West Seattle park comes complete with a play castle, sandbox, and swings, plus an epic dome structure with ropes, obstacles, and cargo nets. Older kiddos can test their mettle on a more difficult climbing course outfitted with rock-climbing holds on several vertical poles—jumping and clambering across *American Ninja Warrior*-style.

DIG!

Miner's Corner
BOTHELL
22903 45th Ave. SE
425-388-6600
www.snohomishcountywa.gov/facilities/facility/details/miners
-corner-57
FREE! ALL AGES

This new 13-acre play area, replete with epically tall slides and basketball courts, lets kids get back to nature with a pond and an awesome sandpit at the edge of the forest-inspired playground. It's outfitted with "ditch digger" tools and a giant rain barrel for creating mud puddles. And be sure to let your little archaeologist in on a secret: there's a dinosaur fossil buried somewhere in the sand.

LOOK!

Alki Playground
WEST SEATTLE
5817 SW Lander St.
206-684-4075
www.seattle.gov/parks/find/parks/alki-playground
FREE! ALL AGES ✕

Ahoy, landlubbers. Kids adore climbing on the tall "whale tail" sculpture at this sweet park and heading off on a make-believe voyage on the playground's very own boat. Taller pirates can have even more fun, as they'll be able to spy the real ocean from their perch on high.

Carkeek Park
BROADVIEW
950 NW Carkeek Park Rd.
206-684-0877
www.seattle.gov/parks/environment/carkeek.htm
FREE! ALL AGES

At this North End park, kids can slide down a truly unique feature: an oversize salmon tunnel slide, a fitting tribute to the scores of salmon that come through this park on their way upriver each year. (For more on salmon-spawning spots, see page 92). Climb the slope on either side, duck inside the fish's open mouth, and down you goooooooo.

Family Fitness and Play Area at the Cross Kirkland Corridor
KIRKLAND
747 6th Ave. S
425-587-3000
www.kirklandwa.gov/residents/community/cross_kirkland
    _corridor.htm
FREE! ALL AGES

Kids take flight at this new Eastside park. Abutting the Google campus (hence earning it the nickname "Google Park"), the spot includes a playground climbing structure, a sand volleyball court, a CrossFit section, a bocce ball court, and a tot-friendly zip line that packs just enough punch to be a kick for parents and preschoolers alike.

Gas Works Park
WALLINGFORD
2101 N. Northlake Way
206-684-4075
www.seattle.gov/parks/find/parks/gas-works-park
FREE! ALL AGES

This is a Seattle classic. Boasting incredible Lake Union and downtown views, Gas Works Park sits on the site of a former gas plant, where industrial behemoths still dot the landscape. Add to this a play barn and the big hill suited for kite flying or rolling down at wild speeds, and you're in for one high-octane afternoon.

SLIDE!

Artists at Play
SEATTLE CENTER
305 Harrison St.
206-684-7200
www.seattlecenter.com/news/detail.aspx?id=1932
FREE! AGES 6–9 AGES 10–14

This one is for the daredevils. Boasting both 52-foot and 38-foot slides, this wildly creative playground—one of the newest in Seattle—sits next door to the MoPOP. Recommended for kids age 5 and older, it also contains an epic 30-foot climbing tower, cargo nets, rope climbs, and swaying bridges that have an awesome view of the Needle.

Jefferson Park
BEACON HILL
801 Beacon Ave. S
206-684-4075
www.seattle.gov/parks/find/parks/jefferson-park
FREE! ALL AGES

Perched atop a hill overlooking downtown Seattle, Jefferson Park boasts a number of steep slides—one an almost-terrifying curving tunnel—that will have kids squealing with glee as they career down the hillside. Zip lines, basketball and tennis courts, a splash pad, and plenty of rolling lawns complete this near-perfect spot.

Westcrest Park
WEST SEATTLE
9000 8th Ave. SW
206-684-4075
www.seattle.gov/parks/find/parks/westcrest-park
FREE! ALL AGES

This recently expanded park boasts five different slides—three options at the playground and two "secret" slides tucked into the hillside by the climbing wall—plus dueling zip lines, walking paths, and an off-leash dog area so Fido can also run like mad.

SWING!

Woodland Park Playground
PHINNEY RIDGE
1000 N. 50th St.
206-684-4075
www.seattle.gov/parks/find/parks/woodland-park
FREE! ALL AGES

This darling play area and park directly west of Woodland Park Zoo recently received an upgrade and now features swings that are some of the city's tallest, at 12 feet. Get to pumping!

PEDAL POWER

No matter if the tykes are two-, three-, or four-wheelin' it these days, cycle-crazy Seattle and the surrounding cities have a bike track or trail to suit.

COURSES & TRACKS

Jerry Baker Memorial Velodrome
REDMOND
6046 NE Marymoor Way
www.velodrome.org
$ AGES 3–5 AGES 6–9 AGES 10–14 ✕

Local cycling enthusiasts take to the velodrome at Marymoor Park on Friday nights, May on into September, as world-class athletes race. Spectators can picnic on the lawn or enjoy the view from the stands; the $5 per person spectacle also draws a bevy of food trucks. If your little speed racers want in on the action, bring 'em to one of the popular Kiddie Kilo races held the first and third Friday of every month from June through September. Kids age 12 and under can try out the velodrome for themselves—race for that checkered flag!

North SeaTac BMX
SEATAC
1855 S. 136th St.
206-243-4411
www.seatacbmx.org
FREE! AGES 6–9 AGES 10–14

Unless it's hosting an official event, this awesome BMX dirt course in the South End is open from dawn to dusk for free riding—just remember to bring your helmet and follow the posted rules. Kids interested in racing can do so for free as a one-time trial; being a spectator at the high-energy races, which usually take place Tuesdays, Thursdays, and Saturdays during the spring and summer, is also free.

MOUNTAIN BIKING

Duthie Hill Mountain Bike Park
ISSAQUAH
SE Duthie Hill Rd. and SE Issaquah-Fall City Rd.
206-296-0100
www.kingcounty.gov/services/parks-recreation/parks/trails
/backcountry-trails/duthie-hill.aspx
FREE! AGES 3–5 AGES 6–9 AGES 10–14

Tucked among the evergreens, this 120-acre park beckons mountain-biking fanatics with over 5 miles of dirt trails and accompanying jumps that make their way through the forest. Obstacles range from beginning- to expert-level, and kids can careen through puddles and over gopher hills before stopping to gape at more experienced riders taking on Voodoo Child, a trail with multiple jumps and a tilted velodrome-style wall. (No bike? No prob. Nearby Compass Outdoor Adventures in North Bend not only rents 'em, but will also drop off the selected bike at the park for you; more at www.compassoutdooradventures .com/bikerentals.)

URBAN TRAILS

Alki Trail
WEST SEATTLE
Runs along Harbor Ave. SW and Alki Ave. SW,
starting at West Seattle Bridge
206-684-7623
www.seattle.gov/transportation/alkitrail.htm
FREE! AGES 3–5 AGES 6–9 AGES 10–14

This lovely paved trail follows the shores of Alki Beach around the point to the iconic lighthouse. Park at or near Seacrest Park (or take the water taxi from Downtown Seattle) and then head north for the best family biking; the path there is separated into biking and pedestrian lanes. This pretty path is bustling on nice days, so expect to ride at a leisurely pace, all the better for frequent stops to peer at the surf and sand. Should you be in need, nearby Wheel Fun Rentals (www.wheelfunrentals.com) rents bikes of all styles and sizes from May to October.

Burke-Gilman Trail

RUNS FROM BALLARD THROUGH FREMONT AND THE UNIVERSITY
DISTRICT, TO NORTH SEATTLE AND BOTHELL
206-684-7623
www.seattle.gov/parks/burkegilman/bgtrail.htm

FREE! AGES 3–5 AGES 6–9 AGES 10–14

Mayhap Seattle's most popular trail, this paved path of more than 18 miles goes from Shilshole Bay in Ballard all the way to the North End city of Bothell, where it connects with another lovely bike path, the Sammamish River Trail. Perhaps the most fun segment for kids is the portion from Fremont to the University District, where the awe-inspiring Gas Works Park (page 72) provides for a perfect midride pit stop.

Green Lake Path

GREEN LAKE
7201 E. Green Lake Dr. N
206-684-4075
www.seattle.gov/parks/find/parks/green-lake-park

FREE! AGES 3–5 AGES 6–9 AGES 10–14

Seattleites flock to this beloved park and the accompanying 2.8-mile paved trail that encircles the lake. At this fantastic family spot, little bikers can stop at the playground, brave the wading pool during the summer months, brake for fishing, or watch the goings-on at the ball fields all while en route on the loop.

Myrtle Edwards Park Trail

WATERFRONT
3130 Alaskan Way
206-684-4075
www.seattle.gov/parks/find/parks/myrtle-edwards-park

FREE! AGES 3–5 AGES 6–9 AGES 10–14

Fronting 1.25 miles of Elliott Bay near Downtown Seattle, the Myrtle Edwards Park path connects with the Elliott Bay Trail, which runs all the way to the cruise-ship terminal in Magnolia, should avid bikers be interested in a longer ride. Little tykes will be well entertained with the short route, however, meandering pleasantly between picnic spots and viewpoints. Head south to connect to the 9-acre Olympic Sculpture Park (page 122), which is worth a gander all its own.

LET'S RIDE

If you are looking to form your own biker gang, consider joining in on the monthly **Kidical Mass** rides run by the Familybike organization (www.familybike.org/kidical -mass-seattle). Legions of petite pedalers and their parents take to the city streets and trails to bike together, ringing their bike bells with abandon and in general having a grand ol' time.

RAINY-DAY ROMPING

When Mother Nature ignores pleas of "Rain, rain, go away," get those restless kiddies out of the house with these imaginative play spaces, gaming arcades, and museums.

ARCADES

GameWorks

DOWNTOWN

1511 7th Ave.

206-521-0952

www.gameworks.com

$$ AGES 6-9 AGES 10-14 ☂ ✕ 🎁

With over 180 interactive games, GameWorks draws gamers tall and small to its downtown digs. Game cards run $5–$50, but check the deals on the website for stellar packages, such as the Sunday Family 4-Pack. For $39.99 your crew will receive four one-hour unlimited-play game cards and a large pizza. The arcade also runs early-bird specials—from 10 a.m. to 12 p.m. on weekends, you'll receive a two-hour game card for $15. There's also a bar and big screens for sports fans.

Round 1 Bowling & Amusement

TUKWILA

Contact information on page 17

$-$$ AGES 3-5 AGES 6-9 AGES 10-14 ⏵ ✕ ⛾

From driving games like Mario Kart DX to rhythm and sports games, plus arcade classics like Skee-Ball, the Round 1 arcade has it all. If you plan on staying awhile, it's worth buying a Time Play card to get unlimited play for a chosen amount of time (instead of forking over cash per game). For more information on bowling at Round 1, see page 17.

Seattle Pinball Museum

INTERNATIONAL DISTRICT

508 Maynard Ave. S

206-623-0759

www.seattlepinballmuseum.com

$$ AGES 6-9 AGES 10-14 ⏵ ✕ ⛾

Home to over fifty vintage pinball machines, this quirky little outpost in the ID provides unlimited access to pinballin' for a flat fee (must be age 7 to play; $12 for ages 7-12, and $15 for age 13 and up). Unleash the littles to their clingy-clangy arcade games while you kick back with a craft beer from the in-house snack stand.

CHILDREN'S MUSEUMS

Imagine Children's Museum

EVERETT

1502 Wall St.

425-258-1006

www.imaginecm.org

$ AGES 0-2 AGES 3-5 AGES 6-9 ⏵ 🏃

With three full floors of fun—including a rooftop playground, dress-up theater, and crafty art studio—Imagine Children's Museum, located about forty-five minutes north of Seattle, is a whimsical place to play and learn. Other highlights include the Construction Studio, filled with hard hats and giant foam blocks, and Imagine WaterWorks, where kids can harness the power of water while pumping, stirring, and squirting their way through the exhibit (take heed and corral little ones into a provided smock!). The roof is especially fun on a sunny summer day, with a dino-dig area, musical instruments to bang on as loudly as kids please, and a wicked-good playground. Admission is half off Thursdays from 3 to 5 p.m. (regular admission is $10 and free for babies 12 months and younger).

KidsQuest Children's Museum
BELLEVUE
4091 Factoria Square Mall SE
425-637-8100
www.kidsquestmuseum.org
$ AGES 0-2 AGES 3-5 AGES 6-9 ☂ ✗

This beloved Eastside museum just moved into new digs in downtown Bellevue and now boasts over 13,500 square feet of interactive fun, including water tables and wind tunnels, a tree house complete with dress-up gear, and even a full-size big rig for pretending to be a trucker. The museum also has a sweet play area for kiddos ages 0–3, replete with train tables, a blanket-fort area, and lots of spots for climbing. Don't miss out on $1 admission the third Thursday of every month from 5 to 8 p.m. (regular admission $9.50); babies age 12 months and under are always free.

Seattle Children's Museum
SEATTLE CENTER
305 Harrison St.
206-441-1768
www.thechildrensmuseum.org
$ AGES 0-2 AGES 3-5 AGES 6-9 ☂ ✗

Filled with exploratory playthings, the Seattle Children's Museum is heaven for kids, and especially so for the toddler set. Sprawling over 22,000 square feet, exhibits range from an art studio and pretend eye clinic, where kids can play doc, to the STEM-based cog section and a global village filled with worldly goods, ranging from rickshaws to drums. Recent updates helped upgrade the Bijou Theatre space and make room for two new exhibits: Seattle Boomtown Jr., which recalls the city's pioneer days with a barbershop, smithy, and school; and the Marbleous Museum, which houses an extensive collection of, you guessed it, marbles. Those looking for discounts would do well to visit late in the day; for the last hour of operation on weekdays, the museum offers pay-what-you-can admission (regular admission is $9.25 and free for babies 12 months and younger).

DAY AT THE MUSEUM

Seattle's myriad museums make for great indoor adventures. For art museums, see **You've Been Framed** (page 119). For cultural museums, see **Cross-Cultural Explorations** (page 34). For history museums, see **Time Travel** (page 104). And science museums are found in **Science & Tech** (page 84).

UNIQUE PLAY SPACES

Arena Sports FunZone Inflatable Playground

ISSAQUAH   REDMOND   SAND POINT

2115 NW Poplar Way   *9040 Willows Rd. NE*   *7751 63rd Ave. NE*

425-270-2030   *425-885-4881*   *206-985-8990*

www.arenasports.net/fun-zone-inflatable-playground

$ AGES 3–5 AGES 6–9 AGES 10–14 👕 🏃 🎁

Held at popular indoor soccer centers, Arena Sports FunZones are always jumpin' during drop-in sessions, offering inflatable slides, bounce houses, and obstacle playgrounds. The Redmond location is open Monday through Friday only; the other locations also offer weekend sessions. Admission is $6 per child for members and $9 for nonmembers. (Parents are free.)

Elevated Sportz

BOTHELL

18311 Bothell-Everett Hwy., Suite 140

425-949-4488

www.elevatedsportz.com

$–$$ ALL AGES 👕 🏃 🎁

No other play space caters to every age bracket quite like Elevated Sportz. Located twenty-five minutes north of Seattle, it houses wall-to-wall trampolines as well as jump-on-in foam pits, a dodgeball area, a basketball court for slam-dunking from on high, and a laser-tag maze, in addition to a multilevel play structure for little kiddos. The uber-popular two-hour "Hoppy Hour" special on weekday mornings is nice on the budget, with unlimited playground access for $5 (available for children ages 0–8) or a combo jump-and-play package (must be at least 3 years old to use the trampolines) for $8 (regular admission fees start at $7–$10 per thirty minutes). Elevated Sportz also offers drop-off date nights for 'rents yearning to dine sans kiddos.

Lil Diggers Playtime at Sandbox Sports
GEORGETOWN
5955 Airport Way S
206-624-2899
www.sandboxsports.net/kids-sandbox
$ AGES 0–2 AGES 3–5 🛝 🎠

This indoor sand volleyball facility turns into a rainy-day rescue during the winter months, opening up its huge sandy courts for frolicking Mondays, Wednesdays, and Thursdays from 9:30 to 11 a.m. and then 11:30 a.m. to 1 p.m. Open to kids age 5 and under, Sandbox Sports is stocked with myriad toys and cars for playing; each kid is $7 per ninety-minute session, which is just enough time to ensure those little diggers are worn out for a nap on the drive home.

Roo's World of Discovery
KIRKLAND
108 Central Way
425-495-0714
www.roosworldofdiscovery.com
$-$$ AGES 0–2 AGES 3–5 AGES 6–9 🛝 🍴 🎠

Inspired by her own journey with a preemie, owner Michelle Landwehr opened this lovely play space designed for children with developmental delays and for introverts who have a hard time in the boisterous setting of many children's spots. Featuring a play area with toys and books, as well as a small shopping boutique with kids' goods, Roo's plays peaceful music and provides many of the comforts of home (Bumbo seats in the bathroom, changing areas, and even a special sensory room for overwhelmed kids). Admission is $20 per family for all-day in-and-out privileges; offered at half off for the last two hours of operation each day.

Wunderkind
Bryant
3318 NE 55th St.
206-854-7186
www.wunderkindseattle.com
$ AGES 0-2 AGES 3-5 AGES 6-9 ⬆ ✕ 🍴

Whoever dreamed up Wunderkind must indeed be one. This café/play space caters to both kids and adults, with two floors devoted to Lego-building, as well as a full-blown café offering espresso in the morn and then wine and beer for that five o'clock somewhere. Both the main floor (created for kids age 4 and under) and the second-floor room (built for older Lego fiends) are viewable from the dining tables, where Mom and Dad can attempt to have an adult conversation before caving in to play themselves.

COMMUNITY GATHERING
Many of Seattle Parks and Recreation's community centers offer toddler play gyms and interactive play spaces at a fraction of the cost of private businesses (the average rate is $3 per session). To find the one nearest you, visit www.seattle.gov/parks/children/play.htm.

BOREDOM BEATERS

Combat the dreaded "I'm bored" complaint with a roundup of quirky, zany, and unique activities gathered from all corners of this guidebook.

1. Meet a troll under a bridge (Fremont Troll, page 164).
2. Try on some Handerpants (Archie McPhee, page 118).
3. Ride in an amphibious truck (Ride the Ducks, page 115).
4. Add to the gum wall (Pike Place Market, page 104).
5. Find a hidden city (Underground Tour, page 106).
6. Discover a 44-foot-wide cowboy hat (Oxbow Park, page 231).
7. Visit with an albino alligator (The Reptile Zoo, page 13).
8. Learn to fly high (Emerald City Trapeze Arts, page 94).
9. Play soccer inside a bubble (Seattle Bubble Soccer, page 21).
10. Peer at a 12,000-year-old fossil (Burke Museum, page 106).
11. Feed a kangaroo (Outback Kangaroo Farm, page 12).
12. Inspect a plane factory (Future of Flight Aviation Center & Boeing Tour, page 85).
13. Gaze at "the world's largest collection of giant shoes" (Giant Shoe Museum, page 109).
14. Visit a cat café (Seattle Meowtropolitan, page 13).
15. Slide down a giant salmon (Carkeek Park, page 71).
16. Zip-line through a wildlife park (Zip Wild Challenge Courses, page 95).
17. Race down (free!) dueling zip lines (Fisher Creek Park, page 259).
18. Wave to Mount Rainier from a steam train (Mount Rainier Railroad and Logging Museum, page 270).
19. Visit an Old West mining town (Cle Elum & Roslyn, page 263).
20. Swim in a saltwater pool on the beach (Colman Pool, page 67).

SCIENCE & TECH

From science museums built for poking and prodding to spots dedicated to trains, planes, and automobiles, these kid-ready centers are infused with the techy tone of the city.

SCIENCE

Living Computer Museum
SoDo
2245 1st Ave. S
206-342-2020
www.livingcomputermuseum.org
$ AGES 6–9 AGES 10–14 ☂

This sister museum to the MoPOP offers a fascinating look at the history of the computer, with makes and models dating back to the late 1960s to test out and play on. Kids will be enthralled by the made-for-families BitZone, where they can learn about electrical circuits and binary decoding. Adults may be even more enthralled with the museum's large selection of throwback games (*The Oregon Trail!*). Kids' admission is just $2 (free for those age 5 and under), and adults are $5–plus, the SoDo location makes this a fantastic pre–Mariners game stop.

Pacific Science Center
SEATTLE CENTER
200 2nd Ave. N
206-443-2001
www.pacificsciencecenter.org
$$–$$$ AGES 3–5 AGES 6–9 AGES 10–14 ☂ ✗ ☕

With options for tots on up to tweens, Pacific Science Center is fit for a daylong family exploration, with immersive and interactive exhibits that range from the Tropical Butterfly House and the Insect Village to the poke-and-prod-ready Tinker Tank and the Saltwater Tide Pool. In warmer weather, the museum's wealth of outdoor exhibits truly delights, with water cannons for spraying and even a high-rail bike, elevated 15 feet off the ground. The on-site IMAX theaters are always worth a look (see page 26), as are the awe-inspiring shows in the planetarium. PacSci also frequently plays host to traveling national exhibits, so be sure to investigate the current offerings before your visit.

Theodor Jacobsen Observatory
UNIVERSITY DISTRICT
4324 Memorial Way NE
www.depts.washington.edu/astron/outreach/jacobsen
  -observatory
FREE! AGES 6-9 AGES 10-14

Take your young stargazer over to the University of Washington campus for one of the semimonthly open houses at this historic observatory. Housed in the second-oldest building on campus, the observatory boasts a 120-year-old refracting telescope, which is put to good use for peeks at the stars and neighboring planets during the nighttime sessions, weather permitting. Open houses are held the first and third Wednesday of the month, April through September.

TRANSPORTATION & TECH

Future of Flight Aviation Center & Boeing Tour
MUKILTEO
8415 Paine Field Blvd.
425-438-8100
www.futureofflight.org
$-$$ AGES 6-9 AGES 10-14 ☂

If you've ever been flummoxed by questions about the mysteries of plane flight, here's your chance for redemption. Located at the Boeing factory north of Seattle, this museum chronicles the history of the airplane and the company itself, with interactive exhibits, such as flight systems displays, and a family zone with a kiddie-size airport and plane for playing pretend. Older kids will especially like it here. Those over 4 feet tall can embark on the engaging tour of the factory to see planes in progress. Kids can also design and print their own 3-D models as part of the

Maker Monday program ($5, or free with museum admission; no age stipulation but better suited to age 8 and up). The tours sell out quickly, so book ahead on the website, where you'll score a $1-$2 discount per ticket (usually $20 for adults, $14 for age 15 and under). Prices also drop during the winter months, making this a wonderful wet-day outing.

Hydroplane & Raceboat Museum
KENT

5917 S. 196th St.

206-764-9453

www.thunderboats.org

$ AGES 3–5 AGES 6–9 AGES 10–14 ☂

Located in a tucked-away office park south of Seattle is the nation's only public museum dedicated to powerboat racing. Packed with historic hydros and speedy racers, the museum is led by superpassionate staffers who are always eager to spin tales about the history of each beloved boat. This definitely is a "do touch" spot. Kids can sit in the driver's seats of many boats, see restorations in progress, and sometimes even join in to help.

LeMay—America's Car Museum
TACOMA

2702 E. D St.

253-779-8490

www.americascarmuseum.com

$-$$ AGES 3–5 AGES 6–9 AGES 10–14 🚼 ☂

Great for a day out with the family car buff, the LeMay museum, about an hour south of Seattle in Tacoma, is filled to the brim with automobiles, from classic hot rods and muscle cars to Model Ts and jalopies dating all the way back to 1903. Little speed demons can test their mettle in the racing simulator or take a gander at real-life NASCAR race cars; littler wannabe drivers can take a pretend spin in the convertible at the colorful Family Zone area. Before you speed off, snap a souvenir pic in the 1923 Buick touring car parked out front, as a remembrance of the day.

The Museum of Flight
SOUTH SEATTLE
9404 E. Marginal Way S
206-764-5700
www.museumofflight.org
$$-$$$ AGES 3-5 AGES 6-9 AGES 10-14 🛒 🍦

The Museum of Flight takes looks at the past, present, and future of flight in fascinating detail, from World War I and World War II planes to the NASA training rocket that is the centerpiece of the new Spaceflight Academy exhibit. Kids will be agape at the sheer number of fighter planes, jets, and prop planes displayed in the airy main atrium (be sure to let them sit in the cockpit of the Blackbird recon plane). Once they're ready to move on, set 'em loose in the Flight Zone—where they can test their piloting skills in a hang-gliding simulator—before heading outside to tour the 1959-era plane used as Air Force One, along with other jets.

TAKE A HIKE
Thanks to its natural beauty, Seattle is stocked with stellar hikes (not to mention the sweet walking sticks, epic puddle jumps, and cool fish sightings that come along with 'em).

IN-CITY TRAILS & NATURE CENTERS

Camp Long
WEST SEATTLE
5200 35th Ave. SW
206-684-7434
www.seattle.gov/parks/environment/camplong.htm
FREE! AGES 3-5 AGES 6-9 AGES 10-14

Housed in a charming brick building, the nature center at Camp Long provides stellar nature programming and is also the jumping-off point for the park's rock-climbing classes and ropes course. This tucked-away 68-acre park is filled with trails and even has cabins for rent (campout!).

Discovery Park

MAGNOLIA

3801 Discovery Park Blvd.

206-386-4236

www.seattle.gov/parks/environment/discovery.htm

FREE! AGES 3-5 AGES 6-9 AGES 10-14 🏃

The Environmental Learning Center (ELC) is just one of the educational spots to stop within Discovery Park, Seattle's largest city park. Allow kids to soak up some nature know-how at the center, then ask one of the informative guides to delve into a quick history of the park. Part of it sits on the site of a former military base, Fort Lawton; outbuildings and officers' quarters remain. With waterfront and woods, meadows and gullies, there is no shortage of spots to explore here. Pick up the 2.8-mile Loop Trail from the ELC. It winds through forests and bluffs before offering gorgeous Sound views near the end.

Schmitz Preserve Park

WEST SEATTLE

5551 SW Admiral Way

206-684-4075

www.seattle.gov/parks/find/parks/schmitz-preserve-park

FREE! AGES 3-5 AGES 6-9

This little-known nature preserve is home to one of the largest old-growth forests in the city, making for fantastic shadowy and shaded hiking. With 1.7 miles of trails that cut diagonally across the park and bound over creeks and streams, this splash-filled saunter is a great one for little kids. A massive "alligator" (a fallen and split tree cleverly painted with scales, teeth, and the like) is just waiting to be discovered along the way.

Seward Park

SEWARD PARK

5900 Lake Washington Blvd. S

206-684-4396

www.seattle.gov/parks/environment/seward.htm

FREE! ALL AGES 🛒 🏃

Bordered by Lake Washington on three sides and boasting one of the most magnificent urban forests you'll ever see, Seward Park offers many walking and hiking trails, including a 2.4-mile paved loop that is oh-so-stroller-friendly. The on-site Environmental Learning Center is home to an Audubon center, as the wild and lush park is known for its collection of birds, including the bald eagles who like to nest here. The center also offers a Toddler Tales & Trails session every Wednesday and Saturday morning featuring a story time followed by a nature walk, plus a Friday evening Owl Prowl for adults and kids age 10 and up to search for the resident owls.

Warren G. Magnuson Park
SAND POINT
7400 Sand Point Way NE
206-684-4946
www.seattle.gov/parks/find/parks/magnuson-park
FREE! ALL AGES 🚶

Magnuson Nature Programs, a fantastic nonprofit dedicated to helping individuals and families explore nature in this equally fantastic 350-acre park, offers guided family nature hikes that focus on different areas of the park, including a wetland walk and a nighttime tour ($3 per person, kids age 2 and under are free). If you venture out on your own, be sure to stop at the Magnuson Community Center (7110 62nd Ave. NE) to pick up an Explorer Pack ($5 per day), full of exploration tools, books, and tips for a fun-filled day; choose either the bird-watching adventure tote or the wetlands discovery pack, and then it's off to adventure.

> **AND SO MUCH MORE**
> Seattle Parks and Recreation maintains thousands of miles of trails within its myriad parks; for more urban hiking ideas, visit www.seattle.gov/parks/trails.asp.

Audubon BirdLoop at Marymoor Park

REDMOND

6046 West Lake Sammamish Pkwy. NE
King County Parks Dept.: 206-477-4527;
 Eastside Audubon: 425-576-8805
www.eastsideaudubon.org/conservation/audubon-birdloop-at
 -marymoor-park
FREE! AGES 3–5 AGES 6–9 🚶

This flat 2-mile loop near the off-leash dog area in Marymoor Park is home to thousands of tweety birds, making for a fun bird-watching expedition. Traipse through the grassy meadow, then follow the trail along the river before heading through lush forest dubbed the Mysterious Thicket—the name alone should inspire a game of hide-and-seek or two.

Bridle Trails State Park

KIRKLAND

5300 116th Ave. NE
425-649-4275
www.parks.state.wa.us/481/bridle-trails
FREE! AGES 3–5 AGES 6–9 AGES 10–14

Don't be surprised if you hear a few neighs if you take a hike along the 28 miles of well-maintained paths within Bridle Trails. Frequented by riders and their equine friends, this 482-acre state park is lush with cool shade on a hot summer's day. There are three marked trails within the park—the 1-mile Raven Trail, 1.7-mile Trillium Trail, and 3.5-mile Coyote Trail—all of which are little-leg-friendly and begin at a central junction near the parking lot. (Bridle Trails is free to enjoy, but like all state-run spots, you'll need to pay to park.)

Cougar Mountain Regional Wildland Park

BELLEVUE

18201 SE Cougar Mountain Dr.
206-296-0100
www.kingcounty.gov/services/parks-recreation/parks/parks
 -and-natural-lands.aspx
FREE! AGES 6–9 AGES 10–14

Spanning more than 3,100 acres, Cougar Mountain Regional Wildland Park calls to hikers and bikers, offering stunning views of old-growth forest, cascading waterfalls, and mossy caves. Head to any of the four main trailheads and poke about, or set off for Coal Creek Falls, one of the best hikes for kiddos, at 2.5 gently sloping miles. Park at the trailhead for the Red Town Trail—off Lakemont Boulevard SE in Bellevue—then walk from there to connect to the Cave Hole Trail and on down to the falls. (Just follow the crowds!)

Franklin Falls Trail

SNOQUALMIE

Trailhead located on Denny Creek FS Rd. 58

www.fs.usda.gov/recarea/mbs/recreation
   /recarea/?recid=17980&actid=50

FREE! AGES 3-5 AGES 6-9 AGES 10-14

The gorgeous waterfalls about 1 mile into this 2-mile loop are the main draw here, but kids will also be flabbergasted by the wagon-wheel ruts made by pioneers that run alongside the trail. The short, rocky descent to the falls can be slippery, so hang tight to especially wiggly kids.

Mercer Slough Nature Park

BELLEVUE

2102 Bellevue Way SE

425-452-6885

parkstrails.myparksandrecreation.com/details.aspx?pid=471

FREE! ALL AGES 🛒

Nestled in the heart of Bellevue, the 320-acre Mercer Slough Nature Park offers a variety of recreational fun, from hiking and biking to blueberry picking and even guided canoe tours. The asphalt Periphery Trail, which outlines the perimeter of the park, is ideal for the stroller set. If you happen to hike to the east side of the park, don't miss stepping into the Mercer Slough Environmental Education Center, which offers great insight into the wetlands and even has a tree house.

Saint Edward State Park

KENMORE

14445 Juanita Dr. NE

425-823-2992

www.parks.state.wa.us/577/saint-edward

FREE! AGES 3-5 AGES 6-9 AGES 10-14 🏃

Once a Catholic seminary, Saint Edward boasts 3,000 feet of undeveloped Lake Washington waterfront and 316 acres of woodland, meadows, and beaches to explore, plus a fantastic classic wooden playground. Stroll over to the historic main building before picking up the #4 Seminary Trail, which winds its way down, steeply at times, to the beach below. Your hard work will be rewarded by stunning lake views and sometimes even an otter sighting.

Twin Falls Trail

NORTH BEND

Trailhead located at the end of SE 159th St.

425-455-7010

www.parks.state.wa.us/555/olallie

FREE! AGES 3-5 AGES 6-9 AGES 10-14

This hike, at Olallie State Park, is one of almost instant gratification—no grumblings of "Are we there yet?" here—as the beautiful route to Twin Falls follows the south fork of the Snoqualmie River for just a mile before climbing up to the viewpoint of the lower falls, which plunge with impressive force over a 135-foot-high cliff. After oohing and aahing for a few minutes, hike the extra quarter mile up to the bridge that spans the canyon and offers views of the upper falls.

SALMON-SPAWNING STOPS

Bear Creek

WOODINVILLE

Tolt Pipeline at Mink Rd. NE, between NE 148th St. and NE 150th St.

www.govlink.org/watersheds

FREE! AGES 3-5 AGES 6-9 AGES 10-14

For a few magical weeks each fall, the salmon return from the sea and head upstream to spawn. Turn your next autumn hike into a salmon-spotting mission: take a picturesque half-mile hike up Tolt Pipeline Trail to peer into Bear Creek to spot the fish beginning to run upstream as early as September.

Longfellow Creek
WEST SEATTLE
28th Ave. SW and SW Dakota St.
www.govlink.org/watersheds
FREE! AGES 3–5 AGES 6–9 AGES 10–14

Salmon love this 4-mile-long creek from October to December every year; stroll along the pedestrian path and see how many you can spot.

Insider tip: Those salmon love to hide under bridges.

Piper's Creek at Carkeek Park
BROADVIEW
950 NW Carkeek Park Rd.
www.govlink.org/watersheds
FREE! AGES 3–5 AGES 6–9 AGES 10–14

At this beloved park, trained "salmon stewards" are on hand every weekend in November and December to answer questions about the coho and chum salmon that make their way up the creek.

THRILLS & CHILLS
From Ferris wheels and go-cart tracks to zip lines and snowy sledding hills, these scream-worthy spots are sure to satisfy your darling daredevil's rush.

ADVENTURE THRILLS

Bellevue Zip Tour
BELLEVUE
14500 SE Newport Way
425-452-6885
www.bellevueziptour.com
$$$ AGES 10–14

With seven different zip lines that range in length from 78 to 458 feet, Bellevue Zip Tour allows kids age 9 and up to go wild amid the wooded canopy of Eastgate Park. Open seasonally, from April to late fall, the tour traverses two suspension bridges, with zip liners reaching speeds up to 35 miles an hour as they're suspended 80 feet aboveground. But it's all very safety-conscious, with a pretour safety session and guides at the ready during the two-and-a-half-hour adventure; youth ages 9–17 are $49 per session, adults $78.

Insider tip: Zip liners ages 9–13 must be accompanied by an adult chaperone.

Emerald City Trapeze Arts
SoDo
2702 6th Ave. S
206-906-9442
www.emeraldcitytrapeze.com
$$$ AGES 6–9 AGES 10–14 🤸

You'll fly through the air with the greatest of ease after just one lesson at Emerald City Trapeze Arts. Kids and adults alike flock to this unique 20,000-square-foot circus arts gym in SoDo, which is fully equipped with a towering trapeze and an expansive catching net. The two-hour beginners' class is open to anyone age 6 and up (250-pound weight limit applies). Students receive a fifteen- to twenty-minute ground tutorial before suiting up to attempt a "knee hang"; once mastered, they can even try a "catch" with one of the instructors, an achievement that is celebrated with the ringing of the gym's cowbell. (If your little trapeze artist develops a fever for more cowbell, the gym also offers circus camps.)

iFly Indoor Skydiving
TUKWILA
349 Tukwila Pkwy.
206-244-4359
www.iflyworld.com
$$$ AGES 3–5 AGES 6–9 AGES 10–14 🤸 🎪

If your little one is keen to jump off couches, beds, and . . . pretty much everything else, head to iFly for an indoor "skydiving" experience like no other. Flyers head into a vertical wind tunnel that simulates the feeling of freefall skydiving, but from a parent-friendly mere feet off the ground. Funny and fun, iFly offers family packages—up to five people can share ten flights for $303. Packages include flight gear, a predive safety session, and a personalized certificate for kids to take home for bragging rights. You must be at least 3 years old to take the leap.

Zip Wild Challenge Courses

EATONVILLE

11610 Trek Dr. E

360-832-6117

www.nwtrek.org/zipwild

$$$ AGES 6–9 AGES 10–14

Crisscrossing through Northwest Trek Wildlife Park's lush tree canopy, Zip Wild offers four different zip-line courses for your Tarzan or Jane, with a Super Kid Course ($21.95 per child) that offers thrills for kids as young as age 5. With elements such as a 30-foot-tall climbing wall, suspended bridges, and cargo nets, other courses boast such daunting challenges as a high-wire tightrope walk and zip lines that have riders traveling as fast as 33 feet per second. For more on the wildlife park, see page 10.

AMUSEMENT PARKS & RIDES

The Seattle Great Wheel

WATERFRONT

1301 Alaskan Way

206-623-8607

www.seattlegreatwheel.com

$-$$ AGES 3–5 AGES 6–9 ✖

Since opening in 2012, the Seattle Great Wheel has quickly become a key landmark, thanks to its picture-perfect spot on Pier 57. The 175-foot-tall Ferris wheel extends 40 feet past the end of the pier, over Elliott Bay, lending itself to truly spectacular views of both city and Sound. The fifteen- to twenty-minute ride includes three revolutions of the wheel, with gorgeous LEDs lighting up the attraction at night. Kids age 3 and under are free, with kids 4–10 priced at $8.50. Adult fare runs $13 each.

Wild Waves & Enchanted Village
FEDERAL WAY
36201 Enchanted Pkwy. S
253-661-8000
www.wildwaves.com
$-$$$ AGES 3–5 AGES 6–9 AGES 10–14 🛒 ✕ 🎪

Make a splash at these neighboring amusement parks: Enchanted Village is packed with wicked coasters, while Wild Waves features waterslides that start from on high—so much so that they can be spotted from the I-5 freeway, prompting countless "Can we stop, puh-lease?" queries from young travelers. Open seasonally May through September, the water park includes a lazy river and swimming lagoon, in addition to slides like Zooma Falls, which adventurers plunge down in inflatable rafts. Enchanted Village boasts an antique carousel, bumper cars, a kiddie coaster, and the largest wooden roller coaster in the state, the Timberhawk Ride of Prey. Tickets vary widely, but in general start at $9.99 for kids under 48 inches tall for the amusement park only ($19.99 for those over 48 inches); packages for a day pass to both parks start at $19.99 for kids under 48 inches ($39.99 for those over 48 inches); kids age 3 and under are free. Season passes and discount packages are available on the website.

GO, GO, GO-CARTS

K1 Speed
REDMOND
2207 NE Bel-Red Rd.
425-455-9999
www.k1speed.com
$$ AGES 6–9 AGES 10–14

For $19.99, junior racers 4 feet tall and up can "arrive and drive" at this indoor speed track outfitted with kid-size carts that reach speeds of 20 miles an hour. (PS: Parents can even shoot pool in between races.) Offered seven days a week during regular business hours, each race lasts about ten minutes; helmets and safety equipment included in price.

Sykart Indoor Racing Center
TUKWILA
17450 W. Valley Hwy.
425-251-5060
www.sykart.com
$$ AGES 6–9 AGES 10–14

The youth track is open to kids age 8 and up for the six-minute race sessions ($12 each) available from 12 to 8 p.m. Friday through Sunday at this high-octane spot complete with a larger adult track and a retro-style café.

Traxx Indoor Raceway
MUKILTEO
4329 Chennault Beach Rd.
425-493-8729
www.traxxracing.com
$–$$$ AGES 3–5 AGES 6–9 AGES 10–14

Kids as young as age 3 can get in on the action at the specially outfitted kids' track ($7–$9 per session depending on age and cart); kids age 11 and over can race around the adult track ($15–$35). Psst—kids who bring in an "A" report card receive half-off pricing Monday through Thursday.

ICE & ROLLER RINKS

Highland Ice Arena
SHORELINE
18005 Aurora Ave. N
206-546-2431
www.highlandice.com
$–$$ AGES 3–5 AGES 6–9 AGES 10–14

This family-owned ice rink is a hot spot for figure skaters and hockey players, as well as birthday and broomball parties. Head to an open session on a Sunday and get the whole crew in for

$16.50 total with the family special; otherwise, public sessions run $6.50–$7.50 per person plus $4 for skate rental (kids under age 6 are free). Now, get out there and stick that double axel.

Lynnwood Bowl & Skate
LYNNWOOD
Contact information on page 16
$-$$ AGES 3–5 AGES 6–9 AGES 10–14 🎁 🎪

This affable bowling alley/roller rink is ever abustle on rainy weekends. Open skating sessions (complete with kid-friendly music blaring) are held all weekend long, with a Saturday midday Learn to Skate session for beginners, plus a late-night, teen-friendly open skate on Wednesday (6–9 p.m.), Friday (7:30–11 p.m.) and Saturday (also 7:30–11 p.m.) evenings.

Sno-King Ice Arenas

KIRKLAND
14326 124th Ave. NE
425-821-7133
www.snokingkirkland.com

RENTON
12620 164th Ave. SE
425-254-8750
www.snokingrenton.com

$-$$ AGES 3–5 AGES 6–9 AGES 10–14 🎁 🎪

Skate to your heart's content at these well-regarded rinks, which play host to ice-skating lessons and hockey matches in addition to open skates. The latter run $6–$8 per person on weekends with cheaper rates on weekdays. "Walkers" are available for $4 each for little skaters just learning to glide. The arenas also offer a one-hour Try Hockey Free class, in which kids ages 4–9 are given a lesson in hockey basics (they'll be shootin' goals in no time).

SNOWBOARDING & DOWNHILL SKIING

Crystal Mountain Resort
CRYSTAL MOUNTAIN
33914 Crystal Mountain Blvd.
888-754-6199
www.crystalmountainresort.com
$$$ AGES 3–5 AGES 6–9 AGES 10–14

A mere two-hour drive from Seattle, Crystal Mountain feels worlds away. With 2,600 skiable snowcapped acres, it's the biggest ski resort in the state. Daily passes are $48 for kids ages 11–15 to roam the slopes, and adults run $72, but little skiers age 10 and under are completely free. In addition to over fifty named runs, Crystal offers scenic gondola tours (wave hi to Mount Rainier as you ascend; the view is incredible on sunny days) and the ever-popular Sasquatch Terrain Park, where adrenaline junkies can shred it among such features as rails, tubes, boxes, and jumps.

Mount Baker Ski Area
DEMING
Mount Baker Hwy.
360-734-6771
www.mtbaker.us
$$$ AGES 3–5 AGES 6–9 AGES 10–14

Just about everyone loves Mount Baker Ski Area, the state's snowiest ski resort located about two and a half hours north of Seattle, but parents of 5th graders especially so. Enroll your 5th grader on the website, and he or she will enjoy free admission to Baker all season long. Kids under age 6 can also enjoy their own discount via the Powder Pups program in which they are admitted for free and up to four registered accompanying adults can ski for half price ($29) right alongside 'em. (Don't worry. Even if you didn't plan ahead to score the parental discount, kiddos under age 6 ski for free every day anyways.)

Stevens Pass
SKYKOMISH
Summit Stevens Pass, US 2
206-812-4510
www.stevenspass.com
$$$ AGES 3–5 AGES 6–9 AGES 10–14

Rip it up at Stevens Pass, about two hours east of Seattle. Adventurous little skiers can join the Kids Club for the day and pal around with other snow bunnies ages 3–6 during a group skiing session offered by the ski and snowboard school. Don't worry, older sibs, there's a place for you too—the Adventure Club for 7- to 12-year-olds is suited to bunny hillers and highfliers alike. (All kids' programs run $59–$129, available as half- or full-day sessions, rental equipment not included; do note that Stevens also offers a free ski program for 5th graders.)

The Summit at Snoqualmie
SNOQUALMIE PASS
1001 SR 906
425-434-7669
www.summitatsnoqualmie.com
$$$ AGES 3–5 AGES 6–9 AGES 10–14

With four base areas to choose from, plus a Nordic center (opposite page) and a tubing hill (page 103), the Summit at Snoqualmie has just about every snow sport covered. Only an hour from Seattle, the mountain offers many beginner and intermediate trails, as well as back bowls and lit terrain for night skiing. Kids age 6 and under ski for a flat $12 rate, while youth tickets (ages 7–12) range from $38 (for night skiing) to $45 (for a full day).

White Pass
NACHES
48935 US 12
509-672-3100
www.skiwhitepass.com
$$$ AGES 3–5 AGES 6–9 AGES 10–14

In addition to the cross-country trails for skiing and snowshoeing (page 102), White Pass offers plenty of runs for boarders and skiers too, with runs that feature stop-and-snap-a-photo views of nearby Mount Rainier. White Pass also offers childcare for kids ages 2–6 ($15 per hour) while the 'rents ski; through that same childcare center, kiddos can also participate in the PeeWee Skee session, an hour-long snow-play and introductory ski program offered for $15. Lift tickets range from $42 (half day) to $63 (full day) for adults, and $29–$43 for junior skiers ages 7–15; kids 6 and under are $5.

SNOWSHOEING & CROSS-COUNTRY SKIING

Snoqualmie Nordic Center
SNOQUALMIE PASS
1001 SR 906
425-434-7669
www.summitatsnoqualmie.com/mountains/nordic
$$ AGES 6–9 AGES 10–14

Located at the Summit at Snoqualmie (opposite page), the Snoqualmie Nordic Center offers not only more than 30 miles of groomed trails for traversing, but also equipment rentals and flat teaching areas where kiddies can get the hang of skiing or 'shoeing before setting off. Multiweek classes are available—the four-week Treasure Trails course is crafted especially for 4- to 6-year-olds—or 'rents and kids age 10 and up can partake in a one-day weekend tutorial for a quick introduction to cross-country ($69 each; private lessons available for younger kids beginning at age 3); day passes to use the trails range from $16 to $21; kids under age 5 are free.

Stevens Pass Nordic Center
SKYKOMISH
Summit Stevens Pass, US 2
206-812-4510
www.stevenspass.com/site/mountain/nordic
$$ ALL AGES

Located about 5 miles beyond the Stevens Pass alpine resort, the Nordic Center maintains over 17 miles of picturesque cross-country and snowshoeing trails, many of which are designated as "beginner level" (try the Main Line trail—it has benches for snack breaks). The center also offers private and group classes to kids as young as 5 and even rents pulks (specially outfitted sleds with runners that parents can tow) so you can bring baby along too. Day passes for adults run $20, while kids ages 7–15 are $15; kids under age 6 are free.

White Pass Nordic Center
NACHES
48935 US 12
509-672-3100
www.skiwhitepass.com/the-mountain/nordic-center.asp
$$ AGES 6-9 AGES 10-14

Open Thursday through Sunday during the winter season, the beautifully groomed trails at White Pass, located about a two-and-a-half-hour drive from Seattle, are fantastic for little nature lovers. Surrounded by the majestic Wenatchee and Gifford Pinchot forests, the center maintains over 11 miles of trails in varying difficulties. Beginners would do well to take the Introduction to Nordic Skiing group lessons on offer; $52 covers a lesson, equipment rentals, and a day pass (offered for anyone age 5 and over). Day passes on their own run $15.

TUBING & SLEDDING

Hyak Sno-Park
SNOQUALMIE PASS
Exit 54 off 1-90 E; follow signs
509-656-2230
www.parks.state.wa.us/647/snow-play-sno-parks
FREE! AGES 3-5 AGES 6-9 AGES 10-14

This state park boasts glorious hills groomed up to five times a week. It's one uber-popular stop, so best to get there early; sledding is free, but parking in the lot requires a Sno-Park permit, which runs $20 per day.

Paradise Snowplay Area
ASHFORD
Near Henry M. Jackson Visitor Center, close to 98368 Paradise-
   Longmire Rd.
www.visitrainier.com/snowplay-area-at-paradise-mt-rainier
   -national-park-sledding-inner-tubing
FREE! AGES 3-5 AGES 6-9 AGES 10-14

This park-ranger-patrolled sledding hill located near the visitor center's upper parking lot is always bustling, and it's no surprise since it's the only official sledding hill in Mount Rainier National Park. (Sledding is free, but a parking fee applies, as in all national parks; "soft" sleds only.)

Summit Tubing Center
SNOQUALMIE PASS
1001 SR 906
425-434-6791
www.summitatsnoqualmie.com/mountains/tubing
$$$ AGES 3–5 AGES 6–9 AGES 10–14

This twelve-lane hill about an hour from Seattle features football-field-length runs plus a tow to make your ascent back up perfectly painless. Tickets for a two-hour session are $5 for kids age 5 and under, $20–$22 for kids ages 6–12, and $22–$24 for adults and teens.

Tubing Park at Leavenworth Ski Hill
LEAVENWORTH
10701 Ski Hill Dr.
www.skileavenworth.com/activities/tubing-ski-hill
$$$ AGES 3–5 AGES 6–9 AGES 10–14

For $20 a person you can unleash the whole crew on the 100-foot tubing hill here, which tends to get snow earlier in the season than the Seattle-area ski resorts. (Leavenworth is about a two-hour drive from Seattle. Find more on this charming town in Weekend Trips, page 268.)

TIME TRAVEL

Step back in time and relive Seattle's journey from pioneer town to tech center with the city's fascinating array of landmark attractions and historical museums.

AWESOME ATTRACTIONS

Hiram M. Chittenden Locks

BALLARD

3015 NW 54th St.

206-783-7059

www.nws.usace.army.mil/home.aspx

FREE! AGES 3-5 AGES 6-9 AGES 10-14

Built in 1917 by the US Army Corp of Engineers, the locks are sure to impress engineers both professional and aspiring. The locks help move boat traffic between Lake Washington and the Sound, which are at different elevations. Boats float on in before being locked in the tank, and then the water level is adjusted—by as much as 22 feet—so they can sail out the other side. The entire process is a spectacle, with kids able to go from one set of locks to another via the over-the-water walkways and also visit the salmon ladder, located on the south side.

Insider tip: The salmon run anywhere from mid-June to October.

Pike Place Market

DOWNTOWN

Main entrance at 1st Ave. and Pike St.

206-682-7453

www.pikeplacemarket.org

FREE! AGES 3-5 AGES 6-9 AGES 10-14

Pike Place Market is one of the oldest continuously operating farmers' markets in the country, having opened on August 17, 1907. For further information on exploring this local treasure, see the full listing in To Market, to Market on page 108.

Smith Tower Observation Deck

PIONEER SQUARE

506 2nd Ave.

206-622-3131

www.smithtower.com

$-$$ AGES 3-5 AGES 6-9 AGES 10-14 ✕

Having recently emerged from an extensive renovation, the circa 1914 Smith Tower, once the tallest building in the West, offers up gorgeous water and city views, as well as peeks at Mount Rainier from its thirty-fifth-story observation deck. Step from the gleaming elevators into the Chinese Room, where kids can take a gander at old newspaper reels with stories about the tower's construction and then sit in the Wishing Chair for good luck before heading outside to the viewing deck. This jaunt is cheaper than a ride up the Space Needle, plus here you'll actually get a view *of* the Needle itself.

Space Needle

SEATTLE CENTER

400 Broad St.

206-905-2100

www.spaceneedle.com

$$-$$$ AGES 3-5 AGES 6-9 AGES 10-14 ⚲ ✕

Designed as the futuristic beacon for the 1962 World's Fair, the Space Needle *is* Seattle, drawing tourists and locals alike up 520 feet to its 360-degree observation deck. Be sure to squeeze in next to a window for the forty-one-second elevator ride, and watch as people, places, and things grow smaller and smaller as you ascend. Once you reach the top, the wraparound deck offers views of Queen Anne Hill to the north, Downtown to the south, Lake Union and Capitol Hill to the east, and, of course, that shimmering Sound and all its boat traffic to the west. Tickets range from $14 for kids ages 5–12 to $22 for adults; each comes with a specific "launch" time. Discount tickets are often available packaged with admission to other local sites, such as the Chihuly Garden and Glass museum (page 121); your trip is on the house should you be dining in the SkyCity restaurant up top (page 247).

Underground Tour

PIONEER SQUARE

614 1st Ave.

206-682-4646

www.undergroundtour.com

$-$$ AGES 6-9 AGES 10-14 ✖

Head underneath the city streets for a fascinating look at Seattle's past by partaking in Bill Speidel's Underground Tour in Pioneer Square, one of the oldest neighborhoods in the city. The first incarnation of the neighborhood was destroyed in the great fire of 1889—and the new construction was built right over the top, preserving approximately twenty-five blocks of historical artifacts and trinkets underground. Kids will love the eerie appeal of the ninety-minute tour, which descends into tunnels under the modern-day sidewalks, with the quippy guides pointing out such fascinating finds as old storefronts, building foundations, and . . . a bathroom complete with an antique toilet. (Let the potty jokes commence.)

HISTORICAL MUSEUMS

Burke Museum of Natural History and Culture

UNIVERSITY DISTRICT

4331 Memorial Way NE

206-543-7907

www.burkemuseum.org

FREE! $ AGES 3-5 AGES 6-9 AGES 10-14 ✦ ✖

Free for all and open late the first Thursday of every month (regular admission is $10 for adults, $7.50 for kids ages 5-18, free for tykes ages 0-4), the Burke Museum is a treasure trove for aspiring archaeologists, featuring such finds as the first dinosaur fossil discovered in the state and a 12,000-year-old giant ground sloth fossil, found during the construction of Sea-Tac Airport. The museum is set to get even more interesting in years to come, with a new building slated to open in 2019. It will feature the Burke's most high-profile find to date: the 8.5-foot-long mammoth tusk unearthed at a South Lake Union construction site in 2014.

Klondike Gold Rush National Historical Park
PIONEER SQUARE
319 2nd Ave. S
206-220-4240
www.nps.gov/klse
FREE! AGES 3–5 AGES 6–9 AGES 10–14 ☂ ✗

This hidden gem of a museum is actually a national historical park and thus is always free for everyone. Kids will get caught up in gold fever as they explore Seattle's role in the rush of the late 1890s, aided by such gander-worthy sights as a replica prospector's cabin, historic mining equipment, and a scale that tells what your weight would be worth in gold. The friendly park rangers are superinformative and love to chat with kids; little ones can even become junior rangers. Ask for a booklet at the front desk, then hunt around the museum to complete the activities before returning the finished booklet in exchange for a ranger badge.

Museum of History & Industry (MOHAI)
SOUTH LAKE UNION
860 Terry Ave. N
206-324-1126
www.mohai.org
FREE! AGES 3–5 AGES 6–9 AGES 10–14 ☂ ✗

Kids age 14 and under are always free at MOHAI, and everyone is admitted sans charge on the first Thursday of every month. Further aiding the interactive and immersive exhibits that honor Seattle's history—which range from a working periscope in the maritime exhibit to a multimedia show that walks guests through the city's 1889 fire—are MOHAI's fantastic Exploration Packs, filled with activities, puzzles, books, and more, to help kids explore the museum (available in two age ranges, 3–7 and 7–10).

TO MARKET, TO MARKET

Offering berries to munch and veggies to crunch, Seattle's seasonal and year-round farmers' markets stem from the granddaddy of them all—the 110-year-old Pike Place Market.

THE ALL-TIME CLASSIC

Pike Place Market
DOWNTOWN
Contact information on page 104
FREE! AGES 3–5 AGES 6–9 AGES 10–14 ✖

Outside of the Space Needle there is probably no more iconic symbol of the city than Pike Place Market. A must-stop on any traveler's or resident's bucket list, the Market is home to a wealth of fruit and produce stands; locally grown flowers; a crafts market; specialty food shops, such as Italian grocer DeLaurenti and the famous Beecher's Handmade Cheese (with its glorious mac 'n' cheese—see page 234); and enough delis, cafés, and restaurants to keep a family munching for years. While you could easily spend weeks exploring every nook and cranny, here is a roundup of the top ten not-to-be missed sights for tykes.

1. **Pic with a Pig:** Near the front entrance to the Market, the iconic 550-pound bronze piggy bank called Rachel is perfect for climbing; clamber on up and say "cheese" for the camera. (Any spare change you drop in benefits the Pike Place Market Foundation.)
2. **Flinging Fish:** It wouldn't be a proper visit without seeing fish fly through the air and into the arms of the personable and funny fishmongers. Other fish stalls may be flinging, but Pike Place Fish Market (located right next to Rachel) is known for it.
3. **Comic Book Trove:** Tucked among the lower-level shops is one of the oldest comic shops in the United States, Golden Age Collectables, which is sure to bring out everyone's inner kid with its extensive collection of comics, toys, and games.
4. **Believe in Magic:** Also on the lower level, the kooky Market Magic & Novelty Shop is any budding magician's dream,

chock-full of novelty and gag gifts as well as magic tricks and props. While you're there, hop across the hall to the Giant Shoe Museum to pop some quarters into the exhibit; curtains roll back to reveal some truly ginormous kicks.

5. **First of Its Kind:** Yes, the first Starbucks ever is found in Pike Place Market. And though it doesn't boast any particularly unique features, it's still worth popping in for a drink just to boast you did.

6. **Cinnamon Heaven:** Take a break for a delicious (and gigantic) cookie from the case at Cinnamon Works. From snickerdoodles to cinnamon rolls, plus fantastic gluten-free and vegan options, the baked goods here have been delighting little cookie monsters for decades.

7. **Crafts Time:** On any given day, the crafts market, which is tucked at the north end of the main level, contains all sorts of locally made goods, from jewelry and pottery to paintings, toys, and puzzles.

8. **Cheese Please:** The aforementioned macaroni and cheese at Beecher's Handmade Cheese, across the street from the crafts market, is indeed divine, but so are the (free!) cheese samples. Snag a cube and let the kids press up against the tall glass windows to watch the cheese making in process.

9. **Eat Your Veggies:** Hand out a couple bucks and allow little shoppers to snag some fresh berries or crisp vegetables from one of the myriad produce stands.

10. **Doughnuts:** As you wrap up your visit, snag a paper bag filled with a dozen hot mini doughnuts from the Daily Dozen Doughnut Co., located a stone's throw from Rachel and the flying fish. Order the cinnamon-sugar flavor so kids can shake, shake, shake that bag all the way back to the car.

Contact information for all the above activities and businesses can be found at www.pikeplacemarket.org.

NEIGHBORHOOD FAVORITES

Ballard Farmers Market

Ballard Ave. NW between Vernon Pl. NW and 22nd Ave. NW
www.sfmamarkets.com/visit-ballard-farmers-market

FREE! ALL AGES ♿ ✕

This charming market, along Ballard Avenue NW on Sundays year-round, features a beautiful array of fresh produce, as well as stellar organic sausages from the folks at Skagit River Ranch, fresh farmstead eggs, and honey from local apiaries. Among the vendors, the team from neighborhood favorite Veraci Pizza (page 239) can often be found slinging pizzas from a portable wood-burning oven, so snag a slice for the kids and saunter on.

Columbia City Neighborhood Farmers Market

37th Ave. S and S. Edmunds St., just off Rainier Ave. S
206-547-2278
www.seattlefarmersmarkets.org/markets/columbia-city

FREE! ALL AGES ♿ ✕

An easy jaunt from Downtown by hopping on the light rail, this market—held every Wednesday afternoon May to October—provides a delightful excuse to explore this charming South End neighborhood (for tips, see guide on page 158) in between picking up fresh or smoked salmon, creamy goat cheese from Tieton Farm & Creamery, and maybe a few Jonboy caramels for the little sweeties in tow.

Fremont Sunday Market

3410 Evanston Ave. N
www.fremontmarket.com

FREE! ALL AGES ♿ ✕

This sprawling year-round Sunday market houses up to two hundred vendors on any given week. It's blissfully at home in funky Fremont, offering farm-fresh fare in addition to antiques and flea market finds, artisan crafts, and funny collectibles.

University District Farmers Market
University Way NE between NE 50th St. and 52nd St.
206-547-2278
www.seattlefarmersmarkets.org/markets/u-district
FREE! ALL AGES 🛒 ✖

Held Saturday year-round come rain or shine, this market
near UW is a veritable cornucopia of people, who mill about
the historic Ave as vendors tout everything from cucumbers to
chrysanthemums. Now in its twenty-fourth year, the market has
seventy-plus vendors and offers a summertime food court and
kids' activities.

Wallingford Farmers Market
Meridian Ave. N and N. 50th St.
www.sfmamarkets.com/visit-wallingford-farmers-market
FREE! ALL AGES 🛒 ✖

Located in the middle of gorgeous tree-filled Meridian Park, the
Wallingford Farmers Market—operating Wednesdays, May to
September—is exceedingly family-friendly. After checking out
the produce stands, let the kids loose on the playground before
peeking at Tilth Alliance's original Children's Garden, which will
be abloom with fruit trees, giant kiwi vines, and vegetables.

PLUS A WHOLE LOT MORE
This list is just the tip of the iceberg lettuce when it
comes to the many markets the city and neighboring
towns have to offer: **www.seattlefarmersmarkets.org**,
www.sfmamarkets.com, and **www.pugetsoundfresh**
.org/markets are all fantastic resources for finding one
near you.

TOUR DE SEATTLE

These favorites offer up landmarks by land *and* by sea. Hop on a sweet emerald-green trolley, hop aboard a boat or kayak, or just hop, skip, and stroll along on a walking tour.

BY LAND

Emerald City Trolley

SEATTLE CENTER

Meets outside MoPOP, 325 5th Ave. N

855-313-3456

www.emeraldcitytrolley.com

$$-$$$ AGES 3-5 AGES 6-9 AGES 10-14 ✕

This emerald-green trolley canvases the downtown streets, stopping at such highlights as Pike Place Market, Pioneer Square, and the piers, in operation from 9 a.m. to 6 p.m., May through September. Pick up the open-air ride at Seattle Center and then ride as long as you like. Kids intrigued by a particular stop? Hop off and explore, then pick up your ride again at any of the trolley's twelve downtown stops. The company offers other touring options, the most popular of which is the $15 Overlook & Locks Tour, which takes a delightful spin around the neighborhoods of Ballard and Fremont, stopping at the Hiram M. Chittenden Locks, the Fremont Troll, and the picturesque Kerry Park.

Seattle By Foot Kids' Tour

DOWNTOWN

Meets at Pike Place Market, 1st Ave. and Pike St.

206-508-7017

www.seattlebyfoot.com

$$-$$$ AGES 3-5 AGES 6-9 AGES 10-14 ✕

Led by co-owners and moms Penny Truitt and Heather Chermak, this delightful two-hour, two- to three-block walking tour is crafted specifically for kids with adults in tow, exploring the wonders of Pike Place Market, the Seattle Art Museum, and points in between, and covering such highlights as pickle and fruit stands, the infamous gum wall, public art, water fountains, and skyscrapers. The private tours are a flat $100 for two to five participants, or $150 for six to ten participants, so gather up a party to drop that per person rate.

Seattle Free Walking Tours
PIKE PLACE MARKET
Meets at Victor Steinbrueck Park, 2000 Western Ave.
425-770-6928
www.seattlefreewalkingtours.com
$$ AGES 6-9 AGES 10-14 ✗

Operating on a pay-what-you-can model (suggested donation is $15–$20 per person), this company offers two distinct tours under the direction of its personable guides: an immersive Pike Place Market option and the Seattle 101 walkabout, which covers Pioneer Square, the Market, and the waterfront piers. The one-hour Market Experience option is fantastic for kiddies, offered at a family-friendly 9:30 a.m. time slot, with samples galore from the food vendors and fruit stands.

Seattle Qwik Tour
VARIOUS LOCATIONS
Pickups from Westlake Center, area hotels,
and the cruise ship terminals
206-743-1884
www.seattleqwiktour.com
$$$ AGES 3-5 AGES 6-9 AGES 10-14

This quirky bus tour may not have been built for kids, but, man, is it well suited to those short attention spans. Leading a ninety-minute tour of city highlights, ranging from the Smith Tower to the *Sleepless in Seattle* houseboat, energetic owner and guide Charles "The Chuckster" Mickelson mixes in humor, history, facts, and stats along the way, not to mention the appearance of a little cowbell and even bubbles. Tours run Wednesday through Sunday, with two daily options during the busier summer months; tickets hover around $32 for kids ages 4–13 and $42 for adults.

EAT IT UP
Nothing keeps kids entertained quite like a nosh or nibble along the way. Take a bite out of Seattle with a truly unique tour of the **Theo Chocolate** factory (3400 Phinney Ave. N; 206-632-5100; www.theochocolate.com /factory-tours) in Fremont. Guests will be walked through the step-by-step process of how cocoa beans become chocolate creations—and they'll get samples—provoking Willy Wonka-style delight in everyone. The tour is $10 per person, and available to kids age 6 and over. Younger kiddos can still experience the factory at Theo's Chocolate Story Time (page 49).

BY WATER

Alki Kayak Tours
WEST SEATTLE
1660 Harbor Ave. W
206-953-0237
www.kayakalki.com
$$$ AGES 10-14

Offering daily tours that focus on the more natural side of Seattle, Alki Kayak Tours explores such points as the Alki peninsula, Elliott Bay, and the head of the Duwamish River, scouting out curious seals and sea lions or nesting bald eagles along the way. Better suited to tweens and teens (who can help paddle!), these picturesque one- to two-hour tours ($69–$89 per person) are also often offered at sunset or by moonlight, to best take advantage of those stunning water views.

Argosy Cruises
WATERFRONT
1101 Alaskan Way
206-623-1445
www.argosycruises.com
$$-$$$ AGES 3-5 AGES 6-9 AGES 10-14

Gather up the crew and climb aboard a big white boat for one of Argosy's sightseeing cruises. With five different tours to choose from on three different bodies of water (Lake Union, Lake Washington, or the glittering Puget Sound), these three-story boats make for one fun-filled ride. Tours range in length from one to two and a half hours, the longest of which is the popular Locks Cruise—a lovely route that takes riders by workboats in Tugboat Alley, and by Seattle's well-known houseboats, then through the famous Hiram M. Chittenden Locks. Argosy also runs a seasonal tour to Tillicum Village on Blake Island—for more information, see page 38.

Insider tip: Book ahead on the website to receive up to $4 off adult admission (in general, tours range from $25 to $40 for adults and from $13 to $16 for youth under age 12. Kids under age 3 are free of charge).

Ride the Ducks
SEATTLE CENTER
516 Broad St.
206-441-3825
www.ridetheducksofseattle.com
$$-$$$ AGES 3-5 AGES 6-9 AGES 10-14

One of the strangest sights in Seattle is also one of the most common, as the amphibious "Duck" bus-boats roll through downtown streets before splashing into Lake Union for a dip. The ninety-minute tour is quirky and whimsical, led by charismatic tour guides who blare music and prompt kids to blow their Wacky Quacker whistles ($2.25 each, and you might as well join in on the fun). Save a few bucks by booking online (adults are $35; kids (4-12) $20; infants (0-3) $4) as tours tend to sell out quickly on hot summer days.

Seattle Ferry Service Sunday Ice-Cream Cruise
LAKE UNION
899 Terry Ave. N
206-713-8446
www.seattleferryservice.com
$-$$ AGES 3-5 AGES 6-9 AGES 10-14

Two words: "ice cream." That's right, this delightful little cruise around busy Lake Union ups the kid-friendly factor with a bevy of treats on board to lick, slurp, and sip during the forty-five-minute jaunt. Departing on the hour, from 11 a.m. to 3 p.m. every Sunday, the tour also includes funky background music and peeks at Dale Chihuly's glass studio, the famous *Sleepless in Seattle* houseboat, and Gas Works Park. It's $12 for adults, $8 for kids ages 5–13, and $3 for kiddos under age 5. (Ice-cream treats range from $2 to $4.)

TOY STORY

These classic local shops definitely have the goods—from plush stuffed animals and gag gifts to hard-to-find board games and locally made treasures.

CLASSIC TOYS

Atomic Boys Shop-O-Rama
WEST SEATTLE
4311 Admiral Way SW
206-938-3255
www.atomicboysseattle.com
AGES 3–5 AGES 6–9 AGES 10–14 ☂ ✕

Inspired by a love of things retro-cool, this West Seattle shop is a delight for both little ones and grown-ups. Boasting party supplies, cards, and local art, in addition to quality toys, Atomic Boys also features a nostalgic candy case—introduce your tykes to a good ol' Charleston Chew while you shop.

Clover
BALLARD
5333 Ballard Ave. NW
206-782-0715
www.clovertoys.com
AGES 0–2 AGES 3–5 ☂ ✕

Calling historic Ballard Avenue NW home since 2004, Sarah Furstenberg's Clover is almost too cute for words, filled with sweeter-than-sweet baby goods and onesies, old-school-style wooden train sets, and dollhouses for the little darling.

Magic Mouse Toys
PIONEER SQUARE
603 1st Ave.
206-682-8097
www.magicmousetoys.com
AGES 3–5 AGES 6–9 ⬆ ✕

Offering Legos and games, plus toys both classic and imported, Magic Mouse Toys has been a stalwart in Seattle since 1977. Convenient for a pregame stop on the way to see the Mariners or Sounders, the two-story wonderland also boasts a science section and puzzle cave, which is filled with options from floor to ceiling.

Red Wagon Toys
MADISON PARK
4218 E. Madison St.
206-453-5306
www.redwagonmadisonpark.com
AGES 3–5 AGES 6–9 ⬆ ✕

This sweet, imaginative shop is a dream, replete with a dress-up corner (furnished with duds for both guys and gals), a staggering number of books, and a charming Dutch-style front door. The store's decor and toy selection change along with the seasons, so there is seemingly always something new to explore.

Top Ten Toys
GREENWOOD
120 N. 85th St.
206-782-0098
www.toptentoys.com
AGES 3–5 AGES 6–9 AGES 10–14 ⬆ ✕

Get lost for the afternoon in this store, where you'll find a vast selection of educational and hands-on toys, as well as such classics as spinning tops, musical instruments, and wooden blocks. Older kids also flock to these warm, inviting spots for such finds as high-tech science kits, art supplies, and building sets.

GAGS & GAMES

Archie McPhee
WALLINGFORD
1300 N. 45th St.
206-297-0240
www.archiemcpheeseattle.com
AGES 3–5   AGES 6–9   AGES 10–14   ☂ ✗

The king of Seattle gag shops, Archie McPhee is a destination unto itself, chock-full of such hilarious and strange products as itty-bitty rubber chickens, Handerpants (underpants for your hands, naturally), and bacon-flavored toothpicks. Let the kids loose with $5 each and see who comes up with the most delightful find on a drippy afternoon.

Blue Highway Games
QUEEN ANNE
2203 Queen Anne Ave.
206-282-0540
www.bluehighwaygames.com
AGES 3–5   AGES 6–9   AGES 10–14   ☂ ✗

Tucked atop Queen Anne Hill, Blue Highway Games is devoted to board games and card games, with an extensive collection of both the rare and mainstream. With tables to try out new games, plus snacks and drinks for sale (and adults-only beer-and-board game nights), this charming little shop encourages gamers to stay awhile.

YOU'VE BEEN FRAMED

Don't panic. With programs designed just for kids, these art galleries and museums will keep your little aficionado too engaged to even think about knocking anything over.

FINE ARTS

Asian Art Museum

Capitol Hill

1400 E. Prospect St.

206-654-3100

www.seattleartmuseum.org/visit/asian-art-museum

$ AGES 6–9 AGES 10–14 ⚓ ✗

Free for kids age 12 and under and just $5 for those ages 13–19, the Asian Art Museum is free for parents too on the first Thursday or first Saturday of every month—so even if you have to bail outside to Volunteer Park after an hour, this one won't torch the budget. The Saturday programs are crafted just for families, with drop-in workshops, arts activities, and special performances, to help kiddos learn about the many Asian cultures represented throughout the museum.

Insider tip: The museum is set to undergo an extensive renovation beginning in early 2017, so check ahead; it will be closed for stretches during the eighteen months of construction.

Bellevue Arts Museum

Bellevue

510 Bellevue Way NE

425-519-0770

www.bellevuearts.org

$-$$ AGES 6–9 AGES 10–14 ⚓ ✗

Held every Saturday from 1 to 3 p.m. in the museum's Forum space, BAM's hands-on Get Crafty program for kids ties into the current exhibitions, with past projects including 3-D flowers and geometric print art with Duplo block stamps ($4 per child, or free with admission). In addition to that program, BAM also cleverly offers Imagination Stations throughout the museum, for little ones to take a break for some doodling in between peering at the precious pieces of art. Kids under age 6 are admitted for free, and families can visit for a flat rate of $30 (for up to two adults and four kids). Or plan your visit for the first Friday of every month, when all get in for free.

Frye Art Museum
FIRST HILL
704 Terry Ave.
206-622-9250
www.fryemuseum.org
FREE! AGES 3-5 AGES 6-9 AGES 10-14 ☂

The first Friday of every month, the Frye partners with Seattle Children's Theatre for its Small Frye: Storytelling + Art program, which brings stories to life through imaginative narrative and dramatic book readings. Designed for kids ages 3-5 and available free of charge, the 10:30 a.m. story time includes arts activities and teachable elements such as counting, shapes, and letters. Given that the rest of the museum is also always free, this friendly spot is a good place to introduce older kids to the marvels of fine art.

Henry Art Gallery
UNIVERSITY DISTRICT
4100 15th Ave. NE
206-543-2280
www.henryart.org
$ AGES 3-5 AGES 6-9 AGES 10-14

This supercool contemporary art museum on the University of Washington campus opens its doors to families on the second Sunday of every month for the innovative ArtVenture program, which offers a different thematic art experience each time around, and often features local artists at the helm. The museum is free for all on the first Thursday of every month, and free all the time for little tykes and then students from kindergarten on up to college.

Seattle Art Museum
DOWNTOWN
1300 1st Ave.
206-654-3100
www.seattleartmuseum.org
$$ AGES 6–9 AGES 10–14 🔨 🍴

Home to the landmark *Hammering Man* moving sculpture out front, SAM works hard to please its littlest visitors, offering Family Fun Workshops and Free First Saturdays (which include arts activities, special performances, and kid-friendly exhibit tours). Also available are the Knudsen Family Room, outfitted with blocks, drums, and more, and an open studio, where kids can create their own art. Kids 12 and under are always free, and everyone gets in sans charge the first Thursday of every month.

Insider tip: The museum is closed on Tuesdays.

GLASS & SCULPTURE

Chihuly Garden and Glass
SEATTLE CENTER
305 Harrison St.
206-753-4940
www.chihulygardenandglass.com
$$–$$$ AGES 6–9 AGES 10–14 ☂

The good news here is kids will be so agog at the vibrant glass works of Seattle's famed artist Dale Chihuly—which burst to life in wild-crazy shapes and bright-loud colors—that they won't even dare think of touching them. The museum is more child-friendly than you might think; it offers free kids' packets with find-its and fill-in-the-blanks to guide them through the museum, a quirky café decorated with some of Chihuly's colorful collectibles, and an outside garden space for getting the wiggles out. This one ain't cheap ($27 for adults, $16 for kids ages 5–12, and free for those 4 and under), but package deals are available for admission to both the Needle and museum ($29 for kids and $46 for adults).

Museum of Glass

TACOMA

1801 Dock St.

253-284-4750

www.museumofglass.org

$-$$ AGES 6-9 AGES 10-14 ☂

Children and glass don't often play well together, but kiddos are ever-welcome at the Museum of Glass one hour south of Seattle, thanks to Kids Design Glass. This innovative and imaginative program allows museum visitors age 12 and under to dream up their own glass creations. After perusing the galleries, they can pick up some crayons and paper in the Education Studio and submit their idea; the museum will then choose some young artists to invite back at a later date for a front-row seat to watch their creature, monster, or thingamajig come to life in the glass studio. Admission is $15 for adults and $5 for kids ages 6-12. Kids age 5 and under are always free.

Olympic Sculpture Park

WATERFRONT

2901 Western Ave.

206-654-3100

www.seattleartmuseum.org/visit/olympic-sculpture-park

FREE! ALL AGES 🛒 ✕

If the very thought of taking your rambunctious toddler to an art museum fills you with dread, think the Olympic Sculpture Park (OSP) instead. With lots of room to picnic and roam, the always-free OSP makes for a natural introduction to the world of fine art. There are plenty of breathtaking large-scale installations for kids to spy (including the well-known bright-red *Eagle*), plus a stunning view of Elliott Bay.

NEIGHBORHOOD ART WALKS

Ballard Artwalk
BALLARD
NW Market St. and Ballard Ave. NW
Occurs the second Saturday of every month from 6 to 9 p.m.
www.ballardartwalk.blogspot.com
FREE! AGES 6–9 AGES 10–14 ✕

Take the kiddos on a cultural walkabout by visiting one of
the city's many stellar art nights. Many of Ballard Avenue's
charming boutiques also stay open late along so you can shop
in between art stops; occurs the second Saturday of every month
from 6 to 9 p.m.

Fremont Art Walk
FREMONT
Fremont Ave. N and N. 35th St.
Occurs the first Friday of every month from 6 to 9 p.m.
www.fremontfirstfriday.com
FREE! AGES 6–9 AGES 10–14 ✕

Here you'll spy an array of outdoor curiosities (the statue of
Lenin, the Troll under the Aurora Bridge, and the Rocket—see
page 164 for more info) in addition to Fremont's funky galleries;
occurs the first Friday of every month from 6 to 9 p.m.

West Seattle Art Walk
WEST SEATTLE
California Ave. SW and SW Alaska St.
Occurs the second Thursday of every month from 6 to 9 p.m.
www.westseattleartwalk.blogspot.com
FREE! AGES 6–9 AGES 10–14 ✕

Highlights of this tour located all along the West Seattle Junction
include painting, prints, and photography, as well as free
nibbles and drinks; occurs the second Thursday of every month
from 6 to 9 p.m.

ITINERARIES

HEY, BABY

AGES 0–4

Strap on that Baby Bjorn—and pack up everything else you can cram into the diaper bag (wait—the pacifier!) for a grand day out with your tiny tot.

Mark an upcoming Wednesday or Thursday on your calendar, then start that day on the Eastside by stopping at **Issaquah Coffee Company** (page 227) for a velvety latte and warm scone, enjoyed while your little one scoots choo-choos around the on-site train table. Next swing by the adorable **White Horse Toys** (page 200), located a short walk away on the other side of Gilman Village, to find a plush new friend for *le bébé*. Then, if it's Wednesday, keep that car parked and stroll over to **Village Green Yoga** for a mom-and-baby hula class taught by **A Honu World of Hula** (317 NW Gilman Blvd., Suite 1 and 2; www.ahonuworldofhula.com; www.villagegreenyoga.com). This laid-back hour-long class, offered most Wednesdays at 11:30 a.m. for a drop-in fee of $10, has mamas swaying in time to traditional Hawaiian tunes while toting little ones in carriers (who have been known to fall asleep during class, thanks to the soothing motions). Or, if it's Thursday, take the short car trip over to Bellevue for the special once-weekly morning Mommy & Me movie screening at **Lincoln Square Cinemas** (page 193)—no need to worry about disturbing fellow moviegoers, should a few tears be shed. And don't worry, dads, you are welcome on either excursion too.

Are your tummies rumbling yet? Head across the I-90 bridge to the Georgetown location of **Flying Squirrel Pizza Co.** (page 237), where the littlest tykes can gum some crust while you tuck into the pizzeria's famous No. 5 creation, topped with braised pulled pork, cotija cheese, cilantro, red onion, and lime juice.

Take a quick drive down scenic Lake Washington Boulevard South and pull out the stroller for a pretty, pizza-calorie-burning hike in **Seward Park** (page 88). The 2.4-mile paved path is a delightful loop past towering trees along the Lake Washington shore. Decide whether to take in the sweet playground there, or head over to **Columbia City** (neighborhood guide on page 158) to poke around the shops. If it happens to be a summer Wednesday between 3 and 7 p.m., stop at the **Columbia City Neighborhood Farmers Market** (page 110) to buy some creamy goat cheese from Tieton Farm & Creamery, then complement it with a fresh baguette from **Columbia City Bakery** (page 210) and a bottle of stellar Washington wine from **PCC** (page 230).

Finally, if it's Wednesday, head for the **Beacon Hill Branch** of **the Seattle Public Library** (page 49) for Family Story Time at 6:45 p.m., where oft-pajama-clad tots can take in a bedtime tale. (Even if it's not Wednesday, it's worth popping into this branch to pick up a sweet board book to read together later.) Let the car ride home lull them to sleep, and then remember that wine, bread, and cheese from earlier? Uncork that bottle and nibble away before calling it a day.

KIDDO ON THE GO

AGES 5–9

Keep that energetic grade-schooler busy, busy, busy with this adventurous day among the sights.

Start the day off right with breakfast at the South Lake Union location of **Portage Bay Cafe** (page 216). Loved by parents for its laid-back setting, the cheery café is even more beloved by kiddos for the famous breakfast toppings bar. Order a pancake or pile of French toast, then top it your way, with fruit, chocolate chips, or whipped cream. Stuffed? Time to burn off that brekky at one of the most adventure-filled playgrounds around: **Artists at Play** (page 72) at Seattle Center. Boasting both 52-foot and 38-foot slides, this park also contains a 30-foot climbing tower, an epic cargo net, a ropes course, and swaying bridges that will delight daredevils.

Since you're right next door, you could pop on into **MoPOP** (page 57) for the rest of the morn, where kids can bang on a big drum, try out a variety of rock 'n' roll instruments, and check out the latest sci-fi exhibit. Then, when the hunger pangs hit, walk across Seattle Center and on over to **Dick's Drive-In** (page 219) in Lower Queen Anne for lunch. As burgers are only $1.40–$3.10, and fries just $1.75, you can probably scrounge enough change out of everyone's pockets if you don't feel like breaking out the plastic at this classic stop.

Queen Anne Hill offers many delights for an afternoon adventure. First, take the car on up to **Kerry Park** (page 178) for a family selfie with the iconic Needle in the background, then take the staircase to **Bayview-Kinnear Park** (page 70), where kids can clamber up the climbing wall and careen down the hillside slides. From there, head farther up the hill to **Blue Highway Games** (page 118), a delightful board- and card-game shop with stay-and-play tables and a café.

Or, if you'd prefer, head to the **University District** (neighborhood guide on page 182) for one of two afternoon activities, depending on that mercurial Seattle weather. If the day is fine, head over to **Agua Verde Paddle Club** (page 63) to rent a few kayaks and thus explore the many nooks and crannies of Lake Washington or Lake Union. But even if it's blustery or wet, don't fret. The **Burke Museum** (page 106), located on the UW campus, is filled with finds for dino dudes, boasting fossils and archaeological curiosities including the now-famous Columbian mammoth tusk that was unearthed a few years back at a Seattle construction site (cool!).

No matter how you've spent your afternoon, wind down from the busy day at **Wunderkind** (page 82) in Bryant, an innovative play space that is part café for the parents (beer and wine are served) and part Lego heaven for kids, with myriad playing tables stocked with blocks dotting the space. Wunderkind is open until 6 p.m. Sunday through Wednesday, but open until 8 p.m. the rest of the week, so stay and play a bit before taking those tuckered-out kids home to bed.

TWEENS 'N' TEENS ABOUT TOWN

AGES 10-14

With hipster hangouts and high-octane activities galore, the Seattle area might just be cool enough to impress your tween or teen. (Fingers crossed.)

Head east of the city, to Bellevue, with your budding teen to start the day at **Gilbert's on Main** (page 193), where you can tuck into a heaping egg scramble paired with the café's house-made bagels and schmear. Little shoppers will want to then head to the many shops and boutiques of **the Bellevue Collection** (page 192), including Zara, Nordstrom, and Uniqlo at Bellevue Square. Nonshoppers can waltz through the grass at **Bellevue Downtown Park** (page 65), then the whole crew can head over a few blocks to Lincoln Square, to the swank **Lucky Strike** (page 192). Your tween or teen will feel oh-so-grown-up at this upscale bowling alley, a 21-plus establishment in the evenings, which offers cool mood lighting and upscale bites even during the day.

Or, if you're feeling more outdoorsy, set off for an adventure at **Bellevue Zip Tour** (page 93) (open seasonally, from April into late fall). Traveling along seven different zip lines that range in length from 78 feet to 458 feet, Bellevue Zip Tour allows kids to go wild among the wooded canopy of Eastgate Park. If the time isn't right (or zip-lining ain't your thang), choose instead from an afternoon of indoor climbing at the Bellevue outpost of **Stone Gardens** (page 22) or skateboarding at **Bellevue Skatepark** (page 23), which has both an indoor facility featuring mini ramps, wall rides, and a launch box, and a 13,000-square-foot plaza outside. Or keep your adrenaline pumping with a trip out to Issaquah for mountain-biking fun at **Duthie Hill Mountain Bike Park** (page 75). Packed with jumps and obstacles, this wild course careens through the forest and offers up the famous Voodoo Child run, with a tilted, curved jump you've just gotta try.

Once you've wrapped your afternoon activity (and cleaned the dirt out of every nook and cranny if you went biking), get dressed up for a night on the town. Now that they've graduated to cloth-napkin-level establishments, treat your tween or teen to a meal at **Icon Grill** (page 235), which offers mean macaroni and cheese that diners of all ages enjoy. From there, take in a movie at **Cinerama** (page 27), a 1960s-era theater that now features one of the biggest and baddest screens in the city, or head for **the 5th Avenue Theatre** (page 41) to catch the latest musical to hit the stage. Or spend your evening wandering around the hipster hood of **Fremont** (neighborhood guide on page 164). It's hard to beat the handheld savory and sweet pies from the walk-up window at **Pie** (open late on Friday and Saturday evenings, more on page 252), which are best enjoyed over views of the twinkling city skyline at **Gas Works Park** (page 72).

BEAT THE HEAT

KEEP YOUR COOL ON A SWELTERING SUMMER DAY

Pack up those swimsuits and load up on sunscreen for a splish-splash-happy day in Seattle.

Already hot out there? Pick up iced lattes and croissants at the Capitol Hill outpost of **Bakery Nouveau** (page 210), then head for the blissful air-conditioning at the **Capitol Hill Branch** of **the Seattle Public Library** (page 49) to take in a story time—offered Monday and Wednesday mornings at 10:30 a.m.—or browse books for a bit. (Tip: all SPL libraries are air-conditioned, so feel free to head to one nearest you.) Or let the kids play in the fountain at **Cal Anderson Park** (page 65) nearby, toddling back and forth between the sweet playground and the cool water. If you're starting to feel sticky in the mounting heat, consider treating yourself to a noontime cone at **Molly Moon's** (page 249), a block south, or with a towering root beer float at **Rachel's Ginger Beer** (page 250), just down the street.

Balance out all that sugar with a cool, crisp sandwich to go from **Baguette Box** (page 240)—the Crispy Drunken Chicken Baguette (also available as a salad) is a saucy delight, with oranges, cilantro, and pickled veggies. Then roll the windows down for a scenic drive out to West Seattle, where you'll find blissful shade at the hidden gem that is **Schmitz Preserve Park** (page 88). This nature preserve is home to one of the largest old-growth forests in the city, making for fantastic picnicking in the shade followed by hiking over the shadowy forest floor.

Once you've worked up a sweat there, it's time to get wet again, this time at nearby **Colman Pool** (page 67) in Lincoln Park. This longtime favorite, right along the Sound, is filled with heated saltwater. It also boasts an epic twirly slide.

While away the rest of the day there, or keep the kids in their suits and let them take a quick snooze while you drive over to Seattle Center for dinner and a movie, summer-style. Pick up burgers smothered in bacon jam or grilled PB&Js for the kids at **Skillet Counter** in the Armory (page 235), where you can also snap up a few of the day's fruit frescas, juices crafted from seasonal fruit. From there, head over to the biggest fountain in the city, the **International Fountain** (page 66), for round three of wet, drippy fun after you munch down some dinner. With a center dome that shoots water as far as 120 feet, this fountain will cool you off in no time flat. Finally, as the sun starts to set, park yourselves on the lawn and enjoy a free outdoor film, courtesy of **Seattle Center Movies at the Mural** (more info on this and other summer outdoor movie spots on page 30), which will wrap up in time for the starry night (and cooler temps) to finally emerge—aah.

RAINY-DAY ROUTE

BEST BETS FOR STAYING BUSY AND DRY

It's no secret that Seattle gets its fair share of rain, but don't let the drip-drops deter you. There are play spaces and programs aplenty to keep those wee ones entertained all rainy day long.

Pick one of two routes, depending on which day has turned soggy. If it's a drippy Tuesday, start your day by ducking into the Wallingford location of **Essential Bakery Café** (page 211) for a cuppa joe for you and a cookie for those rain boot-clad cuties. Then head over to **University Village** (page 182) for one of its free Village Playdays, from 10 to 11 a.m., which include story times, crafts, and activities—held under a covered atrium or in various stores on wet days. While you're there, feel free to poke into **the Confectionery** (page 243) for a piece of candy, or while away an hour or two painting a ceramic mug at **Paint the Town** (page 32). If the kids are still antsy, detour at any point to the nearby **Arena Sports FunZone** (page 80) for its indoor inflatable playground. The facility is filled to the brim with bounce houses, slides, and more during two drop-in sessions on weekdays, 10 a.m.–1 p.m. and 4:30–8 p.m.

Snag a slice of Neapolitan pizza at cozy **Tutta Bella** (page 239) on Stone Way North in Wallingford and discuss your next move. Up the hill, you'll find the **Woodland Park Zoo** (page 12), which offers two benefits on wet days: half-price admission (check www.zoo.org/rainyday for details) and the indoor Zoomazium play space, an incredibly popular spot, with slides, music toys, and interactive activities. Or, down the hill, there's **All Together Skatepark** (page 23), Seattle's only indoor skateboard park, with 7,000 square feet of ledges, banks, stairs, and rails. And should it still be raining cats and dogs by late afternoon, you might do well to visit the actual cats at the **Seattle Meowtropolitan** café (page 13), or check out the one of the best hot chocolates in town at **Chocolopolis** (page 225).

More rain in the forecast? Rally the troops for day two by starting things off on Capitol Hill at **Mighty-O Donuts** (page 247) for something sweet. Then, if you can time it right, pop by the **Frye Art Museum** (page 120) for its free Small Frye program (the first Friday of every month at 10:30 a.m.), which includes storytelling, as well as arts-and-crafts activities. Whether it's Friday or not, though, do stop by **Volunteer Park Conservatory** (page 44). The glass-encased garden is a true haven during the drippy winter months, flush with exotic succulents and cacti, and vivid orchids. Most of the greenhouse is always kept at a balmy and blissful 70 to 80 degrees.

After filling up on Greek food at the kid-friendly **Vios Cafe** (page 157) nearby, the crew has its choice of two spots for the afternoon. If they're game for climbing and clambering, then it's off to the **Seattle Bouldering Project** in SoDo (page 22), a climbing gym with a dedicated kids' area. But if they're more game for games, head south, to Tukwila's **Round 1 Bowling & Amusement** (page 78), which offers billiards, karaoke, and one of the largest arcades in the state, in addition to fourteen lanes of bowling. The massive facility should keep them entertained until either the showers stop or the commuter traffic dies down enough to head home.

THE GREAT OUTDOORS

EXPLORING THE AREA'S NATURAL WONDERS

Attention Sasquatch hunters, lake lovers, and daisy pluckers—head "onward and yonward," like the intrepid Nature Cat, to these can't-miss outdoorsy spots.

Start your day in the mountains before heading back into the metropolis for more. Fuel up with breakfast on the mountain-view patio at **North Bend Bar & Grill** (page 260), then head out on I-90 East to pick between two picturesque hikes. The **Twin Falls Trail** (page 92) follows the Snoqualmie River for just a mile before climbing up to a viewpoint of the lower falls, which plunge over a 135-foot cliff. Or try the **Franklin Falls Trail** (page 91). Sure, the gorgeous waterfalls are the main draw, but kids will also be flabbergasted by the pioneer-era wagon-wheel ruts that run alongside the trail. Hop in for pic!

Rest those legs on the drive back west, then pick up some picnic supplies at **Pasta & Co.** (page 230) in Bellevue before heading to the innovative **Adventure Playground** (page 69) on Mercer Island. This summer-only site within a larger park supplies kids with tools to build their own play areas—tree house, anyone? Alternatively, head across the I-90 floating bridge to **Seward Park** (page 88). Boasting one of the most magnificent urban forests you'll ever see, the park offers almost six miles of trails and view of Lake Washington and the Cascade Mountains. As a third option for your afternoon, set off for the city's central body of freshwater, Lake Union. Rent either kayaks from **Agua Verde Paddle Club** (page 63) or a boat from **the Electric Boat Company** (page 64) and spend the rest of the afternoon touring about the water.

Cap off your day with one last meal outside, on the expansive deck at **Maggie Bluffs** (2601 W. Marina Pl.; 206-283-8322; www.maggiebluffs.com) in Magnolia, where in addition to enjoying salmon fettucine or fish 'n' chips, you'll very much enjoy the stellar water views. Take a show of hands to see who is up for more outdoorsy fun, then order a brownie sundae to go and head over to nearby **Ella Bailey Park** (page 231) to spy a fantastic look at the downtown skyline and Elliott Bay. Hit up the slides at the playground, then park yourselves on the grassy lawn to enjoy that chocolatey dessert together as the sun turns the sky pink and orange and sets over the water.

FREE DAY

AN ENTIRE ITINERARY OF FREE TO-DOS

Filled with museum visits, theater productions, and story times, this lineup may be cheap on price but not on fun.

One of Seattle's greatest spectacles happens to be one of the cheapest. Start your day by whiling away the morning hours at **Pike Place Market** (page 104), where kids can pose with Rachel the pig, watch fish fly, and gawk at the gum wall, all without you ever busting open your wallet. Or, to take an in-depth look at the historic landmark, consider joining one of the **Seattle Free Walking Tours** (page 113), which operate on a pay-what-you-can model. From the Market, head on down to **South Lake Union** (neighborhood guide on page 179) to the delightful **Center for Wooden Boats** (page 63), where freebies await almost every day of the week. The museum itself, filled with schooners, sloops, and sailboats, is always free to visit; Sundays are especially fun as the museum offers free sailboat rides around Lake Union rain or shine. Next door, the **Museum of History and Industry (MOHAI)** (page 107) is free for kids age 14 and under, and free to all the first Thursday of every month. Be sure pick up a kids' packet filled with games and activities to help aid learning among the exhibits.

After a stroll on the picturesque lawn of **Lake Union Park** (page 181)—where there is also a sweet splash pad, should it be hot out—truck the kids over to the **Bill & Melinda Gates Foundation Visitor Center** (page 36) for a teachable moment or two. Through several interactive exhibits kids will learn how people in other parts of the world live. If the aforementioned museums don't quite fit your freebie fantasies, take your pick from any of the following instead—the **Burke Museum** (page 106) is free the first Thursday of every month, as are the **Nordic Heritage Museum** (page 35) and the **Asian Art Museum** (page 119), and the **Klondike Gold Rush National Historical Park** (page 107) is always free. Or, if the sun happens to be shining, head to either the **Olympic Sculpture Park** (page 122) or take a jaunt southward to the beautiful and lush **Kubota Garden** (page 44), a 20-acre estate that offers a mix of Japanese and Western-style plants. Kids love the various koi ponds and pagodas.

Once little tummies start to rumble, head for either the Georgetown or White Center outpost of **Zippy's Giant Burgers** (page 221), where kids eat free on Wednesdays during happy hour (3–6 p.m.). If you're in more of an alfresco mood, pick up a few rustic, wood-fired to-go pizzas from Georgetown's **Via Tribunali** (6009 12th Ave. S; 206-464-2880; www.viatribunali.com), then head to nearby **Oxbow Park** (page 231). The towering cowboy hat and boots on display there should spur some dinnertime commentary from even the most reticent tween or teen.

If it happens to be a summer evening, don't miss out on the bevy of **outdoor movies** (page 29) that pop up around the city, or consider taking in the latest production at **Seattle Public Theater at the Bathhouse** (page 40) along Green Lake, where young thespians stage their newest creations for free.

FREE TIP
Seattle city residents, take note: the Seattle Public Library offers a limited number of **free passes** to such local museums as the **MoPOP, the Museum of Flight**, and the **Seattle Aquarium**, which can be checked out with an SPL library card; go to www.spl.org/library-collection /museum-pass to reserve prior to your next visit.

WINTER WONDERLAND

STEP-BY-STEP GUIDE TO WINTER FUN

Oh, the weather outside may be frightful, but winter in Seattle is still delightful.

Wake the cuties up bright and early for a pancake breakfast at **Chace's Pancake Corral** (page 193) in Bellevue, then head up I-90 for a morning of sledding fun at **Hyak Sno-Park** (page 102). This groomed sledding hill near Snoqualmie Pass has some of the best runs around, and it's free to the public (although parking fees do apply). If the hill is mobbed—and it often is, so go early—there is also a stellar pay-to-tube hill nearby, the **Summit Tubing Center** (page 103).

CHRISTMAS TREE FARM 411

These u-cut favorites offer up plenty of ho-ho-holiday fun.

Carnation Tree Farm
CARNATION
3861 Tolt Ave.
425-333-4510
www.carnationtreefarm.com

Family-owned for over 100 years, this beautiful farm is listed on the National Register of Historic Places and, as such, provides a truly magical environment for tree scouting. Many of its gorgeous Douglas firs and noble firs are well over 12 feet tall. Warm up afterward with some hot apple cider in the cheery gift shop.

Christmas Creek Tree Farm
NORTH BEND
15515 468th Ave. SE
206-637-1415
www.yourchristmastree.com

An easy thirty minutes from the city, this tree farm has it all—a roaring fireplace to enjoy cookies and hot cocoa, a jolly Santa to take pictures with, and u-cut trees as far as the eye can see.

Take the tired kids home for a snooze, then pick one of two itineraries to finish off your day. Your first option is to head to Downtown Seattle, which is filled this time of year with such sights as the flagship Nordstrom **Santa** and the **seasonal carousel** that sets up shop in Westlake Park (www.downtownseattle.com). Fill your bellies with a bowl of classic clam chowder from **Pike Place Chowder** (page 241), then spring for a steaming cup of cocoa from **Chocolate Box** (page 225) to clutch while you walk around the kiddie emporium that is **Boston Baby** (1902 Post Alley; 206-634-0580) to look for sweet stocking stuffers. Then hop on the **Seattle Center Monorail** (page 6) to head over to Seattle Center, where **Winterfest** (www.seattlecenter.com/winterfest) takes over the grounds from late November to January. Activities include skating on the pop-up ice rink and ice sculpting contests.

McMurtrey's Red-Wood Christmas Tree Farm

REDMOND
13925 Woodinville-Redmond Rd.
425-482-6795
www.red-woodfarm.com

Take a charming wagon ride out to this farm's pretty array of fir trees, where the friendly staffers will supply you with a saw and set you in the right direction. Fido is welcome to sniff out his favorite pick here too, as long as he's on a leash.

Trinity Tree Farm

ISSAQUAH
14237 228th Ave. SE
425-466-1800
www.trinitytreefarm.com

This farm has a full day's worth of activities, with train rides for the kiddos, espresso and food stands, and welcoming fire pits to gather round, in addition to a selection of u-pick trees nestled on the hillside.

When you can no longer stand the chill, either head into the **Seattle Children's Museum** (page 79) to run about the exhibits for a spell, take in a show at the **Seattle Children's Theatre** (page 40), or warm up among the winged creatures in the Tropical Butterfly House at **Pacific Science Center** (page 84).

Alternatively, as the winter day begins to wane head to Bellevue for dinner and a show. Either split a large pie at **Pagliacci Pizza** (page 238), or spice things up with tacos from **Cactus** (page 222) in Bellevue Square, then huddle up outside along **Snowflake Lane** (www.bellevue.com/snowflake-lane .php) to experience the nightly "snowfall." The 7 p.m. show, which runs Thanksgiving weekend through Christmas Eve, features toy soldiers and winter characters parading down the street to holiday music as artificial snow falls from above. The event ends with a dazzling light show. Or head over to the **Bellevue Botanical Garden** (page 43) for the dazzling **Garden d'Lights** (www.gardendlights.org), which transforms the popular gardens into a twinkling winter wonderland. Featuring over half a million lights adorning the foliage and walking paths, the display is pure magic for young and old.

SPRING HAS SPRUNG

SPRINGTIME FROLICKING IN THE SOUND

The tulips are blooming, the cherry blossoms are budding, the rain boots are ready—it's time get outside again!

After breaking your fast over warm scones with honey-orange butter at **Chinook's at Salmon Bay** (page 214), choose between two springtime classics for your morning activity: fragrant new flowers or bouncy baby animals. If you have visions of a family portrait in front of a sea of vibrant blooms, pick the former and head north to the **Skagit Valley Tulip Festival** (www .tulipfestival.org), where local farms put on a colorful display of tulips, tulips, and more tulips in their fields. Snap up a few baked goodies in Mount Vernon at the cuter-than-cute **Calico Cupboard Cafe and Bakery** (121-B Freeway Dr.; 360-336-3107; www.calicocupboardcafe.com) to appease the kids during the car ride, then take a leisurely drive through the fields.

EASTER FEASTER

Gather round the restaurant table for a sweet Easter Sunday brunch at these local eateries.

Cafe Flora
MADISON VALLEY
2901 E. Madison St.
206-325-9100
www.cafeflora.com

This lovely vegetarian and vegan café puts fresh spring produce to good use for its annual brunch (think an asparagus eggs Benedict), plus kids get their own dedicated three-course feast.

Palisade
MAGNOLIA
2601 W. Marina Pl.
206-285-1000
www.palisaderestaurant.com

Sample your way through the seafood-centric brunch buffet at this elegant restaurant, then drink in the incredible skyline view from your table. (Though fancy, this eatery is very friendly to kids, who will also be well entertained by the koi pond running through the restaurant.)

Salty's
WEST SEATTLE
1936 Harbor Ave. SW
206-937-1600
www.saltys.com

DES MOINES
28201 Redondo Beach Dr. S
253-946-0636

The brunch buffet at this waterfront classic is always a satisfying experience (a chocolate fountain!), but Easter brunch kicks things up a notch, with all-you-can eat crab, roasted leg of lamb, and a made-to-order shrimp scampi station.

But if the words "baby animals" elicited squeals of delight from the kiddos, head east to Bellevue instead, to **Kelsey Creek Farm** (page 9), where your brood can take a peek at some other broods; chickens, cows, goats, and sheep call this farm home. You're free to wander, or you can schedule a hands-on farm tour with the affable Farmer Jayne to get an up-close look at the little critters.

Pick up supplies for lunch on the go at the nearest **PCC** (page 230) or **Metropolitan Market** (page 229)—if you've spent the morning amongst the flowers, try the Mount Vernon **Haggen** (2601 E. Divison St.; 360-848-6999; www.haggen.com) before turning back southward—then it's off to the **University District**. There, you can stretch out little legs (and enjoy the spring buds in bloom) at the **Center for Urban Horticulture** (page 43). The **University District Farmers Market** (page 111) is also in full swing every Saturday until 2 p.m.; look for spring crops there, such as asparagus, radishes, and peas, from local farms. Hand over a fiver for the kids to try something new. (How about some squeaky cheese curds from Appel Farms?) Before leaving the area, be sure to take in a landmark spring sight: the abundant **cherry blossoms** that grace the campus (www.depts.washington .edu/grounds/arboriculture), usually by mid-March. Finally, cap off your sweet spring day with a fully stacked burger and shake from **Uneeda Burger** (page 220) in upper Fremont, where the expansive patio should just be opening up for the season.

SUMMER FUN

THE PERFECT SUMMER DAY IN SEATTLE

Slip on those wee sandals, pull out the berry pails, and break out the baseball caps. Bask in a glorious sunny day with these highlights.

It's a bright, sunshiny day. Celebrate with a fresh fruit tart or a unique Japanese baked treat at the Interbay location of **Fuji Bakery** (page 211), and while you're there, pull out your phone and check the **Kindiependent** (page 57) website to see if any cooler-than-cool kiddie bands happen to be playing a free outdoor concert at a nearby park; the odds are good this time of year (also try www.spl.org, www.sno-isle.org, and www.kcls.org for library concert tips). If not, then swing the kids by the Seattle Symphony's **Soundbridge** (page 58) at Benaroya Hall so they can jam for a bit before you head for a nearby farm for some **berry picking** (see box on page 140). The **Mercer Slough Blueberry Farm** is the closest in Bellevue, but **Remlinger Farms** in Carnation offers an amusement park and petting zoo to go along with its fields of berries.

If you didn't flee for the berry fields, instead enjoy lunch on the go by hunting down either the **Grilled Cheese Experience** (page 253) or **Maximus/Minimus** (page 253) food trucks (usually located Downtown or in South Lake Union; check the websites for any given day's location)—for a gooey grilled cheese or deliciously sloppy pulled-pork sandwich, respectively—then head to the adventure-filled **Jefferson Park** (page 73) on Beacon Hill for an afternoon of careening down slides, splashing in the spray park, and flying on not just one, but two speedy zip lines fit for creating your own cooling breeze.

From there consider spending the late-afternoon hours with the many Seattleites flocking to Green Lake. With a picturesque **pitch-and-putt course** (page 19), a **playground and wading pool** (page 76), and a **paved walking trail** (page 76), you can sunbathe in pretty much any way you please. But here's guessing once the kids spy the pedal boats and kayaks out on the water, they'll be pulling you toward the **Greenlake Boathouse** (page 64) to rent one.

For dinner, chow down at **Rosita's Mexican Grill** (page 223) nearby, where kids are handed hot handmade tortillas to munch the moment you sit down. Then decide whether you'll burn off those calories by ducking over to Ballard for the evening to sling some Frisbee at the beach at **Golden Gardens Park** (page 62); be sure to bring marshmallows for toasting, in case there's a fire pit free. Or take in a ball game at Safeco Field, home of the **Seattle Mariners** (page 51). You can root, root, root for the home team as you also watch the city lights begin to twinkle from your vantage point in the center field bleachers, the best spot in the stadium for both the view and the price (as cheap as $10 a ticket).

FINGER-LICKING BERRY PICKING

Fill your bucket (and tummies) with ripe, juicy strawberries, blueberries, and more at these picturesque farms outside Seattle. (Be sure check websites for hours and pricing—ye be warned, many farms only take cash.)

Biringer Farm
ARLINGTON
21412 59th Ave. NE
425-259-0255
www.biringerfarm.com

Providing berry lovers with sweet strawberries for over 60 years, this farm is about an hour north of the city. Ride the Jolly Trolley down to the fields and pick away. (Staffers won't even bat an eyelash over berry-stained lips on the way back.)

Mercer Slough Blueberry Farm
BELLEVUE
2102 Bellevue Way SE
425-452-6885
www.ci.bellevue.wa.us/blueberry_farm.htm

Tucked within the larger Mercer Slough Nature Park (page 91), this u-pick farm is conveniently located minutes from downtown Bellevue.

ALL IN THE FALL

FALL IN LOVE WITH THE CITY

Crisp mornings and sunny afternoons in autumn provide a delightful mix of indoor (sweet story times!) and outdoor (leaf stomping!) adventuring.

Depending on how ravenous the family is on this fine fall morning, either gobble up a (really) big and (really) hearty breakfast at the **5 Spot** (page 214) on Queen Anne Hill, or head a few blocks down to charming **Le Rêve Bakery & Café** (page 212)

Mountainview Blueberry Farm

<small>SNOHOMISH</small>

7617 E. Lowell-Larimer Rd.
360-668-3391
www.mountainviewblueberryfarm.com

This picturesque farm about forty-five minutes northeast of Seattle offers 9 acres of blueberries, including a few hard-to-find varieties. Grab a bucket at the stand, then saunter out to the fields, where you'll catch views of the Cascade Range and Mount Baker on a clear day.

Remlinger Farms

<small>CARNATION</small>

32610 NE 32nd St.
425-333-4135
www.remlingerfarms.com

Yes, you can eat the juicy strawberries and raspberries right off the vine at this famed farm (only all-natural fertilizers are used here), but good luck even getting your tykes to the field once they spy the kiddie amusement park, complete with a steam train, canoe ride, and even a mini roller coaster.

for a lighter croissant or tart to pair with the café's stellar lattes. While you're on the Hill, duck into **Queen Anne Book Company** (page 176) to curl up with a book, or if it's Saturday, head to **Once Upon a Time** (page 176) for its weekly 10:30 a.m. story time. Then walk over to the **West Queen Anne Playfield** (150 W. Blaine St.; 206-684-4075; www.seattle.gov/parks/find/parks/west-queen -anne-playfield), where the towering trees that line the ball fields provide piles of leaves for crunching. Psst—before leaving this sweet hood, you would do well to snag a sammie from **Homegrown** (page 240) for your upcoming car ride.

As fall also means school's in, get into the collegiate spirit by taking a jaunt over the Fremont or Montlake Bridges—keep an eye out for the crew teams rowing up the canal and through the cut this time of year—and on to the University of Washington campus. The **Union Bay Natural Area** (3501 NE 41st St.; 206-543-8616; www.depts.washington.edu/uwbg/research/ubna.shtml) is great for bird-watching and boasts views of Lake Washington and Husky Stadium, which would be a truly spectacular sight during a football game. (For info on UW sports tickets, see page 53.) Or head south to the **Washington Park Arboretum** (page 43), which is awash in color this time of year with the myriad maples turning bright shades of yellow and orange.

THE GREAT PUMPKIN PATCH

Peruse these popular patches for your autumn jack-o'-lantern. (Don't forget to check websites ahead of time for the most up-to-date times and prices!)

Bob's Corn & Pumpkin Farm
SNOHOMISH
10917 Elliott Rd.
360-668-2506
www.bobscorn.com

With a trike track, a cow train, an apple cannon, and weekend pony rides in addition to the corn mazes and pumpkin patches, your kids will be asking to go to Bob's time and again.

Fox Hollow Farm
ISSAQUAH
12123 Issaquah-Hobart Rd.
425-996-0575
www.foxhollowfamilyfarm.com

This popular farm is filled not only with pumpkins, but also with kids, thanks to the on-site amusements including train rides, a petting zoo, pony rides, and a hay-bale maze.

Next, head for **Gorditos** (page 222) in Greenwood to pick up the biggest burritos you'll ever attempt to eat, then lug those big ol' entrees even farther north to **Carkeek Park** (page 71), where a true Northwest spectacle awaits at **Piper's Creek** (page 93). During the late fall months, the salmon return from the sea to spawn upriver. Trained "salmon stewards" staff the park during the peak season, so let them answer the incessant "why" questions for a bit, then cap off your adventure in the most fitting way possible: by taking a ride down the salmon tunnel slide at the playground nearby.

Maris Farms
BUCKLEY
25001 Sumner-Buckley Hwy.
253-862-2848
www.marisfarms.com

Featuring a corn maze, an animal barn, and a huge pumpkin patch, plus thrilling s, mine shaft slides, and even corn shooters, this beloved south-end patch, located about forty-five minutes southeast of the city, is pure harvest fun.

Spooner Farms
PUYALLUP
9710 SR 162 E
253-840-2059
www.spoonerberries.com

This photo-op-ready farm is beloved by South Enders for berries in the summer, and then over fifty varieties of u-pick pumpkins come fall.

ONE DAY IN SEATTLE

THE CITY'S GREATEST HITS FOR KIDS

You've got twenty-four hours to see the sights, and while the **City Highlights** (page 2) are a good place to start, it would be rather ambitious to conquer in just one day—instead, keep close to the water for a marine-themed day.

Start your morning with a visit to the historic **Pike Place Market** (page 104), which is much easier to traverse earlier in the day. For breakfast, visit the original Starbucks, just to say you did, then head to **Le Panier** (1902 Pike Pl.; 206-441-3669; www.lepanier.com) for a buttery croissant. Once you've roamed the stalls and shops—see the full Market guide on page 108 for ideas—walk down the Hill Climb steps to find yourself at the **Seattle Aquarium** (page 11), where the kids will happily spend the rest of the morning poking sea anemones and laughing at the silly otters. On your way to snag lunch, make a detour for a ride on **the Seattle Great Wheel** (page 95), situated at the end of a pier. The water and city views cannot be beat from the top of the Ferris wheel.

Pick up fish 'n' chips from **Ivar's Fish Bar** (page 246), on Pier 54 on the Elliott Bay waterfront, then head the 1.3 miles north to the **Olympic Sculpture Park** (page 122). There, enjoy the water and Space Needle views while you munch, then amble about the oversize sculptures or walk down to **Myrtle Edwards Park** (page 76), which boasts fantastic pedestrian and bike paths right along the water.

Hop aboard a **Metro bus** (page 5) headed back toward the Market to pick up the car, then drive to **Alki Beach** (page 61) in West Seattle, your destination for the rest of the afternoon. With biking (**Alki Trail**, page 75), kayaking (**Alki Kayak Tours**, page 114), and a playground replete with a whale tail to climb (**Alki Playground**, page 71), there is lots to choose from here. Whatever you do, make sure to take a midactivity break to enjoy some flavored shave ice at **Marination Ma Kai** (page 233).

For dinner, take votes between **La Rustica** (page 236)—a charming family-run Italian eatery tucked off the beach—or a more casual meal at **Blue Moon Burgers** (page 218) near the lighthouse. Once fed, head 4 miles south for a stop at **Lincoln Park** (8011 Fauntleroy Way SW; 206-684-4075; www.seattle.gov /parks/find/parks/lincoln-park) to watch the sunset as ferryboats go by in the foreground. Then spend the rest of the evening licking up ice cream while engaged in an epic family pinball match at **Full Tilt Ice Cream** (page 248) in nearby White Center.

FORTY-EIGHT HOURS IN SEATTLE

EXPANDED GUIDE TO SEEING THE SIGHTS

Assuming you didn't get waylaid or distracted at all the first day (ha!), a second in Seattle should include hopping a ride to a few of the city's scenic viewpoints and landmarks.

Start round two with a hearty breakfast sandwich from **Serious Pie and Biscuit** (page 181) in South Lake Union, then make your way over to Seattle Center, where there's a bevy of kids' activities in addition to a trip up the iconic **Space Needle** (page 105). There, pick up your ride for the day: the **Emerald City Trolley** (page 112). This cheery green trolley offers hop-on, hop-off service to many of the city's sights, May through September. Visiting in the winter? No sweat—just ride the bus, using the handy **Downtown Seattle Transit Tunnel** (metro.kingcounty.gov /tops/tunnel) instead.

Get on and stay on for the first few stops of the tour, which will take you past the waterfront piers and Pike Place Market— been there, done that—before heading south toward the stadiums and the **International District** (neighborhood guide on page 167). Take the kids on a quick cross-cultural tour of the **Uwajimaya** (page 169) Asian grocery store, which is filled with fascinating imported goods, plus a food court that offers oodles of noodles. From there, head back to the trolley stop and hitch a ride to **Pioneer Square** (neighborhood guide on page 173), where you can take a poll to decide your next adventure: far up or way down? If the former wins, head up thirty-five stories to the **Smith Tower Observation Deck** (page 105). Once the tallest building west of the Mississippi, this historic building offers gorgeous downtown and water views. But if your clan prefers to go below, head for the **Underground Tour** (page 106) instead, which takes visitors underneath the city streets for a peek of the city as it was before the 1889 Great Fire. Before leaving the neighborhood, pop into the **Klondike Gold Rush National Historical Park** (page 107), a hidden museum that plays tribute to the 1890s gold rush through fun, newsy exhibits (plus, it's free).

Convince those now-weary legs to hop back on the trolley, enjoying the rest of the ride as it cheerily rolls by the **Seattle Art Museum** (page 121) and up to **Capitol Hill** (neighborhood guide on page 155) before making its final stop at 5th Avenue and Denny Way. Walk two blocks over to another of Tom Douglas's spots, **Home Remedy** (page 229), where you can satisfy your hunger pangs (the pizza by the slice should do the trick). Then devour your takeout meal on one of the rolling lawns at nearby Seattle Center. If you didn't take an early-morning elevator up the Space Needle, consider doing it at sunset. Otherwise, grab some tickets to whatever is playing at the **Pacific Science Center Boeing IMAX Theater** (page 26) and become fully immersed in the moviegoing experience.

PART 2:

NEIGHBORHOOD GUIDES

Just as all kids possess their own distinct personalities, so do Seattle's diverse set of neighborhoods and suburbs, each claiming its own identity and vibe. Explore the activities *and* eccentricities of these places with this **guide to the best stops and shops**—from delightfully weird **Fremont** (page 164) and oh-so-charming **Queen Anne** (page 176) to friendly enclaves like **Columbia City** (page 158), **Madison Park** and **Madrona** (page 170), and **West Seattle** (page 188).

Farther afield, the suburbs beckon, with diversions for daredevils and pretty parks for picnickers. Hop in the car to explore the kid paradise that is **Bellevue** (page 192), the waterfront towns of **Edmonds** (page 197) and **Kirkland** (page 201), or the thrill-seeker-ready trio of **Tukwila, Kent, and Auburn** (page 206).

Honing in on the heartbeat of each hood, the following field guides contain tips on the **best spots to park**—both your car and yourself, should you decide to stay overnight—plus the **most walkable blocks, favorites for food and drink, and places to play, play, play.**

Elliott Bay

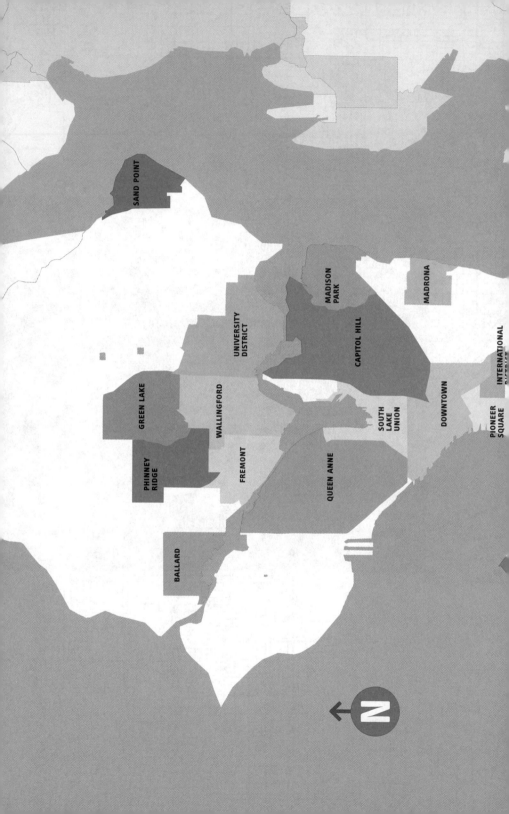

SEATTLE NEIGHBORHOODS

COLUMBIA CITY

SODO

WEST SEATTLE

NEIGHBORHOODS

BALLARD

THE MOOD
This wharf-side fishermen's hangout turned hipster haven is replete with cute boutiques, finger-stickin' sweets, and one heckuva farmers' market.

PARK IT RIGHT THERE
The main attractions of Ballard live near the intersection of NW Market Street and historic Ballard Avenue NW. Metered street parking abounds on Market, but try the neighborhood blocks north of the library (NW 57th St. through 60th St.) or offshoot streets along Ballard Avenue (20th Ave. NW is your best bet) for free, unmetered spots.

STROLLER ALONG
Ballard is made for moseying, especially on Sundays, when the vibrant **Ballard Farmers Market** (page 110) takes over. Kick-start your tour on NW Market Street and 22nd Avenue NW at the airy **Ballard Coffee Works** (page 224) for a quick cuppa joe for the adults, and then over to **Cupcake Royale** (page 244) for a kid-ready sweet before continuing west on Market, where you'll find such cute shops as gift-laden **Annie's Art and Frame** (2212 NW Market St.; 206-784-4761; www.anniesartandframe.com) and record-filled **Sonic Boom Records** (2209 NW Market St.; 206-297-2666; www.sonicboomrecords.com). Then turn that stroller southeast and head for Ballard Avenue NW, which is flush with even more finds.

SHOP HOP
Just past the brick clock tower on the aforementioned avenue, **Clover** (page 116) is a dreamy wonderland filled with wooden train sets, sweet dollhouses, and awesome duds for tykes. A few

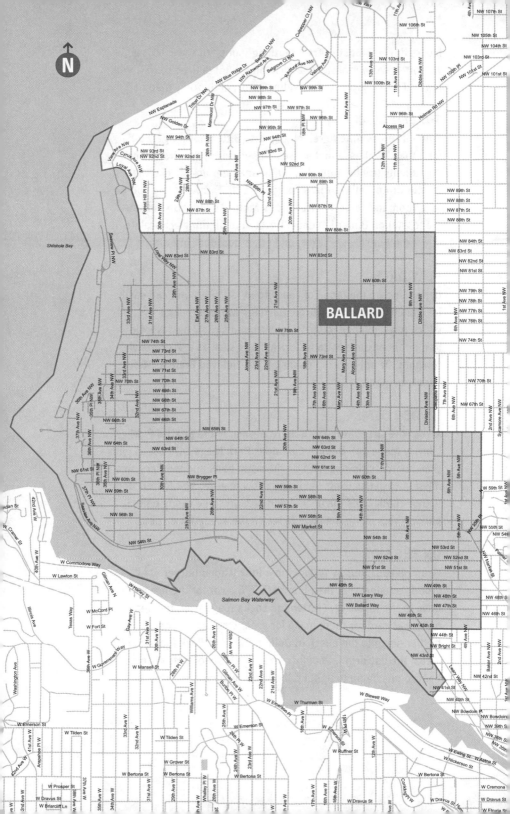

blocks down, **Monster Art & Clothing** (5000 20th Ave. NW; 206-789-0037; www.monsterartandclothing.com) defines quirky, with fun and funky socks, zany greeting cards, and locally made art.

SNACK BREAK

When it comes time to refuel, pop into **Bitterroot** (page 234) for a mac 'n' cheese that arrives topped with your choice of ingredients (try the pulled pork), or snag a quick slice at the counter from **Ballard Pizza Co.** (page 237). But whatever you do, save room for dessert at **Hot Cakes Molten Chocolate Cakery** (page 252) on Ballard Avenue. Devoted to all things chocolate, it offers molten cakes, shakes, and other decadent bites.

PLAY DATE

Depending on the mood of your brood, an afternoon can easily be whiled away at the **Nordic Heritage Museum** (page 35), which pays homage to the neighborhood's roots as a Nordic immigrant enclave, with historical finds such as a Viking-style rowboat. Or opt to take in a flick at the beloved **Majestic Bay Theatres** (page 27).

HIDDEN GEMS

Across the street from the **Ballard Branch** of the **Seattle Public Library** (page 49), **Ballard Commons Park** (page 24) bustles with skateboarders ripping it up on the skate bowl and toddlers on a mission to get soaking wet in the spray feature. Amble next door to **Sweet Mickey's** (page 244) and pick up some candy before parking yourself in the lawn to watch the action for a spell.

ON THE SIDE

Wrap up your tour by picking up a fully loaded burger at **Li'l Woody's** (page 219), then hop back in the car for the five-minute drive to the **Hiram M. Chittenden Locks** (page 104); the beautiful botanical gardens there make for great picnicking. Or sally farther north to the beach at **Golden Gardens Park** (page 62) to watch the day drift into night, when the first-come-first-served bonfire pits begin to light up the sandy expanse.

SLEEP ON IT
Ballard Inn (5300 Ballard Ave. NW; 206-789-5011; www.ballardinnseattle.com), a small sixteen-room hotel housed in a historic building smack in the heart of the neighborhood, is your best bet for staying close-by. (But warn the kids: some suites do share bathrooms.)

CAPITOL HILL

THE MOOD
Just east of Downtown, the hustling Hill will keep tiny tummies satisfied with goodies from bakeries and cafés that exude cool urban vibes, day into very late night.

PARK IT RIGHT THERE
With its commuter bustle and tight quarters, this hood can be short on parking, especially on the weekends. Your best bets are the sleepier streets off the main strip of Broadway, particularly 12th through 14th Avenues between East Pike Street and East Denny Way. Better yet, take **Link** light rail (page 5), which now connects to the Hill from Downtown; the short four-minute ride to the Broadway and East John Street station will save you any parking hassle.

STROLLER ALONG
You could meander for blocks and blocks on Capitol Hill, but the stretch along 10th Avenue between East Pine and East Union Streets is easily accomplished in the seemingly precarious one- or maybe two-hour window when the toddler will agree to stay in the stroller. Saunter southward along that avenue, then once you reach East Union, complete your loop by turning back north on either the charming 11th or 12th Avenues. Other stops of note on the Hill include the kneeling **Jimi Hendrix statue** (located at the northeast corner of Broadway and Pine) and the colorful **rainbow crosswalk** painted on the street at the intersection of 10th Avenue and Pine Street.

CAPITOL HILL

SHOP HOP

On 10th, you'll find **Elliott Bay Book Company** (page 47), a Seattle classic filled with books stacked on gorgeous wood shelves. Time it right and sit in on the free weekly story time for children, on Saturdays at 11 a.m.

SNACK BREAK

Right next door, you'll be met with a tough choice: to sit and sip one of **Oddfellows Cafe & Bar**'s rich and velvety hot cocoa creations (1525 10th Ave.; 206-325-0807; www.oddfellowscafe .com), which come topped with house-made creamy marshmallows, or to head to **Molly Moon's** scoop shop (page 249) for a cone of balsamic strawberry or salted caramel ice cream. (Or choose both.)

PARKS & REC

The ever-popular **Cal Anderson Park** (page 65) boasts one of the most beautiful fountains in the city, perfect for dousing those tired tootsies after your walkabout on the Hill.

ON THE SIDE

Located about a five-minute drive from the main hub, the north end of Capitol Hill is home to kid-friendly eateries and escapades. If the littles have gotten "hangry," head straight for **Vios Cafe** (903 19th Ave. E; 206-329-3236; www.vioscafe.com). This kid-friendly Greek spot has an impressively stocked toy area for kids to play in before gobbling up some fries dunked in whipped feta dip. Near Vios, the **Volunteer Park Conservatory** (page 44) offers a beautiful glass-encased hothouse filled with tropical plants. The larger park's sprawling lawns and play area beg for a picnic—and the neighboring **Volunteer Park Cafe** (1501 17th Ave. E; 206-328-3155; www.alwaysfreshgoodness.com) is happy to oblige, with bacon-and-egg panini, baguette sandwiches, and chewy cookies available for takeout. The park is also home to the **Asian Art Museum** (page 119), which offers free family programs the first Saturday of every month, including arts activities and live performances to help introduce the kiddos to Asian culture and art.

SLEEP ON IT

The **Silver Cloud Hotel Seattle–Broadway** (1100 Broadway; 206-325-1400; www.silvercloud.com/seattlebroadway) is a welcome spot to kick up your heels after a long day, with an indoor pool on-site and a free shuttle to and from Downtown to help you explore with ease.

COLUMBIA CITY

THE MOOD

This South Side enclave is oh-so-friendly to families, with a sweet downtown strip and delish dining that includes a pinball-crazy ice-cream shop.

PARK IT RIGHT THERE

Head for the intersection of Rainier Avenue South and South Ferdinand Street to find yourself in the heart of Columbia City. Go east on Ferdinand to find easy street parking and an inexpensive pay lot ($2 per hour). Or ditch the car completely by hopping aboard **Link** light rail (page 5) from Downtown. Either way, once there, head for the cheery sight of **Geraldine's Counter** (page 214), where you really ought to pop in for a hearty egg scramble or stack of pancakes to start your day.

STROLLER ALONG & SHOP HOP

From Geraldine's, make a delightful little loop through the neighborhood's "downtown" by crossing Rainier and ducking immediately into **Columbia City Bouquet** (4873 Rainier Ave. S; 206-722-2200; www.columbiacitybouquet.com) to gander at the many gifts, flowers, and birthday balloons on offer. Next, saunter north, first to **Gather** (4863 Rainier Ave. S; 206-760-0674; www.gatherconsignment.com), a women's consignment store, and then to **Retroactive Kids** (4859 Rainier Ave. S; 206-932-3154; www.retroactivekids.com). This delightful toy shop is full of nostalgia, including vintage-style games, as well as a book nook and an in-house kiddie salon, Columbia City Cuts (if the race-car chair doesn't convince junior to get a haircut,

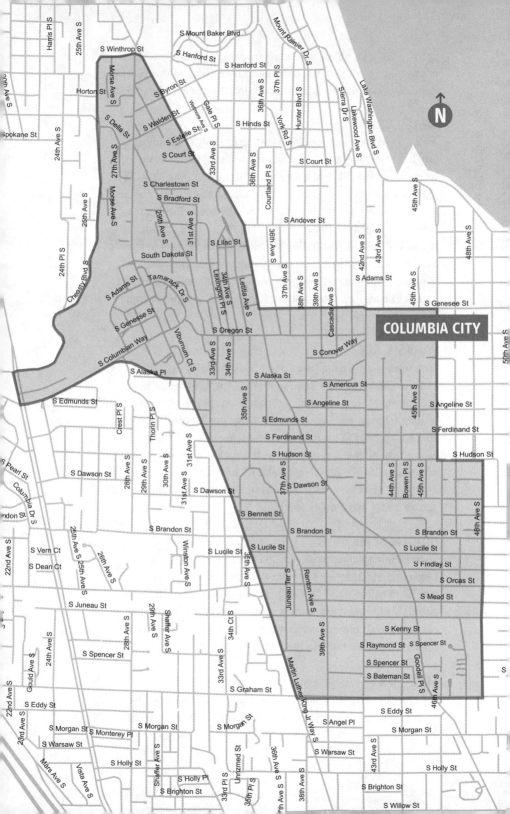

nothing will). Complete your walk by popping into the historic brick building housing the **Columbia City Branch** of **the Seattle Public Library** (page 49) before crossing the street to head back.

SNACK BREAK

Truly one of the most popular bakeries in Seattle, **Columbia City Bakery** (page 210) is always worth a stop for a cookie, croissant, or other baked treat, as is **Tutta Bella** (page 239), a place known not only for wood-fired pizzas but also for handing dough to little ones to play with before the meal. But it's the ever-fun **Full Tilt Ice Cream** (page 248) that is sure to produce squeals of delight. In addition to handmade ice cream in flavors like bourbon maple walnut, orange Creamsicle, and root beer, the ice creamery offers a wealth of raucous pinball and arcade games to play. Hey, Mom and Dad, try not to hog the machines too much, m'kay?

PARKS & REC

With expansive playing fields and hiking trails that crisscross its 57 acres, **Genesee Park and Playfield** (4316 S. Genesee St.; 206-684-4075; www.seattle.gov/parks/find/parks/genesee -park-and-playfield), a five-minute drive northeast of downtown Columbia City, is fit for running and roaming. Stretch those legs with a hike all the way east across the park and be rewarded with views of Lake Washington and its beautiful shores. Need another dose of nature? The amazing **Seward Park** (page 88) is just an additional 2 miles south.

HIDDEN GEMS

Spend some time puttering around **Bike Works** (3709 S. Ferdinand St.; 206-725-8867; www.bikeworks.org), a nonprofit bike shop committed to making cycling accessible and affordable for all. It also runs a youth program, allowing kids to earn their own bikes through volunteer work. So you can often see kids fixing up bikes in the back of the shop.

SLEEP ON IT

It's easiest to stay Downtown and day-trip it to Columbia City—see accommodation recommendations for Downtown on page 163.

DOWNTOWN

THE MOOD

The epicenter for all things business and cultural in the city, Downtown offers up playful toy shops, walking tours, and, of course, some of the most iconic sights in the Northwest.

PARK IT RIGHT THERE

Parking in Downtown Seattle (especially on weekdays) can be a true hassle, so take the guesswork out of the equation and head straight for **Pacific Place** (600 Pine St.; 206-405-2655; www.pacificplaceseattle.com). With six floors of subterranean parking, plus a convenient location in the heart of the city, this mall is a great park-and-peruse spot.

STROLLER ALONG

The downtown core boasts multiple loops you can make depending on the stamina of little legs. For a classic tour, start at the aforementioned Pacific Place and head west on Pine Street, past **Nordstrom** (500 Pine St.; 206-628-2111; www .nordstrom.com) and **Westlake Center** (400 Pine St.; 206-467-1600; www.westlakecenter.com), all the way to 1st Avenue, where you'll run into **Pike Place Market** (page 104). (For those of you who can't help but answer chocolate's call, be aware you'll have to pass **Chocolate Box** en route; more on page 225.) From the Market, you can stroll back on Pike Street, going the opposite direction.

SHOP HOP

Kids can pretty much shop until they drop Downtown. At Westlake Center alone, **Daiso** (400 Pine St., Level 2; 206-625-0076; www.daisollc.com) delights with quirky imported finds from Japan, and just downstairs, little brainiacs fittingly go nuts for **Marbles: The Brain Store** (400 Pine St., Level 1; 206-682-1325; www.marblesthebrainstore.com) and its wide selection of educational games and puzzles. Northwest-owned **Candy Tyme** (400 Pine St., Level 3; 206-623-0454; www.candytyme.com) is not only stocked with over two hundred bins of bulk candy but also offers a bevy Hello Kitty toys and accessories.

SNACK BREAK

Pike Place Market (page 104) is a veritable cornucopia of eats, from the grilled cheese at **Beecher's Handmade Cheese** (page 234) to the fully stacked meatloaf sammich at **Three Girls Bakery** (page 242). Need something sweet to polish off your meal? A jam-kissed crumpet from **the Crumpet Shop** (1503 1st Ave.; 206-682-1598; www.thecrumpetshop.com) will do quite nicely.

PARKS & REC

If you are lucky enough to visit during the summer months, be sure to catch a (free!) concert courtesy of the **Out to Lunch Concert Series** (page 60), held weekdays in such locations as Westlake Park and Occidental Square. Or get your rec on with a walking tour. The **Seattle By Foot Kids' Tour** (page 112) guides families through Downtown Seattle with a kid's viewpoint in mind. Expect to find fountains, parks, *Hammering Man* at SAM, and much more along this jaunt.

PLAY DATE

Check out a story time at the **Central Library** (page 49), housed in a modern glass building akin to an art museum. (Or just explore! Download the library's self-guided tour tips at www.spl .org/documents/audiences/chi/kidsself-guidedtour.pdf.) Nearby, the Seattle Symphony's **Soundbridge** (page 58) is another delight for tykes as young as age 3. Drop by on Fridays between 10 a.m. and 2 p.m. for a musical story time and other related activities (read "jam sessions").

SLEEP ON IT

Downtown is the place to stay and play, with over a dozen options within a six-block radius. With kids in tow, the **Sheraton Seattle Hotel** (1400 6th Ave.; 206-621-9000; www .sheratonseattle.com) and **The Westin Seattle** (1900 5th Ave.; 206-728-1000; www.westinseattle.com) are both hits with indoor pools, or try the **Holiday Inn Seattle Downtown** (211 Dexter Ave. N; 206-728-8123; www.ihg.com/holidayinn/hotels/us/en/seattle /seasc/hoteldetail); conveniently located between Downtown and Seattle Center, the hotel exudes a casual vibe.

FREMONT, PHINNEY RIDGE & GREEN LAKE

THE MOOD

The self-proclaimed "Center of the Universe," Fremont is delightfully kooky–where else can you find a giant troll lurking under a bridge?–while neighboring Phinney Ridge and Green Lake will woo you too, boasting Woodland Park Zoo and the most popular city lake.

PARK IT RIGHT THERE

Kick-start your tour by driving north from Downtown Seattle across the bright-blue **Fremont Bridge** (www.seattle.gov /transportation/bridges.htm), one of busiest drawbridges in the country, then hang a left onto Fremont Place North, which turns into North 36th Street. From there, turn up one of the many residential streets to find free street parking–Evanston, Dayton, and Francis Avenues North are usually good bets.

STROLLER ALONG

From the car, head into the heart of Fremont–North 34th, 35th, and 36th Streets between Phinney and Fremont Avenues North. Heading east on 36th, you'll soon see the **statue of Lenin** (corner of N. 36th St. and Fremont Pl. N), the neighborhood's slightly inexplicable bronze monument to Vladimir Lenin. But your walkabout is far from done. Keep meandering along 36th until it passes under the towering Aurora Bridge; there, tucked underneath, you'll spy the **Fremont Troll** (3405 Troll Pl. N), a huge troll sculpture holding a Volkswagen Bug. Kids (and adults) can clamber on up as much as they please. Loop around to 35th, and it's all downhill to the main attractions.

SHOP HOP

Held every weekend the **Fremont Sunday Market** (page 110)– filled with flea-market finds, a farmers' market, and funny collectibles–makes for fantastic people-watching. Around the corner from the market's main hub, **Destee-Nation Shirt Company** (3412 Evanston Ave. N; 206-324-9403; www .desteenation.com) offers quirky graphic-print T-shirts for the

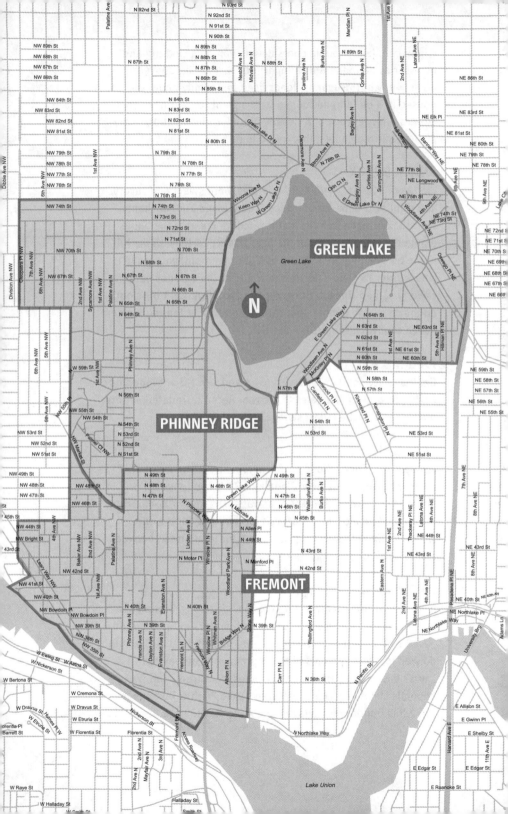

whole fam. Just a couple doors down, women's clothing and accessories boutique **Burnt Sugar** (601 N. 35th St.; 206-545-0699; www.burntsugar.us) lends itself to a family photo op; it's housed in a building festooned with a giant rocket on the roof. (You can now even spot a cleverly placed art installation of the planet Saturn on a neighboring building.)

SNACK BREAK

Pie (page 252) bakes up handheld pies, both sweet and savory, and right next door, **Bluebird Ice Cream** (page 248) enchants with shakes made from its handcrafted ice cream. (The adults would do well to ask about the beer floats.) Farther up the hill, in the burgeoning area known as Upper Fremont, you can get your burger fix—and soak up some sun on the outdoor patio—at cleverly named **Uneeda Burger** (page 220). But don't miss out on the chance to gobble up a Caribbean Roast at the renowned **Paseo** sandwich shop (page 241).

PARKS & REC

Get that slow-roasted sandwich to go and savor it at **Woodland Park**, just outside the gates to the zoo. Recently updated, it now boasts some of the tallest swings in the city—whee!

PLAY DATE

Located on Phinney Ridge at North 50th Street and Fremont Avenue North, the 92-acre **Woodland Park Zoo** (page 12) is a primo stop for animal lovers of any age. The indoor **Zoomazium** is designed just for tiny tykes with fun building blocks and slides, along with musical instruments for jamming in between animal exhibits.

ON THE SIDE

A quick two-minute drive from the zoo, glistening **Green Lake** beckons walkers, joggers, bikers, and boarders to the 2.8-mile paved **trail loop** (page 76) surrounding it. Skateboarders would do well to inform parents of the impressive skate bowl at **Lower Woodland Park** (page 24), across the street, and PGA hopefuls should check out the **Green Lake Pitch & Putt** (page 19), while budding boaters will point the way toward **Greenlake**

Boathouse (page 64), which has been renting kayaks and canoes to adventurers since the 1970s.

SLEEP ON IT
Given that these hoods are easily accessible from the epicenter of the city, it's probably best to stay either in South Lake Union or Downtown—see recommendations on pages 181 and 163 respectively.

INTERNATIONAL DISTRICT & SODO

THE MOOD
Bordered by SoDo—which houses everything from sports stadiums and warehouses to a trapeze school and a computer museum— the International District offers a (delicious) taste of Asia.

PARK IT RIGHT THERE
You'll find the International District, one of the city's oldest neighborhoods, tucked just east of Pioneer Square, centered around the Uwajimaya marketplace located at 5th Avenue South and South Lane Street. The easiest street parking is found north of South Dearborn Street, on Maynard Avenue South, 7th Avenue South, or 8th Avenue South. These spots are snapped up quickly on game days, but the ID is oh-so-accessible via the **Downtown Seattle Transit Tunnel** (King County Metro, page 5) or **Link** light rail (page 5), so consider hopping aboard a bus or train instead.

STROLLER ALONG
From the ornate Chinese archways that cross several streets to the eclectic shops and eateries, there's plenty to keep kids agape during the popular **Chinatown Discovery Tours** (page 37) put on by the **Wing Luke Museum** (page 37). This ninety-minute walking tour canvases the neighborhood's streets, including a stop at the **Panama Hotel** (605½ S. Main St.; 206-223-9242; www.panamahotel.net), a historic inn that provides an eye-opening experience with a see-through glass floor revealing

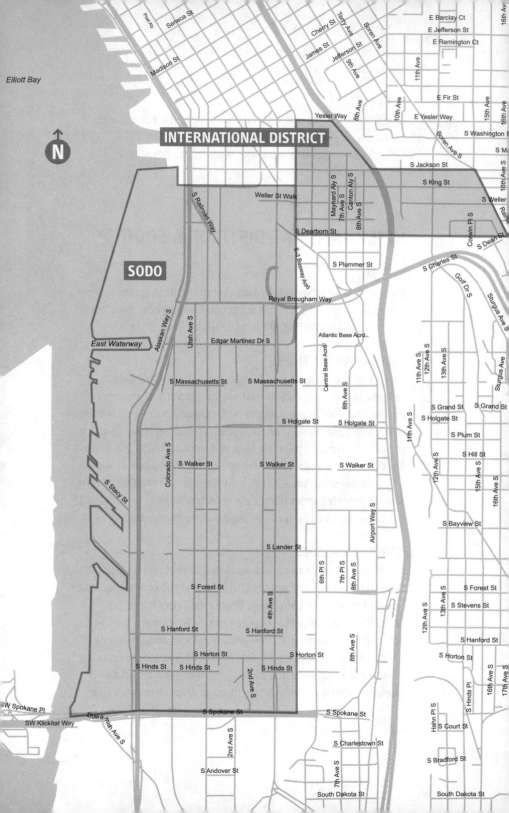

still-left-behind goods stashed in the basement during the internment of Japanese Americans during World War II.

SHOP HOP

Located at 6th Avenue South and South Jackson Street, sweet little **Momo** (600 S. Jackson St.; 206-329-4736; www .momoseattle.com) contains a bevy of fashion finds, gifts, and trinkets. Next door, you can also comb through **Kobo at Higo** (604 S. Jackson St.; 206-381-3000; www.koboseattle.com) for quirky imported knickknacks. Then get lost for hours in **Uwajimaya** (600 5th Ave. S; 206-624-6248; www.uwajimaya .com), a specialty Asian grocery store that also offers home goods, craft supplies (kids go wild for the funny pencil erasers in food shapes), and a food court filled with everything from succulent satay to spicy rice dishes.

SNACK BREAK

Two of the city's best bakeries call this part of the city home. In the ID, **Fuji Bakery** (page 211) serves up Japanese-fusion baked goods, including a matcha-green-tea Danish and a PB&J doughnut, which hungry tykes will devour. In SoDo, not far from the stadiums, it's a sweet and a show for visitors to **Macrina Bakery** (page 212), where kids can peer through the huge glass windows that divide the busy bakers from the eatery.

PARKS & REC

The "parks" that define this neighborhood are unlike any other: Safeco Field, home of the **Seattle Mariners** (page 51) MLB team, and CenturyLink Field, which hosts the NFL's **Seattle Seahawks** (page 54) and the MLS's **Seattle Sounders FC** (page 56). Looking to get on the field? Both Safeco and CenturyLink offer tours of the stadiums' inner workings (tickets are $10–$12 for Safeco Field tours, $8–$14 for tours of the Clink).

PLAY DATE

Yes, you can join the circus at **Emerald City Trapeze Arts** (page 94), where kids age 6 and up can take to the flying trapeze. Schedule a lesson and get swingin'.

HIDDEN GEMS

Those aforementioned SoDo warehouses now house a burgeoning set of businesses, including the **Seattle Bouldering Project** (page 22, which features a dedicated kids' area for little ones to try their hands (and feet) at rope-free rock climbing. In another warehouse, you'll find the **Living Computer Museum** (page 84). An inexpensive romp ($2–$4 for admission), this Paul Allen–owned facility features antique computers dating back to the '60s. The museum also offers myriad vintage gaming consoles to try out during your visit.

SLEEP ON IT

Located directly across the street from Safeco Field, the **Silver Cloud Hotel Seattle–Stadium** (1046 1st Ave. S; 206-204-9800; www.silvercloud.com/seattlestadium) offers you-can't-get-any-closer access to the fields. Plus, it has a rooftop pool for cooling off at day's end.

MADISON PARK & MADRONA

THE MOOD

East of Capitol Hill, natty Madison Park and neighborly Madrona please the tiniest visitors with toy shops, frosted treats, and lakefront parks brimming with sandy fun.

PARK IT RIGHT THERE

From Downtown Seattle, take Madison Street east for about 3 miles until you reach the "downtown" of the hood, which is centered around the actual Madison Park, at the intersection of 42nd Avenue East. Parking is usually no sweat, either on Madison itself or on the neighboring streets.

STROLLER ALONG & SHOP HOP

Pick a theme for your walk—urban safari or pastoral park—by either perusing the shops on Madison or sauntering through the 8.3-acre park (more on that option on page 172). Start your shop hop at the adorable **Red Wagon Toys** (page 117), where the Dutch front door is just the beginning of its charms; those include a dress-up corner and an extensive collection of

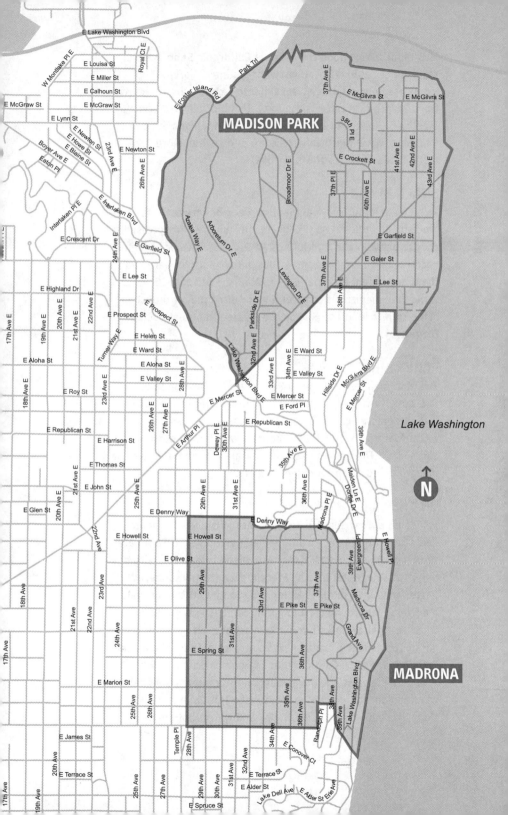

kids' books. Next door, **the Original Children's Shop** (4216 E. Madison St.; 206-328-7121; www.theoriginalchildrensshop .com) has been offering sweet children's clothing, plus haircuts from its in-house salon, since 1993. This block is also home to **Martha E. Harris Flowers & Gifts** (4218 E. Madison St.; 206-568-0347; www.marthaeharris.com) and kitchen store **Cookin'** (4224 E. Madison St.; 206-328-2665).

SNACK BREAK

Pick up a midtour snack at **Madison Park Bakery** (4214 E. Madison St.; 206-322-3238), where kids will be hard-pressed to choose between the colorful frosted sugar cookies or its famous bacon maple bars. For a more substantial snack, either head to **the Independent Pizzeria** (4235 E. Madison St.; 206-860-6110; www.theindiepizzeria.com) for a wood-fired pie, or munch on some chips and guacamole on the (heated!) patio at **Cactus** (page 222).

PARKS & REC

The aforementioned **Madison Park** (4201 E. Madison St.; 206-684-4075; www.seattle.gov/parks/find/parks/madison-park) features grassy fields suited to pickup ball games as well as a 400-foot beach lawn that is mobbed with beachgoers on sunny days. There are also three separate play zones within the playground to suit playground pros of any age.

ON THE SIDE

Just south of Madison Park, dear Madrona is a lovely spot to dedicate a morning or an afternoon. The popular **Hi Spot Café** (1410 34th Ave.; 206-325-7905; www.hispotcafe.com) welcomes diners of all ages for brioche French toast, freshly squeezed juices, and egg scrambles all morning long. With swings galore, **Madrona Playground** (3211 E. Spring St.; 206-684-4075; www.seattle.gov/parks/find/parks/madrona-playground) is also oh-so-conveniently located next door to an outpost of **Cupcake Royale** (page 244). Consider nibbling on your cupcake while watching the glassblowers at work on the company's signature candleholders at the nearby **Glassybaby Hot Shop** (3406 E. Union St.; 206-518-9071; www.glassybaby.com/hot-shop).

If it's a warm one, take refuge on the trails of **Madrona Woods** (853 Lake Washington Blvd.; 206-684-4075; www.seattle.gov/parks/find/parks/madrona-park) or head to **Madrona Park Beach** (same contact as Madrona Woods) on the shores of Lake Washington for a toe dunk. Wrap up the day with a fantastic dinner at **St. Clouds** (page 217), where every kids' meal is finished off with a complimentary ice-cream sundae.

SLEEP ON IT

Given its proximity to Capitol Hill, the most convenient sleeping spots near Madison Park are located there; see page 158.

PIONEER SQUARE

THE MOOD

The oldest neighborhood in the city, Pioneer Square offers the kind of history lessons kids actually like—with a gold rush museum and an eerie-cool tour that goes below the city streets.

PARK IT RIGHT THERE

Parking in this busy neighborhood is quite tricky, but there are a number of garages nearby (try the garage at 1st Ave. and Cherry St.). The easiest way to check out the area is by hopping on **Link** light rail (page 5) and getting off at the Pioneer Square station.

STROLLER ALONG & SHOP HOP

The main hub of Pioneer Square lies at the intersection of 1st Avenue and Yesler Way, where the bright and cheery marquee of **Magic Mouse Toys** (page 117) calls the kiddos inside. There you'll find an abundance of puzzles and games, and a book nook. From there, head south on 1st, past the many eateries and shops—**E. Smith Mercantile** (208 1st Ave. S; 206-641-7250; www.esmithmercantile.com) is a fun stop for American-made products—before turning left on South Main Street. There you'll find **Occidental Square** (117 S. Washington St.; 206-684-4075; www.seattle.gov/parks/find/parks/occidental-square), a busy plaza overflowing with pedestrians and pigeons, which also

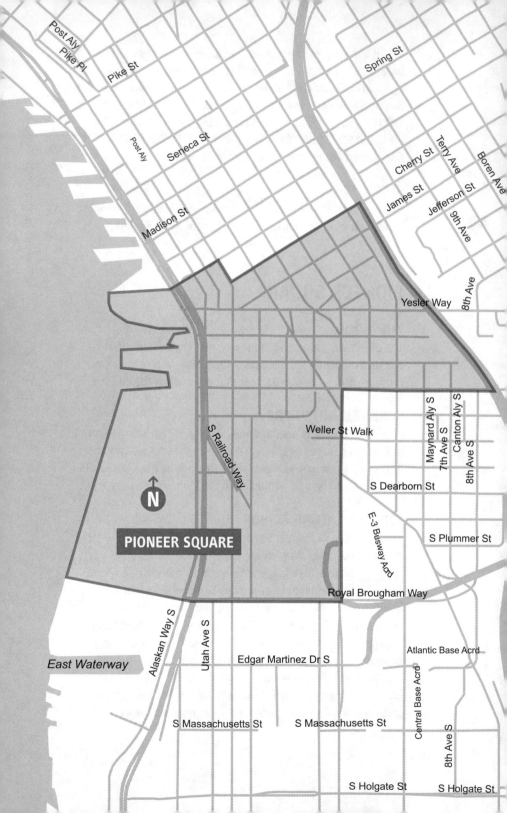

features a memorial to fallen firefighters. Head one more block east to find the little-known **Waterfall Garden Park** (219 2nd Ave. S; 206-684-2489), featuring a 22-foot man-made falls; pull up a chair at one of the patio tables to relax or have a snack.

SNACK BREAK

There are two spots for great grab-and-go sammies in the area. **Grand Central Bakery** (page 212), right by Occidental Square, offers fantastic deli-style options piled high on bread baked in-house. But if it's open, get yourself an Italian sandwich from **Salumi** (page 242), a hole-in-the-wall *salumeria* run by the family of superstar chef Mario Batali.

PARKS & REC

It's a little-known fact, but Pioneer Square is also home to a national park, the **Klondike Gold Rush National Historical Park** (page 107). Helmed by the friendly park rangers, this little museum is free for all and covers Seattle's unique part in the gold rush of the late 1890s.

HIDDEN GEMS

This hidden gem is truly hidden. The **Underground Tour** (page 106) quite literally takes tourgoers under the city streets, for a look at the artifacts and ruins leftover from Seattle's Great Fire of 1889.

SLEEP ON IT

The **Courtyard Seattle Downtown/Pioneer Square** (612 2nd Ave.; 206-625-1111; www.marriott.com/hotels/travel/seaps -courtyard-seattle-downtown-pioneer-square) may be located in a historic 1904 building, but it offers such modern amenities as a gym and an indoor pool.

QUEEN ANNE

THE MOOD

North of Downtown, Queen Anne is a pint-size delight, with book, game, and toy shops dotting the walkable main lane, plus one of the city's most awe-inspiring viewpoints.

PARK IT RIGHT THERE

Head for the intersection of Queen Anne Avenue North and West Boston Street; from there, turn east onto Boston and start playing I Spy a Parking Spot on the residential streets of 1st, 2nd, and 3rd Avenues West (which shouldn't be too hard of a game, really).

STROLLER ALONG & SHOP HOP

The top of Queen Anne provides a walk-and-shop tour that's short enough for little legs to keep up. Starting at that previously mentioned intersection, head first into **Blue Highway Games** (page 118). Filled with rare and unique games, the shop also offers snacks and playing tables, should you want to sit and play awhile. Take a quick detour across the street to **Queen Anne Dispatch** (2212 Queen Anne Ave. N; 206-286-1024; www .queenannedispatch.com) to check out its selection of shoes, accessories, and precious baby clothes. From there head south, where the delights come one after the other. **Queen Anne Book Company** (1811 Queen Anne Ave. N.; 206-284-2427; www .qabookco.com) is everything a neighborhood bookshop should be, staffed by friendly clerks and featuring the sweetest of children's book sections. One more block brings you to **Once Upon a Time** (1622 Queen Anne Ave. N; 206-284-7260; www .onceuponatimeseattle.com), a beloved children's clothing and toy store that even offers classes like toddler yoga. And still one more block will bring you just rewards at the end of your exploration: the hearty, satisfying portions of all-American fare at the **5 Spot** (page 214).

SNACK BREAK

You can also satisfy the family sweet teeth on Queen Anne. **Chocolopolis** (page 225) melts up one of the richest cups of hot cocoa around. (Choose any chocolate bar in the store to be made into your treat.) In a red house replete with a sweet garden patio, **Le Rêve Bakery & Café** (page 212) offers amazing twice-baked

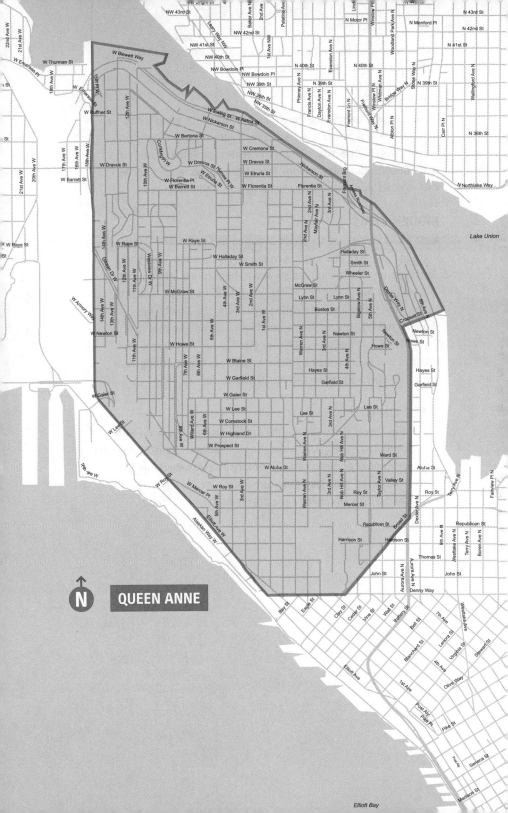

QUEEN ANNE

chocolate croissants and fruit tarts to enjoy. Next door, **El Diablo Coffee Co.** (page 226) serves Cuban coffee and food.

PARKS & REC

On wet days, **Queen Anne Pool** (page 67) provides great indoor fun, but the real action is at **East Queen Anne Playground** (1912 Warren Ave. N; 206-684-4075; www.seattle.gov/parks/find/parks /east-queen-anne-playground) during the opposite weather as kiddos splash and dash in the wading pool and playground.

HIDDEN GEMS

Most likely you've seen a photo snapped at **Kerry Park** (211 W. Highland Dr.; 206-684-4075; www.seattle.gov/parks/find/parks /kerry-park), which is tucked somewhat obscurely into a quiet Queen Anne neighborhood. Once you find it, you'll be awestruck by the impressive view of the Space Needle, the downtown skyline, and Elliott Bay. Take a family photo, then head down the flight of stairs to **Bayview-Kinnear Park** (page 70), where the kids can run wild by making their way across the climbing wall or sliding down slides tucked into the hillside.

SLEEP ON IT

Located in Lower Queen Anne, the family-owned **Maxwell Hotel** (300 Roy St.; 877-298-9728; www.themaxwellhotel.com) is dog- and kid-friendly, and has complimentary bicycles available to check out during your stay. (The convenient location near Seattle Center and **Dick's Drive-In**—page 219—is pretty sweet too.)

SOUTH LAKE UNION

THE MOOD
Home to some of the city's most illustrious tech companies (oh, hey, Amazon), South Lake Union appeals to families, thanks to the body of water it's named for nearby—and all the activities that come along with it.

PARK IT RIGHT THERE
Centered along Westlake Avenue North between Denny Way and Mercer Street, South Lake Union still offers decent street parking, especially in the blocks of 8th and 9th Avenues North at Harrison Street, where ten-hour metered spots are typically available.

STROLLER ALONG
In my humble opinion, South Lake Union is best toured by the **Seattle Streetcar** (page 7). Pick up the cheery little trolley at the Westlake Avenue and Olive Way stop in Downtown Seattle and then hop on and hop off as you please. Stops of note include the Westlake Avenue North and Denny Way, which will drop you in front of **Tutta Bella** (page 239), where you can enjoy some pizza on the deck if it's a sunny day. Another is at the intersection of Terry Avenue North and Harrison Street. There you'll find **Ping Pong Plaza** (www.bustersimpson.net/pingpongplaza), outfitted with an outdoor bronze-and-steel Ping-Pong table for all to enjoy; plan ahead and BYOP (bring your own paddles—and balls). End your streetcar trip at **Lake Union Park** (page 181), a lovely spot to hang after your ride.

SHOP HOP
Outdoor enthusiasts would do well to take a detour to the flagship **REI** store (222 Yale Ave. N; 206-470-4083; www.rei.com), which offers not only retail gear but also an unusual climbing wall. The glass-encased pinnacle is 65 feet of fun, giving intrepid climbers a just reward for reaching the top: a breathtaking view of the Seattle skyline and sparkling Lake Union. Single climbs are available for $25–$50 per person (discounts available to REI members); climbers must be at least age 5.

SNACK BREAK

Time to cast your vote. Breakfast means making a tough choice between a stacked biscuit sammich from chef Tom Douglas's **Serious Pie and Biscuit** (401 Westlake Ave. N; 206-436-0050; www.seriouspieseattle.com) or the fully loaded toppings bar–stocked with fresh fruit, whipped cream, and syrups for your waffle or pancakes–at **Portage Bay Cafe** (page 216). Whichever side loses the breakfast battle can pick between **LunchBox Laboratory** (page 220) and **Blue Moon Burgers** (page 218) later in the day; both eateries offer up big beefy burgers and creative toppings.

PARKS & REC

Lake Union Park (860 Terry Ave. N; 206-684-4075; www.seattle .gov/parks/find/parks/lake-union-park) offers an expansive lakefront lawn to roam, plus a spray pad to cool off in during the summer months.

PLAY DATE

Kids can wiggle, giggle, dance, and jiggle at **PlayDate SEA** (1275 Mercer St.; 206-623-7529; www.playdatesea.com), an 8,000-square-foot indoor play space in this hood. With slides and tunnels, plus a dancing area, toddler section, laser tag, and even puppet shows, this spot is nice for parents too, with a café that offers Stumptown coffee and free Wi-Fi.

SLEEP ON IT

South Lake Union offers quite a few options for hotels. But the **Residence Inn Seattle Downtown/Lake Union** (800 Fairview Ave. N; 206-624-6000; www.marriott.com/hotels/travel /sealu-residence-inn-seattle-downtown-lake-union) offers multiroom suites (hey, sometimes one teeny room is too much togetherness) and is located just steps from the lake.

UNIVERSITY DISTRICT & SAND POINT

THE MOOD

Loaded with botanicals, bookstores, and biking paths, the home of the Huskies offers family fun by land *and* by lake.

PARK IT RIGHT THERE

There are two main sightseeing strips in the U District. First are the shops, theaters, and eateries on University Way NE, known as "the Ave," the highlights of which include **University Book Store** (page 48) and the **Varsity Theatre** (page 26). The Ave also plays host to the **University District Farmers Market** (page 111) every Saturday. For these stops, look for street parking just off the Ave, north of the main intersection at NE 45th Street–on NE 47th, 50th, and 52nd Streets.

STROLLER ALONG

From the bookstore near NE 43rd Street, meander southward down the Ave about a half mile to pick up the famous **Burke-Gilman Trail** (page 76), next to NE Pacific Street. (You'll know it by all the bikers whizzing past.) Follow this section of the trail northeast, and it will take you on a charming tour of the University of Washington campus.

SHOP HOP

If you've got the stamina, you can take the trail 1.6 miles all the way to **University Village** (2623 NE University Village St.; 206-523-0622; www.uvillage.com), the second must-see area of this neighborhood tour. (The upscale outdoor shopping mall has lots of free parking too, if you'd prefer to go by car.) A family could easily spend the day here, painting ceramic mugs at **Paint the Town** (page 32), poking through plants at **Ravenna Gardens** (2600 NE University Village St.; 206-729-7388; www.ravennagardens.com), and perusing wee clothes and cool toys at **Kid's Club** (2630 NE University Village St.; 206-524-2553; www.salonkidsclub.com). The shopping center delivers on goodies too, with **Fran's Chocolates** (page 225) and the darling **Confectionery** candy shop (page 243). A few more buzz-worthy

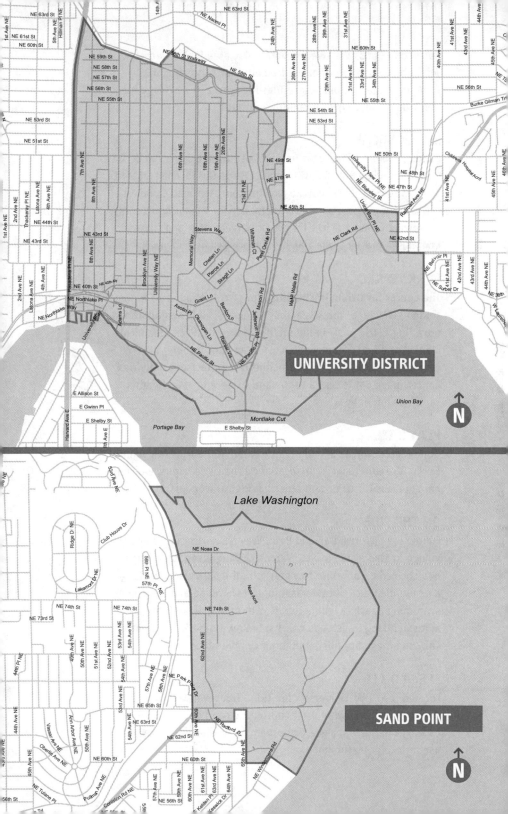

notes: don't miss the sweet covered play area for the preschool set in the Village center or the free outdoor concerts come summer (page 60), plus every Tuesday at 10 a.m. U Village hosts free Village Playdays programming for kids.

SNACK BREAK

Budding foodies will love the unique Asian cuisine options at U Village, including **Blue C Sushi** (page 232) and **Din Tai Fung** (2621 NE 46th St.; 206-525-0958; www.dintaifung.com), the Seattle outpost of a Taiwanese restaurant that is internationally famous for its pork dumplings. Others will love the classic burgers, fries, and shakes from **Burgermaster** (page 218), just a block east from the mall.

PARKS & REC

The **Center for Urban Horticulture** (page 43), about a half mile south of U Village, sprawls across 90 acres of this neighborhood, providing a lush oasis in the middle of the city. Pack up a picnic blanket and find a grassy patch, or head back through the UW campus to the **University of Washington Waterfront Activities Center** (page 65) to rent a canoe and explore the Washington Park Arboretum by water.

PLAY DATE

Got a dino devotee? Spend the afternoon at the truly fascinating **Burke Museum** (page 106), located on the UW campus, which is home to fossils, rocks, and other geological wonders.

ON THE SIDE

Follow the picturesque Sand Point Way NE north from University Village to take a side trip to **Warren G. Magnuson Park** (page 89). Located on a former Navy airfield, the park also sits along a beautiful stretch of Lake Washington shoreline and features a swimming beach, a tennis center with mini golf, and miles and miles of hiking trails. Also nearby: the awesome **Arena Sports FunZone** (page 80) filled with bouncy inflatables.

SLEEP ON IT

Located near UW, **University Inn** (4140 Roosevelt Way NE; 800-733-3855; www.universityinnseattle.com) offers pineapple cupcakes in the lobby every afternoon as well as free bikes to use for exploring the hood.

WALLINGFORD

THE MOOD
Wallingford may be right next door to the busy U District, but it still manages to exude a friendly small-town feel that families adore. (A giggle-worthy gag store and a beloved urban gardening center only add to its appeal.)

PARK IT RIGHT THERE
The neighborhood is centered around the intersection of North 45th Street and Wallingford Avenue North, but it's best to park on the offshoot streets, such as Densmore, Woodlawn, or Burke Avenues North. From there, stroll back up to 45th to start your tour.

STROLLER ALONG & SHOP HOP
Start things off at the charming Wallingford Center, where cute little **Bootyland Kids** (1815 N. 45th St., Suite 208; 206-328-0636; www.bootylandkids.com) is filled with organic and sustainably made baby and kids' clothes, as well as a handpicked collection of natural toys. Then, depending on the kids' current sugar levels, decide whether to make a stop at the **Trophy Cupcakes** (page 245) across the hall. Back outside on 45th, go east to take a brief detour into **the Sock Monster** (1909 N. 45th St.; 206-724-0123; www.thesockmonster.com) to spy dozens upon dozens of colorful and patterned socks before heading west to **Kids on 45th** (1720 N. 45th St.; 206-633-5437; www.kidson45th.com), which offers killer consignment deals on kids' clothing, toys, and gear. Next up, you'll encounter **Alphabet Soup** (page 46), one of the sweetest kids' bookshops in all the lands before arriving at **Archie McPhee** (page 118). Teeny tykes will most likely be struck by a case of the giggles over the silly gag goods here, which could include some Handerpants (hand underpants) or Glow-in-the-Dark Finger Tentacles. Be sure to ask the staffers about the most recent sighting of the Wallingford Beast, a mythical creature that apparently haunted the neighborhood back in the 1930s and still visits Archie McPhee on occasion.

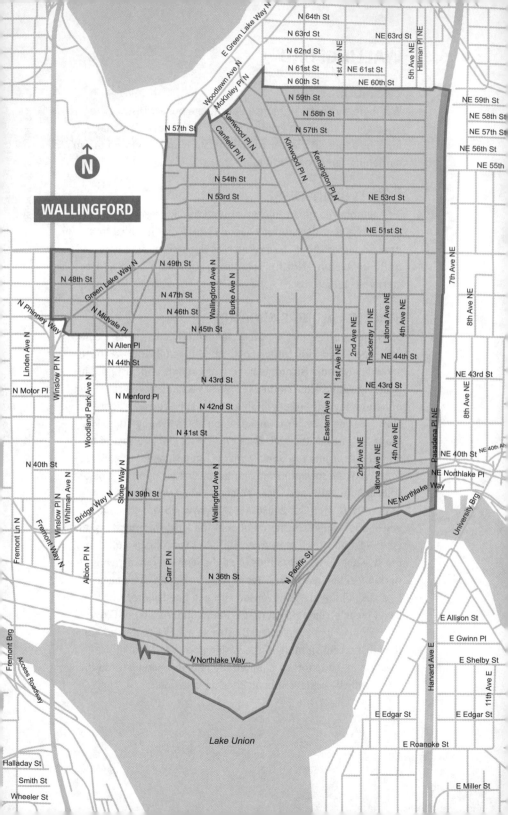

SNACK BREAK

Yes, you definitely did drag the kids past another outpost of **Molly Moon's** ice-cream shop (page 249) on your shopping tour. (Oh, you went in? Good on ya.) **Fainting Goat Gelato** (1903 N. 45th St.; 206-327-9459; www.faintinggoatseattle.com) features another creamy treat you can feel good about, as their Italian-style gelato is crafted from organic milk. (Try the fig vanilla or peanut butter flavors.) If you are looking for a truly satisfying pile of spaghetti, try out **Bizzarro Italian Cafe** (page 235), which is festooned with fun and funky decor.

PARKS & REC

Wallingford Playfield (4219 Wallingford Ave. N; 206-684-4075; www.seattle.gov/parks/find/parks/wallingford-playfield) is a popular neighborhood gathering place. Featuring an expansive playground (don't miss out on the giant tube slide), this park is wet and wild come summertime, thanks to the fun wading pool.

PLAY DATE

Mosaic Community Coffeehouse (page 227)—a hidden gem located in the basement of a church—is a real refuge come rainy season, thanks to its in-house playroom.

HIDDEN GEMS

Tucked north of the main drag, Meridian Park plays host to both the **Wallingford Farmers Market** (page 111) and the gardens of **Tilth Alliance** (page 46). The latter provides (awesome) gardening programs for kids, who can tour Tilth's gardens as well as attend workshops and classes.

SLEEP ON IT

Given its close proximity to the University District, it's probably easiest to stay in a hotel there (see page 184) and then hop over to Wallingford for the day.

WEST SEATTLE

THE MOOD

This close-knit community draws young families and outdoor enthusiasts with its ultrawelcoming, laid-back vibe and gorgeous beachfront locations.

PARK IT RIGHT THERE

Connected to the mainland by the West Seattle Bridge, the heart of this neighborhood is the **Junction** (4210 SW Oregon St.; 206-935-0904; www.wsjunction.com), located at California Avenue SW and SW Oregon Street. Parking can usually be found northward on California, or on side streets such as 41st, 42nd, and 44th Avenues SW. But do watch the signs, as some spots are for residents only.

STROLLER ALONG & SHOP HOP

Take a spin down California to see the highlights of this district. First, pop into **Fleurt** (4536 California Ave. SW; 206-937-1103; www.fleurtseattle.com), a fragrant floral boutique that also carries cards, gifts, and paper goods. Then stop at **Click! Design That Fits** (4540 California Ave. SW; 206-328-9252; www .clickdesignthatfits.com) to check out the wooden blocks, coloring books, and other stylish kids' items. (Surely you need a baby onesie with a Seattle neighborhood map on it after all this exploring, right?) Step around the corner on SW Alaska Street to **City Mouse Studio and Store** (4218 SW Alaska St.; 206-909-0189; www.citymouse.com), one part photo studio, another part fantastic kids' clothing boutique. Then, back on California, get lost in **Curious Kidstuff** (page 32), an arts-and-crafts supply store that offers classes for toddlers to elementary schoolers. The emporium also carries toys, trinkets, and other treasures.

SNACK BREAK

Homey and cozy **Bakery Nouveau** (page 210) offers fresh pastries and espresso from its space at the Junction, and also churns out wood-fired pizzas during lunchtime. The neighborhood outpost of local chain **Tacos Guaymas** (4719 California Ave. SW;

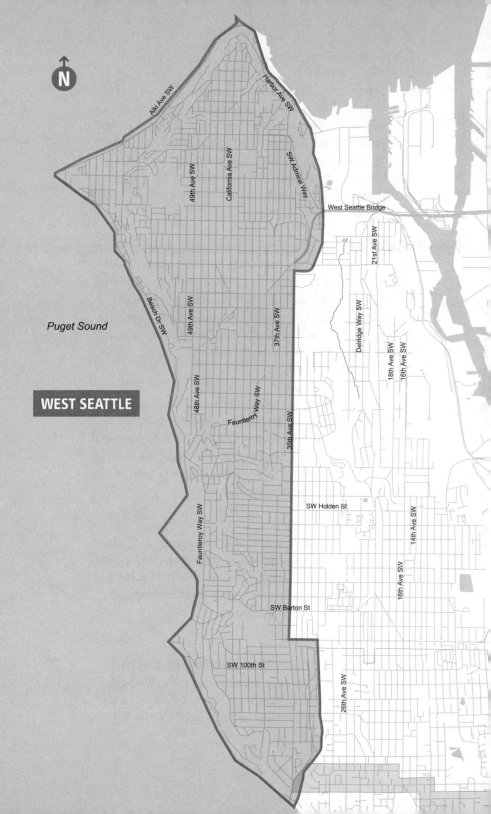

206-935-8970; www.tacosguaymas.com) provides easy grab 'n' go burritos, and **Great Harvest Bread Co.** (4709 California Ave. SW; 206-935-6882; www.greatharvestwestseattle.com) makes a mean sandwich, with deli meat, veggies, and cheese all piled on its freshly baked bread. Order the sammies to go and then head for the **Junction Plaza** (42nd Ave. SW and SW Alaska St.; 206-684-4075; www.seattle.gov/parks/find/parks/junction-plaza) to enjoy them on a sunny day. But whatever you do, brave the line at **Husky Deli** (page 249) for a cone piled high with creamy house-made ice cream.

PARKS & REC

The much-beloved **Lincoln Park** (page 145) offers supersoaker fun for kiddos, with beachfront access alongside the Fauntleroy ferry terminal, as well as a summertime wading pool and playing fields. It is also home to the famous **Colman Pool** (page 67). This unique saltwater pool sits right on the beach, offering stunning water views from, well, the water.

PLAY DATE

"Splatter room." Those two words alone draw budding artists into **West Seattle Art Nest** (page 34), a delightful space that encourages creativity through open crafting. You can create with abandon for a flat $10-$15 per hour rate—and yes, that includes the "splatter" space, where kids are encouraged to paint on the walls, the floor, the ceilings—you name it.

HIDDEN GEMS

Featuring its own ropes course, cabins for rent, and public rock climbing, **Camp Long** (page 87) has all the ingredients for a fun family day. Butting up against the West Seattle Golf Course, the oft-overlooked park features myriad hiking and walking trails that meander through the shady forest.

ON THE SIDE

Though often thought of in conjunction with the rest of West Seattle, **Alki Beach** (page 61) is a destination in its own right, and can be appreciated in many ways. Enjoy it by sea on a trip with **Alki Kayak Tours** (page 114); enjoy it by bike while pedaling along the **Alki Trail** (page 75); or enjoy it by beachcombing and frolicking at **Alki Playground** (page 71).

SLEEP ON IT

Stay near the Junction at **the Grove–West Seattle Inn** (3512 SW Alaska St.; 206-937-9920; www.grovewestseattle.com), and you'll also be just a few steps from Camp Long and the local treasure that is **West Seattle Bowl** (page 17).

SUBURBS

BELLEVUE

THE MOOD

This kid-friendly Eastside burb is a city in its own right. The classy, cosmopolitan shopping district is balanced by parks, nature trails, and even an in-city blueberry patch.

THE MAIN ATTRACTIONS

Bellevue and its many neighborhoods reach from Lake Washington, to the west, to the popular **Crossroads Bellevue** mall (15600 NE 8th St.; 425-644-1111; www.crossroadsbellevue .com), to the east. But just mention the city's name and locals immediately think of the stores at **the Bellevue Collection** (575 Bellevue Way NE; 425-454-8096; www.bellevuecollection.com), the sophisticated and swank shopping area downtown, which acts as the landmark meeting spot for its citizens. It's also the best and easiest parking in the area, with several free garages that encircle the malls.

STROLLER ALONG

From there, take a delightful spin around downtown by first sauntering south on Bellevue Way NE to NE 4th Street, where you'll find the gorgeous **Bellevue Downtown Park** (page 65), which features rolling lawns and a mesmerizing reflecting pond (little hands won't be able to resist a splash or two). Continue south to shortly find Main Street, which contains an adorable cadre of stores and eateries. Then pick up Bellevue Way NE again and head north to **Bellevue Arts Museum** (page 119). The beautiful museum offers child-centric Get Crafty Saturdays every week in its atrium; for $4, kids of all ages can participate in crafts correlated to the current exhibits. With finished masterpiece in hand, walk one block up to **Lincoln Square** (700 Bellevue Way NE; 425-454-8096; www.bellevuecollection.com) to knock down some pins at **Lucky Strike** (21-plus only after 8 p.m.; 700 Bellevue Way NE; 425-453-5137; www.bowlluckystrike.com), the fanciest bowling alley you are ever likely to encounter. Or take in a flick at **Lincoln Square Cinemas** (700 Bellevue Way NE; 425-450-9100; www.cinemark.com). From there you're just a skybridge walk away from where you parked the car.

SHOP HOP

Bellevue Square itself is flush with national kids' brands, such as **Janie and Jack** (www.janieandjack.com), **the Lego Store** (stores.lego.com), and **Gymboree** (www.gymboree.com), but downtown is home to a few local favorites too. **Hopscotch Consignment Boutique** (136 105th Ave. NE; 425-462-4751; www.hopscotchconsign.com) offers great deals on lightly used children's clothing and shoes. On Main Street, better stop in at **Wee Tots Children's Store** (10245 Main St., Suite 103; 425-502-7182; www.shopweetots.com) to peruse the posh collection of baby and toddler gear, as well as nursery furniture and decor.

SNACK BREAK

Start your day with a toasted scratch-made bagel at **Gilbert's on Main** (10024 Main St.; 425-455-5650; www.gilbertsonmain .com). The bustling little eatery boasts easy counter ordering and a patio. **Chace's Pancake Corral** (1606 Bellevue Way SE; 425-454-8888) is another classic stop for syrupy stacks of pancakes in the a.m. Later on, consider picking up a slice of pizza at **Pagliacci Pizza** (page 238) inside the Bellevue Square mall, and then washing it down with a perfectly frosted cupcake from **PinkaBella Cupcakes** (page 245) or a scoop of gelato from **D'Ambrosio Gelato** (403 Bellevue Square; 425-451-4919; www .dambrosiogelato.com).

PARKS & REC

A mere five minutes from all that shopping, the **Bellevue Botanical Garden** (page 43) features lush, natural beauty in the form of a rhododendron glen, a fuchsia section, and a Japanese garden—all free to explore. A bit farther south, the **Mercer Slough Nature Park** (page 91) offers a wide variety of recreational activities, from hiking and biking to guided canoe tours. In the summer, the fields turn blue as the u-pick blueberry bushes ripen.

PLAY DATE

There are play spaces aplenty in this suburb, including the awesome indoor playground that is **Funtastic Playtorium** (4077 Factoria Square Mall SE; 425-623-0034; www.funtasticplaytorium.com), flush with slides, a climbing apparatus, and cushy playthings. **Dabuda Playhouse & Cafe** (13427 NE 20th St., Suite 120; 425-305-7123; www.mydabuda.com), a new favorite, is designed for kids ages 6 months to 6 years old and offers a café for parents to kick back with a cuppa joe while junior climbs the jungle gym. And having just moved into a new location downtown, the popular **KidsQuest Children's Museum** (page 79) just got even cooler, now boasting over 13,500-square-feet of exhibit space for kids to roam.

SLEEP ON IT

Take your pick among the twenty-plus hotels located within a few blocks of downtown Bellevue; the recently refreshed **Seattle Marriott Bellevue** (200 110th Ave. NE; 425-214-7600; www.marriott.com/hotels/travel/seamb-seattle-marriott-bellevue) is a good midrange choice.

BOTHELL & WOODINVILLE

THE MOOD

The growing North End suburbs of Bothell and Woodinville are flush with nature-inspired playgrounds, busy biking trails, and paddle-happy river adventures.

THE MAIN ATTRACTIONS

Once-sleepy Bothell is enjoying a renaissance, thanks to a recently reinvigorated downtown corridor that now boasts one of the coolest hotels around, the **McMenamins Anderson School** (more on page 197). Head for the intersection of Bothell Way NE and Main Street to start your tour. There is usually abundant parking on side streets.

STROLLER ALONG

Head south and cross State Route 522 to first reach the **Park at Bothell Landing** (9919 NE 180th St.; 425-486-7430; www.ci.bothell.wa.us/249/parks-recreation), a lovely spot for an afternoon sojourn with a playground, historical museum, gazebo, and lots of paths to wander. The park meanders along the banks of the Sammamish River, and should your crew feel the urge to hop in, head to **WhatsSup Stand-Up Paddle & Surf** (9929 NE 180th St.; 425-417-8637; www.whatssup.net) to rent a kayak or paddleboard and float the river. Or, see all those bikers whizzing by along the opposite bank? They're all headed for Woodinville wine country via the **Sammamish River Trail** (206-296-0100; www.kingcounty.gov/services/parks-recreation). You can access this trail via the wooden bridge on the landing and then stroll to your heart's content.

SHOP HOP

Quaint and oh-so-charming, the **Country Village Shops** (23718 Bothell-Everett Hwy.; 425-483-2250; www.countryvillagebothell .com) provide lots to look at. Roosters roam the grounds between shops, which include **Kate Quinn Organics** (425-952-4206; www.katequinnorganics.com), an organic baby-and-tot clothier; **Bella and Max** (425-488-8200; www.bellaandmax .com), another sweet kids' clothing boutique, which also features an in-house hair salon for tykes; and **Tickled Pink** (206-554-1632; www.tickledpinkspa.com), a day spa built especially for little gals. This bright spot offers BFF and Me manis and pedis, and birthday party packages. **Toys That Teach** (425-481-2257; www.toysthatteachbothell.com) is packed with fun toys and games for all ages and phases. And if you have a budding thespian, be sure to check out the current roster of classes happening over at **Adventure Children's Theatre** (425-739-9433; www.zeroandsomebuddy.com). Head to the back of the shopping center to find the fun center: an old-school **playground** replete with a pirate ship to climb on, a picnic area, and a chicken coop. Here you'll also find summertime pony rides and a mini train kids can board on weekends year-round and every day in the summer, for their own village tour.

SNACK BREAK

In Country Village you can find succulent-smoky barbecue at **Carolina Smoke BBQ** (23806 Bothell-Everett Hwy.; 425-949-8672; www.carolinasmoke.com), and just listen for the bell a-ringin' to let you know there's a hot batch of corn popping at **King's Kettle Korn** (www.countryvillagebothell.com/kings-kettle-corn-0). Back in downtown Bothell, **Amaro Bistro** (18333 Bothell Way NE; 425-485-2300; www.amarorestaurant.com) offers seasonally focused gourmet Italian cuisine and a fantastic kids' menu, while **Julio's Restaurant** (10023 NE 183rd St.; 425-485-1769; www.julios restaurantwa.com) crafts incredibly fresh Mexican fare from local ingredients.

HIDDEN GEMS

In the rural passageway between Bothell and Woodinville are two gems worth a visit. The newish **Miner's Corner** play area (page 70) boasts a nature-inspired playground with play stumps and logs, plus walking trails, a basketball court, and a huge sand pit. Nearby, you may be surprised to find some of the area's best walking at **Brightwater Center** (22505 SR 9; 206-296-0100; www.kingcounty.gov/services/environment /brightwater-center/trails.aspx). A series of trails, ponds, and wetlands canvas the campus of the Brightwater wastewater treatment facility. (No, really.)

ON THE SIDE

Nationally acclaimed for its wineries and its growing number of distilleries (take note for the next time you have a sitter), Woodinville is also home to sprawling sports fields and adventure activities, like the climbing and challenge course **Adventura** (14300 NE 145th St.; 866-981-8665; www.adventura play.com). **Molbak's Garden + Home** (13625 NE 175th St.; 425-483-5000; www.molbaks.com) draws gardeners from far and wide who wander the 15-acre property or take in a free gardening workshop, many of which are made just for kids. And you can take your fisherkid to **Gold Creek Trout Farm** (15844 148th Ave. NE; 425-483-1415; www.goldcreektroutfarm .com), a fully stocked u-fish trout pond that supplies all the gear and bait you'll need to hook a fish, making it a fantastic spot for beginners.

SLEEP ON IT

It's now a no-brainer where to nod off in Bothell. Book a stay at the newly opened **McMenamins Anderson School** (18607 Bothell Way NE; 425-398-0122; www.mcmenamins.com/andersonschool). The hotel, housed in a historic school, turned classrooms into guest suites. It also features an indoor pool, an on-site movie theater, and three restaurants, not to mention the outdoor fire pits.

EDMONDS & SHORELINE

THE MOOD

Nestled just north of Seattle, scenic Shoreline and historic Edmonds sure are charmers, with beaches for castle building, sand flinging, and kite flying, and downtown shops for peering and perusing.

THE MAIN ATTRACTIONS

Though Edmonds sprawls east into residential neighborhoods, its downtown lies near the Puget Sound waterfront and the bustling ferry terminal that shuttles riders to and from Kingston on the Kitsap Peninsula. It is usually easy to find three-hour street parking on the east end of Main Street near 6th and 7th Avenues South.

STROLLER ALONG

From Main Street, take a quick loop around the shops before heeding the call of the water and strolling down toward the ferry terminal. There, you can join other walkers on a delightful beachside and boardwalk stroll south, which will take you past the Edmonds Yacht Club and the kid-friendly **Anthony's Beach Cafe** (456 Admiral Way; 425-771-4400; www.anthonys .com/restaurants/detail/anthonys-beach-cafe)—outfitted with a genius patio-side sand pit for littles to play in while the adults munch. Then it's onto the shoreside **Marina Beach Park** (470 Admiral Way; www.edmondswa.gov), home to a brand-new play structure.

SHOP HOP

Back in downtown Edmonds, get thee to **Teri's Toybox** (420 Main St.; 425-774-3190) for its delightful array of games, toys, and puzzles before heading next door to **Belly & Co.** (422 Main St.; 425-778-7600; www.bellyandcompany.com), an upscale baby boutique that carries such lines as Uppababy, Aden + Anais, and Petunia Pickle Bottom. Around the corner, the indie **Edmonds Bookshop** (111 5th Ave. S; 425-775-2789; www.edmondsbookshop.com) stocks hard-to-find titles and darling picture books for kids. Then head north to pop into **Nama's Candy Store** (page 243) for a sweet treat. You can eat it right away or stash it in your pockets to enjoy during a flick at the beloved **Edmonds Theater** (page 26), which shows first-run flicks for just $6 a kid.

SNACK BREAK

Red Twig Bakery Café (117 5th Ave. S; 425-771-1200; www.redtwig.com) opens up its glorious patio on nice days, making for a relaxing spot to enjoy stellar panini, wraps, and salads. Nearby, **Canarino Gelato** (203 5th Ave. S, Suite 4; 425-243-9635; www.canarinogelato.com) serves silky gelato and fruity sorbetto. Let the kids pick from twenty-four different flavors, while the adults enjoy an affogato pick-me-up, a scoop of gelato topped with two shots of espresso. Down on the waterfront, **Spud Fish & Chips** (174 Sunset Ave. S; 206-678-0984; www.spudfishandchips.com) sits right next door to **Evviva Woodfired Pizza** (178 Sunset Ave. S; 425-299-0142; www.evvivapizza.com), which many locals claim is the best pie in the entire region.

PARKS & REC

Flanking the ferry terminal, **Brackett's Landing North** and **South** (50 and 100 Railroad Ave.; www.edmondswa.gov) offer beautiful sandy stretches right along the Sound. Spread out a blanket and plan on staying awhile. Between the ferries going to and fro, scuba divers coming in and out of the offshore marine preserve, and the myriad kites in flight on any given day, there's plenty of people-watching to be had.

HIDDEN GEMS

Discover a new sport—with **WhirlyBall** (page 21). The 4,000-square-foot world headquarters for this fast-and-furious sport is located a few miles inland. A cross between basketball, hockey, and pelota, WhirlyBall allows players as young as age 8 to ride in go-cart-esque WhirlyBugs as they chase down the ball, pick it up in a handheld scoop, and fling it in the goal.

ON THE SIDE

Tucked south of Edmonds, the city of **Shoreline** also offers plenty of beachy fun, especially with the marquee **Richmond Beach Saltwater Park** (2021 NW 190th St.; 206-801-2700; www .shorelinewa.gov). With a towering skybridge that takes visitors over the railroad tracks to the sandy beach, the park has fantastic tide pools, huge driftwood logs for climbing on, and a whole lot of choo-choos going by to entertain your little conductor.

SLEEP ON IT

Wake up to the sounds of the lapping ocean and the ferry horn with a stay at the **Best Western Plus Edmonds Harbor Inn** (130 W. Dayton St.; 425-771-5021; book.bestwestern.com). It's just two blocks off the water and just three blocks from the superb cuppa joe found at the **Waterfront Coffee Company** (101 Main St.; 425-670-1400; www.waterfrontcoffeeco.com).

ISSAQUAH

THE MOOD

Located on the forested fringes of Cougar Mountain, Issaquah is a woodland wonderland, plying visitors with outdoorsy activities, a sweet zoo, and laid-back hangouts.

THE MAIN ATTRACTIONS

Downtown Issaquah is divided into two main sections: the quaint and classic Front Street—find free public parking on the street near the Issaquah Train Depot—and the darling little shopping center that is **Gilman Village** (317 NW Gilman Blvd.;

425-392-6802; www.gilmanvillage.com) about a mile north, where there are plenty of parking lots.

STROLLER ALONG & SHOP HOP

Gilman Village is fit for window-shopping and strolling. First stop is **Issaquah Coffee Company** (page 227), where you can linger over a latte while the kids are entertained by the train table. Nearby, **Mudhouse Pottery Painting** (page 31) lets kids create their own painted ceramic masterpiece. Or call ahead to sign your little dancer up for a free class at **the Musik Nest** (Suite 50; 425-427-0984; www.themusiknest.com), a fantastic music and movement school for kids under age 8. Then pop in for an educational moment at **the Recology Store** (Suite 22; 425-392-0285; www.cleanscapes.com/about_us/store), a recycling-awareness space, which offers cool upcycled goods and how-to tips from the friendly staffers. And last, but certainly not least, prepare yourself for a delightful time spent browsing the usual and unusual toys at **White Horse Toys** (Suite 13; 425-391-1498; www.whitehorsetoys.com).

SNACK BREAK

Issaquah Cafe (1580 Gilman Blvd.; 425-391-9690; www.issaquah.cafesinc.com) offers big ol' breakfasts and comfort-food lunches in a friendly everyone-is-welcome space. Just a few minutes south, **XXX Root Beer** (page 251) is where the locals hang, and it's easy to see why—the diner is outfitted in 1950s-style decor and offers classic burgers, shakes, and, of course, root beer floats crafted with house-made soda. On Front Street, don't be surprised to spot a line of hungry hikers outside **Stan's Bar-B-Q** (58 Front St.; 425-392-4551). You should join them if you're in the mood for a smoky beef brisket or pulled-pork sandwich.

PARKS & REC

Older kids will want to be sure to throw the bikes in the back of the car. **Duthie Hill Mountain Bike Park** (page 75) delights with trails that canvas their way through forest and feature obstacles. (Catch some air, dudes!) Issaquah boasts not only forests and trees (the hiking in Cougar Mountain Regional Wildland Park is always good—see page 90), but also the gorgeous and glittering

Lake Sammamish; there are two swimming beaches and extensive walking trails at **Lake Sammamish State Park** (page 62).

PLAY DATE

Just west of the state park, the **Cougar Mountain Zoo** (page 10) is quiet and relaxed, its smaller size perfect for little legs. An array of endangered species can be found here, ranging from reindeer and cranes to Bengal tigers and, of course, cougars.

HIDDEN GEMS

Kicking off its route at the cute Issaquah Depot Museum across the street from Stan's Bar-B-Q, the **Issaquah Valley Trolley** (page 7) offers rides in a cheery 1920s-era electric car from May to September.

SLEEP ON IT

Located a hop, skip, and jump from the zoo, the **Hilton Garden Inn Seattle/Issaquah** (1800 NW Gilman Blvd.; 425-837-3600; www.hiltongardeninn.hilton.com) and the **Homewood Suites by Hilton Seattle-Issaquah** (1484 Hyla Ave. NW; 425-391-4000; www.homewoodsuites.hilton.com) offer cozy and casual accommodations.

KIRKLAND

THE MOOD

With swell stops all along Lake Washington, picturesque Kirkland embodies lakeside living at its finest.

THE MAIN ATTRACTION

The main hub of Kirkland lies right along the lake, at the intersection of Market Street and Central Way, with key businesses radiating outward from there. You can find street parking just north, along 3rd, 4th, and 5th Avenues, and then take a walk from there.

STROLLER ALONG

Along the lake with rolling lawns and even a historical building or two, **Heritage Park** (111 Waverly Way; 425-587-3350; www.kirklandwa.gov/depart/parks) is built for strolling, and it boasts some of the best sunset views in the area. Saunter south and you'll also find **Marina Park** (25 Lakeshore Plaza Dr.; 425-587-3350; www.kirklandwa.gov/depart/parks), where you can walk the pier and let the kids stop at the small sandy beach before heading for the shops downtown.

SHOP HOP

Right across the street from the marina, **Simplicity ABC** (107 Park Ln.; 425-250-1186; www.simplicityabc.com) will draw you in with its cheery window displays, then deliver a fun and innovative toy collection inside. Around the corner and east a block and a half, **Kirkland Bicycle** (208 Kirkland Ave.; 425-828-3800; www.kirklandbikes.com) rents out bikes to cyclists big and small, should a lakeside ride be calling your names (start at $35 per twenty-four-hour rental, first-come, first-served with limited availability of smaller-size bikes, more options for kids 8 and up). And make sure to take your tiny train lover by **Eastside Trains** (217 Central Way; 425-828-4098; www.eastsidetrains.com), a model railroad shop that is seemingly constantly in motion as trains chugga-chugga along the tracks set up throughout the store.

SNACK BREAK

Snag some picnic supplies at **Homegrown Sustainable Sandwich Shop** (page 240), which crafts fresh sandwiches, salads, and soups using local ingredients. Or take a deep dive into a piping-hot pie from **Zeeks Pizza** (124 Park Ln.; 425-893-8646; www.zeekspizzakirkland.com). The Thai One On, topped with chicken, bean sprouts, cilantro, and peanut sauce, is an especially popular choice ($16.95–$25.99). For dessert, pick up a pack of brightly colored macaroons from **Lady Yum** (111 Lake St.; 425-285-9628; www.ladyyum.com).

PARKS & REC

If the kids still haven't had their fill of the outdoors, head 2.5 miles north of downtown to the beautiful sandy stretches of **Juanita Beach Park** (page 62). Nestled along the quiet Juanita Bay, the park offers a play area, ball fields, and even a fishing area. Kirkland is also frequently associated with **Bridle Trails State Park** (page 90), a favorite for hikers, bikers, and equestrians, with over 28 miles of beautifully maintained trails.

PLAY DATE

Jump those jiggles out at **Pump It Up** (11605 NE 116th St.; 425-820-2297; www.pumpitupparty.com), a play space filled with bouncy inflatables. As if that weren't enough, there's a thrice-weekly Bubble Jump, where kids are showered with bubbles at intervals during the two-hour session ($8 per child; $6 for siblings, available to age 6 and under). Sharing the same parking lot, the Rainbow Play Systems showroom, called **Pacific Northwest Kids** (11801 NE 116th St.; 425-821-8779; www.rainbowplay.com; www.pnwkids.com), offers up its indoor playground equipment (including trampolines!) for youngsters to try out during open play sessions on weekdays ($5 per child).

HIDDEN GEMS

As you pass by the **Kirkland Performance Center** (350 Kirkland Ave.; 425-893-9900; www.kpcenter.org), be sure to check the schedule. **StoryBook Theater** (page 40) often performs its charming kiddie musicals, based on classic fairy tales, at the hall. A creative plot twist or two will keep both parents and kids at the edge of their seats.

SLEEP ON IT

The upscale **Heathman Hotel** (220 Kirkland Ave.; 425-284-5800; www.heathmankirkland.com) in downtown Kirkland is quite accommodating to families, offering complimentary bike rentals and transportation services to sights within 10 miles, as well as supreme cuisine from the award-winning Trellis restaurant.

REDMOND

THE MOOD

Home to Microsoft's headquarters, a sweet town center, and the expansive Marymoor Park, Redmond offers a little somethin'-somethin' for everyone from tots to tweens.

THE MAIN ATTRACTION

The heart of Redmond is the two-story open-air shopping mall **Redmond Town Center** (7525 166th Ave. NE; 425-869-2640; www.redmondtowncenter.com), at the intersection of NE 74th Street and 164th Avenue NE. The extremely walkable downtown is accessible from there, so snag a spot in one of the adjacent lots.

STROLLER ALONG & SHOP HOP

In Redmond Town Center, tykes will undoubtedly be drawn to the fountain in the main courtyard, which is well used on warm days. If it's too chilly for that, let them roam and run indoors at the **Giggle Jungle** play space (7330 164th Ave. NE, Suite E165; 425-558-3600; www.gigglejungle.com). Score an all-day pass to the bright inflatables and slides for $10 ($8 for a sibling). At **Paint Away** (page 31), kids can dabble in ceramic painting or glass fusion (where layers of glass are melted together to create fun art). **Uncle's Games** (7325 166th Ave. NE, Suite F150; 425-497-9180; www.unclesgames.com) offers hard-to-find board games and cool puzzles, plus an open play area where you and your kids can duke it out over your favorite game before bopping over to **the Comic Stop** (7525 166th Ave. NE, Suite D145; 425-881-0291; www.comicstoponline.com) to check out the latest adventures of your favorite superheroes. Wrap up your tour by sinking into a cushy seat at **iPic Theaters** (16451 NE 74th St.; 425-636-5601; www.ipictheaters.com), a luxury movie theater that offers reserved seating, reclining lounge chairs, and even gourmet food brought right to your seat. (Do check ahead, as most evening showings are adults only.)

SNACK BREAK

Quick nibbles at Redmond Town Center include frosted treats from **PinkaBella Cupcakes** (page 245) and fresh-from-the-oven treats from **Cow Chip Cookies** (7330 164th Ave. NE; 425-376-2548; www.cowchipcookies.com). Across the street from the mall, the cow theme continues at **Tipsy Cow Burger Bar** (16345 Cleveland St.; 425-896-8716; www.tipsycowburgerbar.com), this time with absolutely huge burgers, plus fries, shakes, and beer on offer. One block to the east the famous **Flying Apron** bakery (16541 Redmond Way; 206-442-1115; www.flyingapron.com) is a must-stop for the gluten-free and vegan crowd. And then about a mile farther down Redmond Way, you'll find **Pomegranate Bistro** (page 216), where the Northwest-meets-Southern food is top-notch, morning, noon, and night.

PARKS & REC

Life in Redmond revolves around the activities held at **Marymoor Park**, which plays host to outdoor concerts, movies (see page 29), and touring events like Cirque du Soleil. The park also is home to walking and biking trails, and the **Jerry Baker Memorial Velodrome** (page 74). Local cyclists and curious spectators flock to this outdoor track on Friday nights, May on into September, for the high-speed races.

ON THE SIDE

Appease the family computer geeks with a visit to mecca: the free-admission **Microsoft Visitor Center** (15010 NE 36th St., Building 92; 425-703-6214; www.microsoft.com/en-us/visitorcenter) on the tech giant's sprawling Redmond campus offers an insider peek at both the history and future of the company. (You can also test out the latest Xbox games and Surface tablet devices while you're there too.)

SLEEP ON IT

Located within Redmond Town Center and just across the street from Marymoor Park, the **Residence Inn Seattle East/Redmond** (7575 164th Ave. NE; 425-497-9226; www.marriott.com/hotels /travel/seard-residence-inn-seattle-east-redmond) is right where you want to be.

TUKWILA, KENT & AUBURN

THE MOOD

With lightning-quick horse races, indoor skydiving, and high-sticking hockey matches, these South End suburbs can provide an adrenaline rush for all ages.

THE MAIN ATTRACTIONS

As these burbs cover almost 75 square miles, the natural meeting points are the malls, namely **Westfield Southcenter** in Tukwila (2800 Southcenter Mall; 206-246-0423; www.westfield.com/southcenter) and the outdoor **Kent Station** (417 Ramsay Way; 253-856-2301; www.kentstation.com). Both sites have ample parking in their free lots.

STROLLER ALONG & SHOP HOP

In Tukwila, Westfield Southcenter bustles with shops such as hometown **Nordstrom** (100 Southcenter Mall; 206-246-0400; www.nordstrom.com), plus enough entertainment options to keep the kids occupied for days. For bowlers, there is fam-favorite **Acme Bowl** (page 16) across the street from the mall. Inside the shopping center you'll find **Round 1 Bowling & Amusement** (page 17), which also includes an expansive gaming arcade. Also nearby are a **Family Fun Center** (page 15), where you can hit some balls in the cage or take in a game of mini golf, and **iFly** (page 94), where the adventurous of your brood can take to the pretend skies with a skydive in a wind tunnel. A quick twenty-minute drive away, Kent Station is super-stroller-friendly, with a movie theater, plus shopping and dining options that all encircle a sweet outdoor square. Buy tix to a flick, or snap up seats to a **Seattle Thunderbirds** (page 55) hockey match at the nearby ShoWare Center, then fuel up with a bowl of chowder or some piping-hot fish 'n' chips at **Duke's Chowder House** (240 W. Kent Station St.; 253-850-6333; www.dukes chowderhouse.com).

SNACK BREAK

In the mood for something sweet? Pop into the **Dilettante Mocha Café** (page 225) at Kent Station for a velvety hot cocoa, which can be enjoyed by the outdoor fireplace on the patio. If you happen to be in Kent in the a.m., don't miss out on breakfast at **Wild Wheat Bakery Cafe & Restaurant** (202 1st Ave. S.; 253-856-8919; www.wildwheat.wordpress.com)—all breads are baked in-house, which makes any of the French toast options truly divine.

HIDDEN GEMS

Tucked into an obscure Kent office park, the **Hydroplane & Raceboat Museum** (page 86) is the nation's only public museum devoted to powerboat racing and, as such, has a truly devoted set of docents who are happy to chat about their favorite racing story. South Enders in the know also flock to the **Seattle Chocolates Factory Store** in Tukwila (1180 Andover Park W; 877-427-7915; www.seattlechocolates.com) for free samples of chocolates and $5 bags of "muffles" (bars with slight imperfections that still taste oh-so-good).

ON THE SIDE

Emerald Downs (page 55), about 5 miles south of Kent, in Auburn, is way more family-friendly than you might think a horse track would be, with sprawling grounds for kids to run on and a bounce house. The superchill atmosphere usually allows little horse lovers to get an up-close look at the Thoroughbreds in the paddock before the race begins.

SLEEP ON IT

There are several hotels surrounding Westfield Southcenter; the **Courtyard Seattle Southcenter** in Tukwila (400 Andover Park W; 206-575-2500; www.marriott.com/hotels/travel/seasc-courtyard -seattle-southcenter/) receives bonus points for the indoor pool and hot tub.

PART 3:

BEST EATS, SWEETS & SIPS

From flaky pastries crafted in cozy bakeries to fresh-caught seafood served at waterfront restaurants, the eating is oh-so-good in Seattle. And when it comes time to chow down—whether for a family night out or a quick stop to refuel in between activities—the city's myriad cafés offer up such signature (and kid-friendly!) dishes as crispy fish 'n' chips, juicy burgers, and hearty chowders, as well as fresh sandwiches, salads, and more.

So gather up the gang for snack time. The following sections map out the **best bites in town for families and foodies alike,** listing those locally owned or locally loved places that satisfy such kiddie cravings as **bubbly and cheesy pizza** (page 237), **slurpy noodles** (page 232), and **sticky-sweet treats ranging from cupcakes to ice cream** (page 243). You'll also get the dish on the best **coffeehouses** (page 224) to visit with kids, the best bets for **grab-and-go takeout** (page 228), the city's best **mac 'n' cheese dishes** (page 234), the **funnest food trucks for kids** (page 253), and can't-miss **Seattle classics** (page 246). Eat up!

Elliott Bay

BAKED GOODS

Offering fresh-baked breads, sticky-sweet treats, and macaroons for *votre petit*, these warm, cozy bakeries invite you to sit down and stay awhile.

Bakery Nouveau

CAPITOL HILL

137 15th Ave. E

206-858-6957

www.bakerynouveau.com

$

WEST SEATTLE

4737 California Ave. SW

206-923-0534

Led by baker extraordinaire William Leaman, this warm and homey bakery churns out insanely good pastries, breads, desserts, sandwiches, and even wood-fired pizzas from its two city locations. The larger West Seattle locale is particularly family-friendly, with a drool-worthy display case piled high with macaroons, cookies, and more. (Helpful hint: grab a loaf of the oat-and-date bread for toast tomorrow.)

Columbia City Bakery

COLUMBIA CITY

4865 Rainier Ave. S

206-723-6023

www.columbiacitybakery.com

$

Ask Seattleites for recommendations on the best bread in town, and Columbia City Bakery will come up time and time again. Grab a hot-from-the-oven loaf—favorites include the potato baguette and traditional-style ciabatta—and let the kids snag a goodie from the selection of morning buns, cinnamon twists, and lemon bars. Seating is limited in the cozy space, but the bakery's location is ideal for walking with treat in tow; the Retroactive Kids toy shop (page 158) is just three doors down.

Coyle's Bakeshop

GREENWOOD

8300 Greenwood Ave. N

206-257-4736

www.coylesbakeshop.com

$

This pop-up hit turned brick-and-mortar bakery is one sweet spot. Owner Rachel Coyle serves lighter-than-air lemon chiffon cake, warm scones, sugary cookies, and other pastries in her petite, airy bakeshop, in addition to loose-leaf teas and piping-hot espresso drinks. Whether you park yourself in a window seat to enjoy your treats or snag it all to go, do not leave without ordering a few buttery "cretzels," Coyle's unique fusion of a croissant and pretzel served with the bakeshop's apricot whole-grain mustard for dipping.

The Essential Bakery Café

GEORGETOWN	MADISON VALLEY	WALLINGFORD
5601 1st Ave. S	*2719 E. Madison St.*	*1604 N. 34th St.*
206-876-3746	*206-328-0078*	*206-545-0444*

www.essentialbaking.com

$

With a fantastic selection of muffins, scones, and bars, in addition to rolls, buns, and loaves, this bakery taps into a long tradition for its delicious goods, using local, organic, and natural ingredients whenever possible. The Wallingford and Madison Valley cafés are especially happy spots to hang, with expansive patios, cozy seating, and large windows to let the sun shine in.

Fuji Bakery

INTERBAY	INTERNATIONAL DISTRICT
1030 Elliott Ave. W	*526 S. King St.*
206-216-3616	*206-623-4050*

www.fujibakeryinc.com

$

Kids will be amazed (maybe even into silence!) at the interesting baked goods at this Japanese artisanal bakery, from smoked-salmon brioches to matcha-green-tea Danishes. The unique European-meets-Asian style suits adventurous little eaters. But don't worry—even the pickiest kid can't resist the PB&J doughnut, filled with raspberry jam and topped with dark and white chocolate, plus peanut sprinkles.

Grand Central Bakery

BURIEN	EASTLAKE	PIONEER SQUARE
626 SW 152nd St.	1616 Eastlake Ave. E	214 1st Ave. S
206-436-1065	206-957-9505	206-622-3644

www.grandcentralbakery.com

$

Bread lovers should take note of Grand Central's hearth-style loaves (the Italian-style Como is not to be missed), which are put to delicious use in the café's wide array of breakfast and lunch sandwiches. The Eastlake outpost boasts free parking in an adjacent garage, and the Pioneer Square shop—located in a historic building, replete with a cobblestone patio—is an ideal stop before a trip to nearby Magic Mouse Toys (page 117).

Le Rêve Bakery & Café

QUEEN ANNE
1805 Queen Anne Ave. N, Suite 100
206-623-7383
www.lerevebakery.com

$

Housed in a cherry-red house on Queen Anne Hill with a verdant garden patio that the littles can roam, Le Rêve charms visitors from first glance. The bakery dishes out both breakfast and lunch, in addition to French-style fruit tarts and extraflaky twice-baked croissants.

Macrina Bakery

BELLTOWN	QUEEN ANNE	SODO
2408 1st Ave.	615 W. McGraw St.	1943 1st Ave. S
206-448-4032	206-283-5900	206-623-0919

www.macrinabakery.com

$

Owned by master bread-maker Leslie Mackie, Macrina Bakery offers an impressive selection of hand-formed loaves at each of its three outposts, from apricot-nut sourdough bread to chewy, salty pretzel rolls. The airy SoDo café is especially fun for kids, as it houses the company's bread-making facilities, all on display through giant windows inside. Sip a latte while the littles watch the expert bakers knead, shape, and bake up some dough.

Rosellini's

BALLARD

1413 NW 70th St.

206-706-4035

www.rosellinis.com

$

This sweet, snug little bakery tucked on a residential street in Ballard has become revered for brightly colored macaroons and *kouign-amann* pastries, a croissant-like Breton cake that features a crackling caramelized exterior and rich, buttery interior. Kids love the roomy Adirondack chairs on the front stoop—seek one out while you munch.

The Wandering Goose

CAPITOL HILL

403 15th Ave. E

206-323-9938

www.thewanderinggoose.com

$-$$

If you're seeking a warm, fluffy biscuit breakfast, look no further than the sweet Wandering Goose atop the Hill. Here, the made-from-scratch, Southern-inspired biscuits are topped with such innovative ingredients as the fried oysters and cured pork belly seen in the Hangtown Fry ($13); kid-friendly options—like the Big Trouble sammie ($5) slathered with peanut butter, banana, and a drizzle of local honey—will also delight. Psst—plan to arrive on the earlier side as the line can grow long for these biscuits by mid- to late morning.

BREAKFAST

As certain tiny tykes are getting you out of bed oh-so-early anyway, you might as well get a big, hearty breakfast out of the deal. Fuel up for the day with these syrupy and savory brunch stops.

5 Spot
QUEEN ANNE
1502 Queen Anne Ave. N
206-285-7768
www.chowfoods.com/5-spot
$-$$

It's go big and go home stuffed at the 5 Spot atop Queen Anne Hill. Well-known for huge portions (think a slice of coffee cake the size of a baby's head), the restaurant also offers up new choices year-round, changing its menu, vibe, and decor seasonally to match a regional American cuisine.

Chinook's at Salmon Bay
INTERBAY
1900 W. Nickerson St.
206-283-4665
www.anthonys.com/restaurants/detail/chinook-at-salmon-bay
$-$$

Featuring unbeatable views of the beautiful harbor and the bobbing boats at Fishermen's Terminal, this restaurant loves kids. Crayons and coloring paper appear almost the second you sit down, as well as a basket of warm homemade scones served with honey-orange butter. Enjoy a wide range of seafood options here, or, if you arrive between 8 and 9 a.m., order the early-bird special—eggs, bacon, red potatoes, scones, and coffee for just $9.95. Do note: this spot is open for brunch on weekends only.

Geraldine's Counter
COLUMBIA CITY
4872 Rainier Ave. S
206-723-2080
www.geraldinescounter.com
$-$$

One of those magical places where you can eat breakfast all day long, Geraldine's Counter boasts all the charm of an old-school diner. It's replete with cozy booths and a high-top bar, complemented by red swivel stools—and it has the culinary chops to please everyone in the fam. Get the decadent French toast the place is known for ($10.25, featuring a different topping each day); you can order up a half order for the half-pints too ($7.50).

Hale's Brewery
FREMONT/BALLARD
4301 Leary Way NW
206-782-0737
www.halesbrewery.com
$-$$

Breakfast in a brewery—with kids? It may sound odd, but this is one of the most kid-friendly weekend brunches in town. Treat the table to a house-made cinnamon roll topped with vanilla-bean Chantilly cream-cheese frosting ($5.25), and then enjoy a hearty pub-style favorites, such as corned beef hash ($10.25), biscuits and gravy ($8.75), or eggs Benedict topped with house-smoked salmon ($10.75).

The Hi-Life
BALLARD
5425 Russell Ave. NW
206-784-7272
www.chowfoods.com/hi-life
$-$$

This laid-back Ballard restaurant, housed in a converted 1911 firehouse, dishes out homey, seasonally focused breakfast dishes seven days a week. Families dig the eatery's signature crushed red potatoes, as well as a wealth of kiddie options, including the Hi-Life Biscuitwich ($5 for a fluffy biscuit sandwich with scrambled egg and cheddar cheese) and the It's a Mickey Cake ($5.50), a big mouse-shaped pancake topped with Vermont maple syrup.

Pomegranate Bistro
REDMOND
18005 NE 68th St.
425-556-5972
www.duparandcompany.com/pomegranate-bistro
$$

Owned by renowned caterer Lisa Dupar, Pomegranate Bistro blends the best of the Northwest with the South, offering up classic comfort food in an inviting space. The Southern fried chicken and waffles ($15) and lemon-and-ginger oatcakes ($13) are sublime, and the kids' brunch special—scrambled eggs, bacon, fruit, and toast—is delish ($9).

Portage Bay Cafe

BALLARD	SOUTH LAKE UNION	UNIVERSITY DISTRICT
2825 NW Market St.	*391 Terry Ave. N*	*4130 Roosevelt*
206-783-1547	*206-462-6400*	*Way NE*
RAVENNA		*206-547-8230*
900 NE 65th St.		
206-529-3252		

www.portagebaycafe.com
$-$$

In addition to being known for using local, organic ingredients, Portage Bay Cafe is home to epic breakfast toppings bars. Order a stack of classic ($11.50), buckwheat ($13), or vegan banana pancakes ($13.50), or oatmeal cobbler French toast ($14), then belly up to the bar to add seasonal fruit, nuts, whipped cream, and organic maple syrup. Kid-size pancakes and waffles are $6.

Serendipity Cafe & Lounge
MAGNOLIA
3222 W. McGraw St.
206-282-9866
www.serendipitycafeandlounge.com
$-$$ 👫

This charming café features a designated kids' area stocked with a play kitchen and a vast array of toys, so adults can sit back and sip their lattes in peace. Menu choices range from classic scrambles, Benedicts, and pancakes to more innovative options, such as the American Dream ($10.50), a plate of mac 'n' cheese topped with bacon crumbles, tomatoes, spinach, and two over-easy eggs. The kids also have a variety of options here (think oatmeal, b'fast burritos, and pancakes), each for $6.50.

St. Clouds
MADRONA
1131 34th Ave.
206-726-1522
www.stclouds.com
$-$$

On weekends families flock to this sweet shingled restaurant in the heart of Madrona for delectable fare served up with an easy-breezy attitude. Curl up in a cozy booth and let the kids dive into some chocolate chip pancakes ($6, served with milk or juice) while you browse a menu that includes a collard-green-and-pesto egg scramble ($10.75) and a seasonal vegetable omelet ($12.50).

BURGERS & FRIES

This tried-and-true combo is always a kid-pleaser (there is ketchup involved, after all). Belly up to these burger bars for some fun in a bun.

Blue Moon Burgers

CAPITOL HILL
523 Broadway Ave. E
206-325-2000
FREMONT
703 N. 34th St.
206-547-1907
www.bluemoonburgers.com
$-$$

SOUTH LAKE UNION
920 Republican St.
206-652-0400
WEST SEATTLE
2504 Alki Ave. SW
206-257-4298

With juicy, run-down-your-arm drippy burgers, a dedicated gluten-free fryer, and stellar vegetarian options (both black-bean and falafel patties), Blue Moon satisfies just about anyone's burger hankering. The Fremont and Alki locations are particularly picturesque, with waterfront patios. Also, don't miss the fries here (both regular and sweet potato), in flavors such as curry and garlic Parmesan.

Burgermaster

BELLEVUE
10606 NE Northup Way
425-827-9566
BOTHELL
18626 Bothell-Everett Hwy.
425-486-8980
EVERETT
7909 Evergreen Way
425-347-5700
www.burgermaster.biz
$-$$

MOUNT VERNON
2030 Freeway Dr.
360-899-4075
NORTH SEATTLE
9820 Aurora Ave. N
206-522-2044
UNIVERSITY DISTRICT
3040 NE 45th St.
206-525-7100

If there's anything kids love more than a drive-thru, it's a drive-in. Slinging chargrilled burgers, salty fries, and fish 'n' chips since 1952, Burgermaster is an inexpensive and satisfying stop for a quick bite (kids' burger combos are less than $5; adults from about $10 to $13). So park your car, crawl in the backseat with the kids, and order up a peanut-butter shake (about $3) to get the party started.

Dick's Drive-In

CAPITOL HILL	LAKE CITY
115 Broadway Ave. E	12325 30th Ave. NE
206-323-1300	206-363-7777
CROWN HILL	QUEEN ANNE
9208 Holman Rd. NW	500 Queen Anne Ave. N
206-783-5233	206-285-5155
EDMONDS	WALLINGFORD
21910 SR 99	111 NE 45th St.
425-775-4243	206-632-5125
www.ddir.com	

$

First opened in 1954, this fast-food place is a true Seattle classic, churning out burgers and fries in six locations across the metropolis. It's also ridiculously cheap to fill up the whole crew here—fries are $1.75 and a double-patty burger will set you back just $3.10. (Do note that most Dick's locations are no longer drive-ins but instead have walk-up windows, so they are excellent for quick pickups or parking lot picnics.)

Li'l Woody's

BALLARD	CAPITOL HILL
2040 NW Market St.	1211 Pine St.
206-257-5259	206-457-4148
www.lilwoodys.com	

$

This casual burger joint doesn't mess around, hand-forming each Northwest grass-fed beef patty that goes into its wildly creative burgers. Tykes can tackle—or split—the Li'l Woody ($4.50 for a quarter-pounder topped with Tillamook cheddar, ketchup, mayo, chopped onions, and pickles). And don't forget to order some Crack ($6) for the table, a big basket of hand-cut fries served with a side of milkshake for dipping.

LunchBox Laboratory

BELLEVUE   SOUTH LAKE UNION
989 112th Ave. NE, Suite 105   *1253 Thomas St.*
425-505-2676   *206-621-1090*
www.lunchboxlaboratory.com
$$

Let the kids play chef at LunchBox Laboratory, a delicious spot where diners are encouraged to build their own wild-and-crazy burgers ($10.99 and up). Choose from such innovative ingredients as a "dork" (duck plus pork) or "churken" (chicken plus turkey) patty, sweet chili mayo, and candied balsamic onions. Kids especially love the restaurant's signature corndogs, called Dogsticks ($8.99 for three).

Red Mill Burgers

BALLARD   INTERBAY   PHINNEY RIDGE
3058 NW 54th St.   *1613 W. Dravus St.* *312 N. 67th St.*
206-784-1400   *206-284-6363*   *206-783-6362*
www.redmillburgers.com
$-$$

This place seems to ever bustle with families popping in and out for big ol' burgers. And rightly so, with Red Mill being chiefly known for the generous stacks of pig on its signature Bacon Deluxe burger, as well as for crispy, crunchy onion rings. This is a cash-only spot, so be sure to have some green on hand. The Phinney Ridge location is the largest, and thus the best bet for snagging a table. (One note: these burger shacks are closed on Mondays.)

Uneeda Burger

FREMONT
4302 Fremont Ave. N
206-547-2600
www.uneedaburger.com
$$

You need a burger? Well then, head to this cozy-chic spot perched atop Fremont, just a few blocks from Woodland Park Zoo (hint, hint). Choose a burger off the big chalkboard menu (topped with portobello mushrooms, the Crispy Emmer Veggie Burger will have vegetarians rejoicing), snag a luscious hand-crafted milkshake, and then, in sunny months, head out to the spacious patio, where the kids can frolic until the sammies are ready.

Zippy's Giant Burgers

GEORGETOWN

5633 Airport Way S

206-466-5954

www.zippysgiantburgers.com

$

WHITE CENTER

9614 14th Ave. SW

206-763-1347

This mom-and-pop diner is known for its retro vibe and—you guessed it—really, really big charbroiled burgers. While the adults attack the Big Mouth ($9.50 for three patties and triple the cheese) or Rae's Black Bean Veggie burger ($5.50), order up the Zippy the Yum Yum Burger Boy's Wacky Meal ($4.95) for the kids, which arrives with a quarter-pounder, fries or tots, and a Capri Sun. Plus, talk about a midweek pick-me-up: kids age 11 and under eat free at Zippy's during happy hour (3–6 p.m.) on Wednesdays.

BURRITOS & TACOS

With pretty outdoor patios, cheesy 'dillas, and chips and guac galore, these Mexican eateries are all *niño*-approved.

Agua Verde Paddle Club

UNIVERSITY DISTRICT

1303 NE Boat St.

206-545-8570

www.aguaverde.com

$-$$

Nestled along the picturesque shores of Portage Bay, near UW, Agua Verde is part restaurant and part kayak-rental shop, boasting an extremely popular patio for dining on warm days. Order up some icy *bebidas* and a platter of nachos to share ($8 for the signature nachos, topped with pinto beans, jack cheese, nopal cactus, and sour cream), then top it your way with your choice of three smoky house-made salsas from the salsa bar. For more details on snagging a kayak or paddleboard, see page 63.

Cactus

BELLEVUE	MADISON PARK	WEST SEATTLE
535 Bellevue Square	4220 E. Madison St.	2820 Alki Ave. SW
425-455-4321	206-324-4140	206-933-6000
KIRKLAND	SOUTH LAKE UNION	
121 Park Ln.	350 Terry Ave. N	
425-893-9799	206-913-2250	

www.cactusrestaurants.com

$-$$

Cactus is well-known for innovative Southwest and Mexican cuisine and lovely patio dining in stellar locations. Particularly well suited for kiddos during the brunch and lunch hours (dinner gets mobbed with the happy-hour crowd), the restaurant offers fare that's perfect for sharing. Kids will gobble up the cinnamon-y Navajo fry bread ($4), and the guacamole with chips and salsa ($7) is not to be missed.

Gorditos

GREENWOOD

213 N. 85th St.

206-706-9352

www.gorditosmexicanfood.com

$

This hole-in-the-wall is famous for its absolutely ginormous burritos, so much so that the family-run eatery has started a photo wall featuring newborn babies posed next to its Burrito Grande. (Spoiler alert: they are the same size.) At $6.75 for an easily shareable regular burrito—stuffed with your choice of meat, black beans, Mexican rice, and chunky salsa—this is one good value. The smaller kids' bean-and-cheese burrito rings up at only $3.50.

La Carta de Oaxaca

BALLARD

5431 Ballard Ave. NW
206-782-8722
www.lacartadeoaxaca.com

$$

For truly authentic Mexican fare, head to the beloved La Carta de Oaxaca in Ballard. This teensy spot seems to ever bustle with hustling servers and hungry diners chowing on such unique dishes as yellow curry empanadas or chicken topped with mole negro sauce. While some fare may be a little far-out for finicky eaters, a helping of the made-to-order guacamole and chips should still appease.

Pecado Bueno

EASTLAKE	FREMONT	WEST SEATTLE
2356 Eastlake Ave. E	*4307 Fremont Ave. N*	*4523 California*
206-687-7423	*206-457-8837*	*Ave. SW*
		206-402-5107

www.pecadobueno.com
$-$$

Pecado Bueno elevates the neighborhood taqueria by using local produce and all-natural proteins, with all three of its locations shelling out fresh fare like the *torta*, a grilled roll topped with mayo, black beans, Havarti cheese, and ranchero sauce with an egg and your choice of meat. Kids will be happy to chow down on a quesadilla filled with black beans or even butternut squash—consider it your parenting win for the day.

Rosita's Mexican Grill

GREEN LAKE

7210 Woodlawn Ave. NE
206-523-3031
www.rositasrestaurant.com

$$

Located just steps from the lake, Rosita's is the place to stop with "hangry" kids. In addition to huge portions of enchiladas, tacos, and burritos, the *niños* will love the fresh house-made corn tortillas that arrive hot off the grill as soon as you're seated. The menu also offers up such kid-friendly options as chile rellenos ($10) and tamales ($9.50).

COFFEE & DRINKS

Outfitted with toy chests, game areas, and great sips, these friendly coffeehouses further solidify Seattle's rep as Coffee Town, USA.

Ballard Coffee Works & Seattle Coffee Works

BALLARD
(BALLARD COFFEE WORKS)
2060 NW Market St.
206-340-8867
www.seattlecoffeeworks.com
$

DOWNTOWN
(SEATTLE COFFEE WORKS)
107 Pike St.
206-340-8867

Made for the coffee aficionado, this coffee shop takes the approach of a winery, with a tasting area, called the Slow Bar, where you can try coffee varietals from around the world, brewed up by baristas using several different methods. The spacious and airy Ballard café has a dedicated kids' area stocked with toys, tucked-away rooms for playing board games, and lots of large tables for spreading out.

Cloud City Coffee

MAPLE LEAF
8801 Roosevelt Way NE
206-527-5552
www.cloudcitycoffee.com
$ 🚶

Beloved by neighborhood locals and for good reason, Cloud City Coffee invites you to sit and stay awhile, with comfy couches, free newspapers, board games, and a kids' play corner, in addition to coffee roasted in the Northwest and house-made breakfast and lunch treats. Plus, once you're caffeinated up, you can take a one-block jaunt to the stellar Maple Leaf Reservoir

HOT CHOCOLATE HEAVEN

Take your little chocolate lover to one of these local
outposts for a rich and velvety hot cocoa treat.

Chocolate Box
PIKE PLACE MARKET
106 Pine St.
206-443-3900
www.sschocolatebox.com

Specializing in locally made chocolates, such as Theo and Forté, the
Box knows hot cocoa. Each year, typically in March, the shop hosts a
Hot Chocolate Festival offering thirty-one days of new hot chocolate
combinations; favorites include s'mores, Nutella, and spiced gingerbread.

Chocolopolis
QUEEN ANNE
1527 Queen Anne Ave. N
206-282-0776
www.chocolopolis.com

Select any chocolate bar in the shop for the friendly staffers to melt into
cocoa. The kids' hot chocolate ($3) has half the amount of chocolate,
so it's not quite as intense. Don't forget to add a house-made vanilla
marshmallow or two.

Dilettante Mocha Café
BELLEVUE, CAPITOL HILL, DOWNTOWN (THREE LOCATIONS), KENT, AND SEA-TAC
AIRPORT (TWO LOCATIONS)
www.dilettante.com

Crafted from molten chocolate and steamed milk, the white hot chocolate
($3.75) from this Seattle classic is decadent and oh-so-dreamy.

Fran's Chocolates
BELLEVUE, DOWNTOWN, GEORGETOWN, AND UNIVERSITY VILLAGE
www.franschocolates.com

Each cup of perfectly crafted hot cocoa comes topped with a dollop of
whipped cream, plus a square of Fran's signature chocolate on the side.

Park (just look for the landmark water tower decorated with maple leaves!), where everyone can burn off some excess energy at the playground on the south end of park.

El Diablo Coffee Co.
QUEEN ANNE
1811 Queen Anne Ave. N, Suite 101
206-285-0693
www.eldiablocoffee.com
$ 👫

This charming coffeehouse, next door to the kid-friendly Queen Anne Book Company, specializes in Cuban coffee, offering up intense *cubanos*, *cortaditos*, and *cafés con leche* for the adults, plus several kinds of hot chocolate (the cinnamon-spiced Mexican variety is a favorite) and a sweet toy corner for the cuties.

Firehouse Coffee
BALLARD
2622 NW Market St.
206-784-2911
$

With a separate playroom that can be closed off from the rest of the shop with a sliding door, Firehouse is a dream location for mamas and papas. Kids can run, jump, and play to their hearts' content (without disturbing other patrons), while the adults enjoy coffee from local roaster Caffé Vita and free Wi-Fi.

Green Bean Coffeehouse
GREENWOOD
8525 Greenwood Ave. N
206-402-5150
www.greenbeancoffee.org
$

This inviting nonprofit coffee shop in the North End offers up Caffè Lusso coffee, fresh-made smoothies, and locally baked treats in a pleasant space accented by big windows. Kids will be begging to stay here, thanks to the giant train table stocked with choo-choos and props, plus a bevy of board games and books to flip through. If you happen to be in the hood on a Tuesday morning, check out the 10 a.m. story time.

Issaquah Coffee Company

ISSAQUAH
317 NW Gilman Blvd., Suite 46
425-677-7118
www.issaquahcoffee.com
$

This place defines cozy, with comfy couches, lounge chairs, and a cabin-y vibe, plus an outdoor patio, perfect for sunny days. Kids will be delighted by the train table and frequent pooch sightings (this is one dog-friendly stop). The café also boasts Stumptown coffee, great gluten-free goodies from the Flying Apron bakery, and fruity smoothies.

Mosaic Community Coffeehouse

WALLINGFORD
4401 2nd Ave. NE
206-632-4560
www.mosaiccoffeehouse.com
$

A tucked-away gem located on the basement floor of a church, this community-centric shop uses a pay-what-you-can policy for drinks. The real draw for parents, though, is the sizeable playroom, separated from the main space by double doors and decorated with cheery wall decals. With a slide, dollhouses, play kitchens, and toys, this is a popular stop on a rainy morning. (One note: the café is closed on weekends and hours are variable seasonally.)

Sip & Ship

BALLARD	GREENWOOD
1752 NW Market St.	*7511 Greenwood Ave. N*
206-789-4488	*206-783-4299*
www.sipandship.com	
$	

This whimsical shop is one part gift spot, one part shipping stop, and one part coffee shop, offering great lattes, savory sandwiches, and sweet toy areas in both of its Seattle locations. Located in an upstairs loft area in the shop, the Ballard Sip & Ship's play area is particularly sweet; latch the gate and let the littles play I Spy using all the goings-on below.

MARKETS & TAKEOUT

No downtime? No problem. These gourmet markets and takeout spots are prepped for grab-and-go chow.

Central Market

MILL CREEK
15605 Main St.
425-357-3240
www.central-market.com

SHORELINE
15505 Westminster Way N
206-363-9226

These high-end grocery stores boast the delis of your dreams, complete with handcrafted sandwiches, house-made soups, and a salad bar that goes way beyond greens—with noodles, naan, and more, in addition to hot items including rotisserie chicken and pizza. Grab each kid a box and let them go to town (bar items are sold by the pound, so feel free to mix and match).

DeLaurenti Specialty Food & Wine

PIKE PLACE MARKET
1435 1st Ave.
206-622-0141
www.delaurenti.com

Tucked in the bustling Pike Place Market, this grocery is devoted to all things Italian, with a wide array of imported noodles, sauces, and cookies in addition to house-made ravioli, pesto, and more. Grab a basket and curate a feast from the cheese-and-meat deli counter, which is also stocked with premade pasta salads and briny olives. The café section offers pizza by the slice, just-baked cookies, crisp salads, and incredible panini to go.

Home Remedy

DOWNTOWN

2121 6th Ave.

206-812-8407

www.tdhomeremedy.com

This bustling little market is filled with provisions from one of Seattle's favorite chefs, Tom Douglas. In addition to fine-food provisions and take-and-bake options, such as chicken potpie, lasagna, and soft pretzels, all sourced from Douglas's nearby restaurants, Home Remedy offers piping-hot pizza by the slice and a gargantuan salad bar, as well as made-to-order rice bowls, sandwiches, and its popular Indian-style burritos.

Metropolitan Market

KIRKLAND	QUEEN ANNE	SAND POINT
10611 NE 68th St.	*100 Mercer St.*	*5250 40th Ave. NE*
425-454-0085	*206-213-0778*	*206-938-6600*
MAGNOLIA	SAMMAMISH	WEST SEATTLE
3830 34th Ave. W	*Opening in 2017*	*2320 42nd Ave. SW*
206-283-2710	*228th Ave. SE*	*206-937-0551*
	and SE 4th St.	

www.metropolitan-market.com

This locally owned grocery store has one heckuva deli, featuring fresh pastas and salads, an antipasto bar, and take-home comfort foods such as Buttermilk Blue mac 'n' cheese and prime rib potpie. Kids will love the carving stations, where the white coat–clad butchers carve your pork or prime rib to order.

Michou

PIKE PLACE MARKET

1904 Pike Pl.

206-448-4758

www.michoudeli.com

Situated along the cobblestone streets of Pike Place Market, this bustling grab-and-go deli serves up fantastic panini-style sandwiches, pizza, soups, salads, and desserts. Salads are sold by the pound and are often crafted from ingredients sourced just a few stalls away.

Pasta & Co

BELLEVUE
10218 NE 8th St.
425-453-8760
www.pastaco.com

UNIVERSITY VILLAGE
4622 26th Ave. NE
206-523-8594

Find all the makings of a meal at this snug neighborhood shop stocked with gourmet take-home options, plus provisions like olive oil, fresh bread, and cheeses. The side salads are stellar here. Choose from such rotating favorites as chipotle potato salad, red pepper couscous, and radiatore pasta with pesto (a kid favorite!).

PCC Natural Markets

BOTHELL, COLUMBIA CITY, EDMONDS, FREMONT, GREEN LAKE (TWO LOCATIONS), ISSAQUAH, KIRKLAND, REDMOND, VIEW RIDGE, AND WEST SEATTLE
www.pccnaturalmarkets.com

With eleven locations, this fantastic co-op is ideal for picking up a fresh picnic lunch. Head to the gourmet deli and let kids pick their favorites from the glass case (such as Parmesan chicken fingers, pesto zucchini noodles, and fresh strawberry shortcake, just to name a few), snag a piece of fruit (kids age 12 and under get a fruit or veggie free!) and a fizzy, locally crafted Dry soda, and off you go.

PRETTY PICNICS

You've canvased the market and stocked up on supplies; now spread out a blanket at one of these sweet spots.

Ella Bailey Park

MAGNOLIA

2601 W. Smith St.

www.seattle.gov/parks/find/parks/ella-bailey-park

Sprawling lawns, a playground, and an awe-inspiring view of Downtown Seattle on a clear day.

Gas Works Park

WALLINGFORD

2101 N. Northlake Way

www.seattle.gov/parks/find/parks/gas-works-park

Cool, old industrial equipment to explore and a lakefront location with views.

Golden Gardens Park

BALLARD

8498 Seaview Pl. NW

www.seattle.gov/parks/find/parks/golden-gardens-park

A sandy, serene beach with a playground, fire pits, and tide pools for the kiddies.

Oxbow Park

GEORGETOWN

6430 Corson Ave. S

www.seattle.gov/parks/find/parks/oxbow-park

A funky neighborhood haunt featuring 22-foot-high cowboy boots and a 44-foot-wide cowboy hat.

Volunteer Park

CAPITOL HILL

1247 15th Ave. E

www.seattle.gov/parks/find/parks/volunteer-park

A beautiful reservoir and lawn area surrounded by giant trees and a climbable water tower.

NOODLES & RICE

Whether the kids swoon for slurpy, saucy pasta or think rice is nice, sate their cravings with these fun local favorites for Asian and Italian cuisines.

ASIAN

Blue C Sushi

BELLEVUE	FREMONT	TUKWILA
503 Bellevue Square	3411 Fremont Ave. N	468 Southcenter Mall
425-454-8288	206-633-3411	206-277-8744
DOWNTOWN	LYNNWOOD	UNIVERSITY VILLAGE
1510 7th Ave.	Alderwood Mall,	2675 Village Ln. NE
206-467-4022	3000 184th St. SW	206-525-4601
	425-774-4223	

www.bluecsushi.com

$-$$

You'll need just two words to talk your kids into visiting Blue C Sushi: "conveyor belt." Kids go crazy for the goods circling around the restaurant, which are handily color-coded by prices, ranging from $2 to $5.50 per dish. Give the tykes a spending cap and let 'em pick their own. In addition to sushi classics like avocado, spicy tuna, and California rolls, there are kid-friendly faves, such as crispy chicken rolls, edamame, and potato katsu (which look an awful lot like good ol' French fries).

Judy Fu's Snappy Dragon

MAPLE LEAF

8917 Roosevelt Way NE

206-528-5575

www.snappydragon.com

$$

A popular Chinese food stop for over 20 years, Snappy Dragon is serious about noodles. The chewy and delicious egg noodles are made in-house (and can even be hand-rolled and cut to order for an extra $2.50); be sure to try 'em in the excellent chow mein ($9.75–$10.25). Casual and very welcoming to kids, with coloring pages and crayons at the table, this place is always a family hit.

Marination

CAPITOL HILL
(MARINATION STATION)
1412 Harvard Ave.
206-325-8226
COLUMBIA CITY (SUPER SIX)
3714 S. Hudson St.
206-420-1201
www.marinationmobile.com

$-$$

DOWNTOWN (MARINATION)
2000 6th Ave.
206-327-9860
WEST SEATTLE
(MARINATION MA KAI)
1660 Harbor Ave. SW
206-328-8226

With its beginnings as a food truck (you can still spot Big Blue slinging chow around town), Marination now has four brick-and-mortar eateries as well, blending Korean and Hawaiian flavors with aplomb in such dishes as miso-ginger-chicken tacos ($2.75 each), fried rice with kimchi and a fried egg ($7), and kalua pork sliders topped with crisp slaw and served on Hawaiian sweet rolls ($2.75 each). The West Seattle location, at Alki, is particularly fun with a bayside patio and shave ice ($3.75 for the kids' size) on offer for those sweltering summer days.

Pho Bac

DOWNTOWN
1809 Minor Ave.
206-621-8816
INTERNATIONAL DISTRICT
1314 S. Jackson St.
206-323-4387
$

PHO VIET
1240 S. Jackson St.
206-568-0882
RAINIER VALLEY
3300 Rainier Ave. S
206-725-4418

When the weather turns gray and drizzly, Seattleites flock to Pho Bac for steaming bowls of comforting pho, a traditional Vietnamese soup packed with silky rice noodles, fresh cilantro, and strip loin that cooks right in the broth ($8–$9). Slurp some up at one of the easygoing eatery's four locations, and be sure to add on an order of Chinese doughnuts for $2—the warm breadstick-like treats are great for dunking.

MAC 'N' CHEESE, PLEASE!

Creamy, gooey, and, of course, oh-so-cheesy, macaroni and cheese has some kind of hold on kids (okay, count the adults in on that one too). Satisfy all your cheese cravings at one of these outposts.

Beecher's Handmade Cheese
BELLEVUE, PIKE PLACE MARKET, AND SEA-TAC AIRPORT
www.beechershandmadecheese.com

Perhaps Seattle's most popular version, the rich, velvety mac 'n' cheese ($5.02 for 8 ounces) from Beecher's is made with the company's own Flagship and Just Jack cheeses and penne pasta.

Bitterroot
BALLARD
5239 Ballard Ave. NW
206-588-1577
www.bitterrootbbq.com

This cozy Ballard barbecue joint's famous mac 'n' cheese ($12) allows kids to play chef, coming with your choice of two toppings piled atop the creamy noodles; choose from the likes of pulled pork, bacon, and sliced hot links.

Cafe Flora
MADISON VALLEY
2901 E. Madison St.
206-325-9100
www.cafeflora.com

Thai Curry Simple
INTERNATIONAL DISTRICT
406 5th Ave. S
206-327-4838
www.thaicurrysimple.com
$

This family-run hole-in-the-wall in the ID features a daily curry special, ranging from sweet panang to spicy red (check the floor-to-ceiling chalkboard for the day's deets). Also on the menu are noodley favorites such as pad thai and the kid-friendly pad see ew, packed with chicken, broccoli, and a sweet sauce

Made-to-order and topped with herbed bread crumbs, the kids' mac at this lovely vegetarian and vegan restaurant is so popular it was included in the café's own cookbook.

Icon Grill
DOWNTOWN
1933 5th Ave.
206-441-6330
www.icongrill.com

The swoon-worthy Ultimate Macaroni & Cheese ($17) is crafted from four different kinds of cheese, tomato "snow," crunchy bread crumbs, and a final topping of molten cheese. (There's also a truly decadent Hog Wild Mac N 'Chz version topped with BBQ pulled pork and caramelized onions for $19.)

Skillet

BALLARD	CAPITOL HILL	DOWNTOWN	SEATTLE CENTER
2034 NW 56th St.	*1400 E. Union St.*	*2050 6th Ave.*	*305 Harrison St.*
206-922-7981	*206-512-2001*	*206-512-2002*	*206-428-6311*

www.skilletfood.com

Made from Muenster, cheddar, and Parmesan cheeses, the retro-cool macaroni and cheese from this upscale diner is finished with wagon-wheel pasta and a chili-cheese-corn-chip crust ($14). A Tillamook cheddar version is available for the kiddos ($5).

($7.95). Inexpensive—most dishes are under $10—and with casual seat-yourself seating, this charming café always brings bright and fresh flavors to the table.

ITALIAN

Bizzarro Italian Cafe
WALLINGFORD
1307 N. 46th St.
206-632-7277
www.bizzarroitaliancafe.com
$$

A longtime favorite not far from Woodland Park, Bizzarro is aptly named, replete with fun and funky decor—"Is that a bike hanging from the ceiling?"—that is so engaging you may need to remind the kids to actually eat. Home to one of the best lasagnas in town ($18 per serving) and a delectable clam linguini kissed with house-cured pancetta ($19), the restaurant is especially popular for Sunday family dinners, when its handmade meatballs and marinara are served as a special treat ($19.25).

La Rustica
WEST SEATTLE
4100 Beach Dr. SW
206-932-3020
www.larustica.moonfruit.com
$$-$$$

Just off the beaten path in Alki, this snug and sophisticated Italian restaurant is run by husband-and-wife duo Giulio and Janie Pellegrini. As such, the eatery exudes a warm, friendly vibe and churns out authentic Italian suppers. The outdoor garden patio is probably the best bet for kids, as is ordering the piping-hot margherita pizza ($12.95) topped with basil and garden-fresh tomatoes.

Perché No Pasta & Vino
GREEN LAKE
1319 N. 49th St.
206-547-0222
www.perchenopastaandvino.com
$-$$

At this eatery just steps from Green Lake, it's not unusual to see owners David and Lily Kong chatting up customers or refilling drink cups; the eatery thus exudes an inviting attitude the minute you step through the door. The fare is just as inviting, with house-made gnocchi, creamy risotto, and Italian-style gelato.

PIZZA

Turn to these inviting pizzerias next time you need a piping-hot pie. Many offer kid-friendly perks (dough to play with!) and grown-up-ready gourmet toppings too.

Ballard Pizza Co.

BALLARD	FREMONT/BALLARD	SOUTH LAKE UNION
5107 Ballard Ave. NW	4010 Leary Way NW	500 9th Ave. N
206-946-9960	206-946-9966	206-623-3583

www.ballardpizzacompany.com

$

With locations in Ballard, South Lake Union, and "Frelard" (where the hoods of Fremont and Ballard meet), these grab 'n' go spots from revered local chef Ethan Stowell are made for those moments when you need pizza pronto. Take your pick from the huge, perfectly charred individual slices ($3.50–$4 each) at the big counter, which staffers reheat in the massive wood-burning oven, then cozy up in a booth or, at the Frelard location, unleash the littles in the play area, replete with building blocks and a chalkboard wall for scribbling.

Flying Squirrel Pizza Co.

GEORGETOWN	MAPLE LEAF	SEWARD PARK
5701 Airport Way S	8310 5th Ave. NE	4920 S. Genesee St.
206-397-3540	206-524-6345	206-721-7620

www.flyingsquirrelpizza.com

$-$$

This pizzeria is known for its inventive and intrepid topping combinations; think a pulled-pork pie topped with cotija cheese, cilantro, red onion, and lime juice ($12–$23) or the lemon, herb, and garlic–roasted potato pizza with blue cheese ($10.50–$22). Better yet for families are the fun and funky atmosphere and easy attitude toward kids; the Seward Park location exudes a boisterous family-reunion-style mood nightly.

Pagliacci Pizza

SEATTLE LOCATIONS INCLUDE BALLARD, CAPITOL HILL, COLUMBIA CITY
FREMONT, LAKE CITY, MADISON VALLEY, MAGNOLIA, NORTH SEATTLE,
QUEEN ANNE, SAND POINT, UNIVERSITY DISTRICT, AND WEST
SEATTLE; ADDITIONAL LOCATIONS IN BELLEVUE, EDMONDS, KENMORE,
KIRKLAND, MERCER ISLAND, AND SHORELINE
www.pagliacci.com

$-$$

This local pizza chain has been beloved by locals since its
inception as a teensy takeout stop back in 1979. And it's
well deserved too, as Pagliacci ups the pizza ante with local
ingredients and seasonally inspired toppings, such as asparagus
in the spring, squash in the fall, and vine-ripened tomatoes in
the summer. Some cafés are carry-out only, so check the website
first; the Madison Valley location is the best bet for kids, outfitted
with a nook that looks into the busy, bustling kitchen.

Proletariat Pizza

WHITE CENTER
9622-A 16th Ave. SW
206-432-9765
www.proletariatpizza.com

$-$$

Churning out a rotating menu of thin-crust pizzas including such
favorites as the Roasted Garlic Special (mellow roasted garlic
cloves, red onion, and feta cheese, $22) from its wood-fired
oven, Proletariat is quite aptly named; the White Center pizzeria
is the type of unfussy place where no one bats an eyelash if
some tomato sauce hits the floor or a soda is spilled. After
chowing down, little gamers would do well to head to the back,
where a treasure trove of arcade games is hidden.

Ridge Pizza

PHINNEY RIDGE
7217 Greenwood Ave. N
206-687-7621
www.ridgepizza.com

$-$$

Ridge Pizza is truly devoted to its neighborhood, with its thick, chewy pizza pies named after other neighborhood favorites, such as the Woodland Park Zoo. (In case you're wondering, the Zoo is topped with artichoke hearts, roasted garlic, and goat cheese, $19–$28.) Adding to the inviting atmosphere are a plethora of arcade games and a vintage shuffleboard table for kids to entertain themselves while waiting for the 'za.

Tutta Bella Neapolitan Pizzeria

BELLEVUE	ISSAQUAH	WALLINGFORD
15600 NE 8th St.,	715 NW Gilman Blvd.	4411 Stone Way N
Suite J1	425-391-6838	206-633-3800
425-502-7402	SOUTH LAKE UNION	
COLUMBIA CITY	2200 Westlake Ave.,	
4918 Rainier Ave. S	Suite 112	
206-721-3501	206-624-4422	
www.tuttabella.com		
$-$$		

Specializing in authentic Naples-style pizzas, Tutta Bella immediately offers parents a helping hand by handing pizza dough to little ones to play with in addition to Wikki Stix or crayons and coloring pages. Kids will also get a kick out of their own personal-size Bambino pizza ($6), arriving crisp and lightly charred from the wood-burning oven, with melted provolone and mozzarella cheeses. Psst—with the exception of the Bellevue location, the pizzerias all boast beautiful patios for alfresco dining.

Veraci Pizza

BALLARD	WEDGWOOD
500 NW Market St.	7320 35th Ave. NE
206-525-1813	206-452-5013
www.veracipizza.com	
$-$$	

The superfast Veraci pizzerias are the brick-and-mortar extensions of owner Marshall Jett's popular traveling wood-burning pizza oven, which often pops up at local farmers' markets. With thin-crust pizzas available by the slice or by the pie at the walk-up counter, Veraci also offers gluten-free crust options ($3.75 extra), as well as stellar salads and authentic gelato.

SANDWICHES, SALADS & SOUPS

These hot spots deliver the best things in between sliced bread, plus cozy soups and crisp salads.

Baguette Box
CAPITOL HILL
1203 Pine St.
206-332-0220
www.baguetteboxseattle.com
$-$$

Baguette Box certainly thinks out of the box, with its inventive Vietnamese and Asian-fusion sandwiches, the most famous of which is the Crispy Drunken Chicken Baguette ($8.95), made from battered chicken, tangy sauce, and caramelized onions (also available as a cool, crisp salad for $10.50). It's a drippy-sloppy-yummy mess the whole fam will love (grab lots of napkins!). For an extra $4 it's well worth ordering the box meal, if just for the homemade banana cake that comes with it.

The Great Northwest Soup Co.

DOWNTOWN	EASTLAKE	SOUTH LAKE UNION
1323 4th Ave.	*1201 Eastlake Ave.*	*340 Westlake Ave. N*
206-859-6498	*206-582-3503*	*206-420-8351*

www.greatnwsoupcompany.com
$

With a revolving selection of nine to twelve daily options and over a hundred original recipes, this place serves up soul-soothing soup in an easy grab-and-go setting with options fit for just about everyone, whether you like brothy or creamy, spicy or mild. Faves for kiddie appetites include the classic chicken noodle, tomato pesto and ravioli, and turkey potpie. Order a Combo 1 for $8.99 and also get a grilled cheese sammie for dunking.

Homegrown Sustainable Sandwich Shop
BELLEVUE, CAPITOL HILL, DOWNTOWN, FREMONT, KIRKLAND, MERCER ISLAND, QUEEN ANNE, REDMOND, SAMMAMISH, AND SOUTH LAKE UNION
www.eathomegrown.com
$$

Utilizing local, sustainable, and often organic ingredients, Homegrown is a great spot for a guilt-free lunch. The kiddie peanut butter and jelly served on whole grain bread ($3–$6) is just as much of a delight for adults, or go for the café's Rogue Cobb salad crafted with Rogue Creamery blue cheese, cage-free eggs, and nitrate-free bacon ($13.95) or signature Chicken Cherry Pecan sandwich, topped with grilled chicken, cherries, pecans, kale, and sage aioli ($6.15–$12.30).

Paseo

FREMONT
4225 Fremont Ave. N
206-545-7440
www.paseorestaurants.com
$ 🏃

SODO
1760 1st Ave. S
206-420-7781

If you eat one Seattle sandwich, Paseo is the place for it. The Caribbean Roast ($9.75)–slow-roasted pork on a toasted baguette slathered with aioli, crisp romaine, cilantro, and pickled jalapeños, and crowned with caramelized onions–has made countless local "best" lists. Its glory is well deserved, though vegetarians seem equally fanatical about the Onion Obsession Sandwich ($8.50 for caramelized onions atop a baguette with garlic tapenade). Seating is limited at the original Fremont location, so grab it to go and enjoy your sloppy sammies outside where it doesn't matter if the juices run all the way down your arm.

Pike Place Chowder

DOWNTOWN
600 Pine St.
206-838-5680
www.pikeplacechowder.com
$-$$

PIKE PLACE MARKET
1530 Post Alley
206-267-2537

With Seattle comes seafood, and with seafood comes chowder. It's little wonder then that Seattleites flock to Pike Place Chowder on cold, drippy days to fortify themselves with piping-hot bowls of creamy soup. A breeze with kids (just order at the counter and claim a table), the café offers crisp salads and sandwich rolls—such as the stellar Dungeness crab roll, with mayo, celery, lemon, and secret seasonings, plush fresh crab meat, of course—as well as a revolving cast of daily chowders. Favorites include classic New England clam, smoked salmon, and seared scallop; for the fish-averse, the chicken-and-corn chowder is also top-notch.

Salumi Artisan Cured Meats
PIONEER SQUARE
309 3rd Ave. S
206-621-8772
www.salumicuredmeats.com
$-$$

Lovingly owned and operated by the Batali family (as in celebrity chef Mario), Salumi has garnered an almost cultlike devotion for its beautifully cured meats. On weekdays, the family puts all of its salami, coppa, and prosciutto to good use in the Italian-style sandwiches ($8.50–$11.75) served out of its teensy storefront. Warning: there is nearly always a long line (go early!). But kids should be entertained enough by the hustle and bustle (not to mention Nonna Batali, who crafts gnocchi by hand in the storefront window on Tuesdays) to give you plenty of time to snag your sandwiches before dashing outside to devour them.

Three Girls Bakery
PIKE PLACE MARKET
1514 Pike Pl.
206-622-1045
$

Tucked among the myriad stalls in Pike Place Market on the east side of Post Alley, Three Girls Bakery is piled high with sweet treats, such as croissants and rugelach, but the real draw comes at lunchtime when the bakery starts serving up its signature meatloaf sandwich ($9). Showcasing a thick slice of homemade meatloaf, plus mayo, mustard, lettuce, tomatoes, and onions, this one will stick with you the rest of the day. The bakery also whips up a wicked BLT and a grilled ham-and-cheese that kids love.

SWEETS

Please those sweet teeth with sugar shops that woo with such decadent delights as strawberry balsamic ice cream, molten chocolate cakes, and handheld pies fresh from the oven.

CANDY

The Confectionery

UNIVERSITY VILLAGE

4608 26th Ave. NE

206-523-1443

www.theconfectionery.com

$

A treasure trove of gumdrops, lollipops, and more, this family-owned store is sweeter than sweet, with a traditional old-school candy-shop vibe (think bright-pink walls and pretty candies displayed in glass jars), a dynamite chocolate truffle case, and premade favor bags for parties. Selections are sold by the pound (minimums apply for some candies).

Nama's Candy Store

EDMONDS

102 5th Ave. N

425-771-4606

www.namascandystore.com

$

Stocked with shelves upon shelves of candy, Nama's is known for its stellar selection of fudge and the darling seasonal window displays that have passersby stopping in their tracks. Fanciful and fun, the shop also pays homage to its seaside locale with oh-so-chewy saltwater taffy.

Sweet Mickey's
BALLARD
2230 NW 57th St.
206-402-6272
www.sweetmickeys.com
$

Both the young and young at heart love this cheery candy shop tucked next to a cute park; it offers ice cream, handmade fudge, and truffles, as well as nostalgic throwback candy, such as cherry sour balls, cola gummies, wax bottles, and licorice coins (all $10–$12 per pound).

CUPCAKES

Cupcake Royale

BALLARD	DOWNTOWN	QUEEN ANNE
2052 NW Market St.	*108 Pine St.*	*1935 Queen Anne*
206-701-6238	*206-443-8674*	*Ave. N*
CAPITOL HILL	MADRONA	*206-285-1447*
1111 E. Pike St.	*1101 34th Ave.*	WEST SEATTLE
206-701-9579	*206-701-6240*	*4556 California*
		Ave. SW
		206-701-6266

www.cupcakeroyale.com
$

This charming sextet of shops offers decadent and dreamy cupcakes in classic combos and wildly popular seasonal flavors, like toasted coconut lime, strawberry rhubarb, and the Valentine's Day special, Death by Chocolate. The shop also offers scratch-made ice creams (some feature cupcake chunks!), as well as espresso, pastries, shakes, and pints to go. Little ones always flip for the heavenly ice cream sammies or the petite-sized Babycake cupcakes and cake pops. Visitors to the Ballard and Capitol Hill locations would do well to sample a brioche doughnut from in-house, offshoot bakery Rodeo Donut (www .rodeodonut.com) too.

PinkaBella Cupcakes

BELLEVUE
320 Bellevue Square
425-453-2253
ISSAQUAH
936 NE Park Dr.
425-392-0287
LYNNWOOD
Alderwood Mall, 3000
   184th St. SW
425-640-9801
www.pinkabellacupcakes.com
$

REDMOND
Redmond Town Center, 7330
   164th Ave. NE
425-861-0300
TUKWILA
1002 Southcenter Mall
206-243-8892

These lovely little outposts serve up such inventive cupcakes as the Bacon Blast (chocolate cake topped with maple frosting, toffee, chocolate crumbles, and bacon bits) and the Pineapple Upside Down Cake (complete with pineapple cake, caramelized brown sugar, and brown sugar buttercream frosting). Eat up!

Trophy Cupcakes and Party

BELLEVUE
The Bravern, 700 110th Ave. NE
DOWNTOWN
Pacific Place, 600 Pine St.
Phone number for all: 206-632-7020
www.trophycupcakes.com
$

UNIVERSITY VILLAGE
2612 NE Village Ln.
WALLINGFORD
1815 N. 45th St.

Trophy's confections are almost too pretty to eat, frosted with buttercream and crafted in such lovely flavors as peanut butter and jelly, lemon meringue pie, and strawberry lemonade. Owned and operated by cupcake maven Jennifer Shea, Trophy's four spots are warm and welcoming, decorated in the company's trademark teal hue.

DOUGHNUTS

Frost

BELLEVUE	EVERETT	MILL CREEK
Lincoln Square, 700 Bellevue Way NE, No. 140 425-274-4600 www.frostology.com $	2811-B Colby Ave. 425-258-6111	15217 Main St. 425-379-2600

Frost kicks the tried-and-true doughnut up a notch with such gourmet options as salted caramel, Aztec chocolate, and white chocolate raspberry truffle flavors, but never fear, all the classics are still here too. Let the kids belly up to the long glass bar to peer and peek at their picks, then order that maple bar or apple fritter, and kick back in the adorable pink-and-chocolate-brown digs.

ICONIC EATS

Every town has its beloved bites. Head to these longtime classics for a true taste of Seattle.

Ivar's Acres of Clams

OVER TWENTY AREA LOCATIONS INCLUDING BELLEVUE, EDMONDS, NORTHGATE, NORTHLAKE, AND THE WATERFRONT
www.ivars.com

Founded by a true Seattle character, Ivar Hagland, Ivar's has been an institution since 1938, and you'll spot its outposts all over the city, including at Safeco Field, inside Sea-Tac Airport, and along Lake Union. But the Ivar's Acres of Clams overlooking Elliott Bay is the premier stop for the full Ivar's experience, with a cozy, approachable dining room and stellar fish 'n' chips.

Salty's

DES MOINES	WEST SEATTLE
28201 Redondo Beach Dr. S 253-946-0636 www.saltys.com	1936 Harbor Ave. SW 206-937-1600

Mighty-O Donuts

BALLARD | CAPITOL HILL | GREEN LAKE
1555 NW Market St. | 1400 12th Ave. | 2110 N. 55th St.

Phone number for all: 206-547-0335
www.mightyo.com

$

This is one doughnut you can feel good about. Mighty-O excels at fluffy cake doughnuts and yeast-raised twists and fritters crafted from scratch with only organic ingredients (they're also dairy- and egg-free!). The Ballard location is especially good for families, with large spacious tables and lots of seating for sprawling out with your box of treats.

This restaurant is known for its prime waterfront spots on Alki and Redondo Beach, with the Alki location also boasting breathtaking views of the Seattle skyline. A bit too fancy at dinnertime for little tykes, Salty's has a famous brunch buffet that is an easier bet; kids especially love the chocolate fountain, complete with fruit, marshmallow, and Rice Krispies treat "dippers."

SkyCity

SEATTLE CENTER
400 Broad St.
206-905-2100
www.spaceneedle.com

Here's one for the bucket list. This truly unique restaurant is located near the top of the 605-foot-high Space Needle. As if that weren't cool enough, the restaurant also rotates 360 degrees about every hour to show off pretty much every view of the city possible. (Kids also love leaving notes and drawings on the ledge for other diners to spot as the restaurants spins 'round.) Though quite fancy, the three-course weekend brunch ($19.95 for kids; $49.95 for adults) is both the best value and the best time to take the tykes.

Top Pot Hand-Forged Doughnuts & Coffee

SEATTLE LOCATIONS INCLUDE BALLARD, CAPITOL HILL, DOWNTOWN, FIRST HILL, QUEEN ANNE, SOUTH LAKE UNION, WEDGWOOD, AND WEST SEATTLE; ADDITIONAL LOCATIONS IN BELLEVUE, ISSAQUAH, KIRKLAND, MILL CREEK, REDMOND, AND RENTON

www.toppotdoughnuts.com

$

Top Pot's seventeen locations are all incredibly inviting, replete with wood-trim touches, espresso drinks, and, of course, warm doughnuts, which run the gamut from filled to frosted. The flagship café on 5th Avenue in Downtown Seattle is well suited to a drizzly day, outfitted with floor-to-ceiling bookcases, towering windows, and a second-story loft that begs for a family campout with a card game.

ICE CREAM

Bluebird Ice Cream

CAPITOL HILL	FREMONT	PHINNEY RIDGE
1205 E. Pike St.	3515 Fremont Ave. N	7400 Greenwood
206-588-1079	206-588-6419	Ave. N

www.bluebirdicecream.com

$

These ice-cream parlors are real treats, offering nanobrewed craft sodas and beers in addition to small-batch ice cream. The Fremont location boasts an old-school soda-fountain vibe, with a darling marble bar. Belly on up to it and order a luscious double scoop, sweet shake, or frothy float. (Just keep the porter beer float with coffee ice cream to the grown-up side of the bar.)

Full Tilt Ice Cream

BALLARD	UNIVERSITY DISTRICT
5453 Leary Ave. NW	4759 Brooklyn Ave. NE
206-297-3000	206-524-4406
COLUMBIA CITY	WHITE CENTER
5041 Rainier Ave. S	9629 16th Ave. SW
206-226-2740	206-767-4811

www.fulltilticecream.com

$

Full Tilt is full-on fun, rocking not only a changing selection of handmade ice cream—if it's available, try the chocolate peanut butter—but also a wealth of pinball machines and arcade games (plus beer for the 'rents). With a retro-cool vibe that permeates from the old-school tunes playing on the stereo, along with the eclectic mix of old-school sodas, this place is sure to please just about everyone—even those never-impressed-nowadays tweens and teens.

Husky Deli
WEST SEATTLE
4721 California Ave. SW
206-937-2810
www.huskydeli.com
$

This quirky and quaint little mom-and-pop shop has been serving up ice cream for over 80 years, and clearly the owners have been doing it right—with such flavors as blackberry cheesecake, root beer, and Nutella, all made in-house. Be prepared to stand in line (which grows very long on hot days), and be sure to reward your patience with a double scoop ($5.50–$8.50) once you reach the counter.

Molly Moon's

CAPITOL HILL	QUEEN ANNE	UNIVERSITY VILLAGE
917 E. Pine St.	*321 W. Galer St.*	*2615 NE 46th St.*
206-708-7947	*206-457-8854*	*206-525-5140*
MADRONA	REDMOND	WALLINGFORD
1408 34th Ave.	*16272 Cleveland St.*	*1622½ N. 45th St.*
206-324-0753	*425-869-7654*	*206-547-5105*
NORTH CAPITOL HILL		
522 19th Ave. E		
206-735-7970		

www.mollymoon.com
$

The kids will be chanting for more after just one lick of the perfectly churned ice cream from this local treasure. Now with seven scoop shops 'round town, Molly Moon's offers ten "always" flavors and four rotating options. Tried-and-true favorites include balsamic strawberry, salted caramel, and

THREE CHEERS FOR ROOT BEER

Creamy and fizzy, the old-fashioned root beer float is pure bliss on a hot day. Slurp down a frosty one at one of these local faves.

Dick's Drive-In

CAPITOL HILL, CROWN HILL, EDMONDS, LAKE CITY, QUEEN ANNE, AND WALLINGFORD
Contact information on page 219

At just $2.50, a classic root beer float from this treasured Seattle burger shack will surely do the trick.

Rachel's Ginger Beer

PIKE PLACE MARKET	CAPITOL HILL
1530 Post Alley	*1610 12th Ave.*
www.rachelsgingerbeer.com	

melted chocolate made with Theo chocolate. Ice-cream fiends also just can't seem to get enough of scout mint, crafted from Thin Mints.

Parfait

BALLARD
2034 NW 56th St.
206-258-3066
www.parfait-icecream.com
$

Crafted "farm to cone" from local organic milk, cage-free eggs, and herbs and berries grown on the plot outside this cheery shop, Parfait's incredibly fresh-tasting ice creams come in lovely flavors that will satisfy your grown-up tastes, such as rosemary almond brittle, Meyer lemon, and a to-die-for honey flavor made with the sweet local honey from the Ballard Bee Company. The kids will flip for the old-school push-up pops and the cookie ice-cream sammies.

Rachel's floats ($8) are crafted from your choice of vanilla, strawberry, or vegan coconut ice cream and the shop's signature ginger beer—a sweet-tart concoction made in-house from ginger, lemons, sugar, and water.

XXX Root Beer
Issaquah
98 NE Gilman Blvd.
425-392-1266
www.triplexrootbeer.com

This quintessential drive-in makes its signature float ($6.35) with Darigold vanilla ice cream and house-made root beer, which has been crafted from the same family recipe since the 1930s.

MORE DESSERTS

A la Mode Pies
Phinney Ridge
5821 Phinney Ave. N
206-383-3796
www.alamodeseattle.com
$

Conveniently located across the street from the zoo (hint, hint), this warm and inviting café is filled with the fragrant wafting smells of roasted coffee and fresh-baked pies. Available in flavors such as bourbon butterscotch, sour cherry, and white-chocolate banana, A la Mode's treats are available by the pie, by the slice, or as kid-ready Pie Babies and LolliPies (on a stick).

Hot Cakes Molten Chocolate Cakery

BALLARD

5427 Ballard Ave. NW

206-453-3792

www.getyourhotcakes.com

$

CAPITOL HILL

1650 E. Olive Way

206-258-2591

Devoted to all things ooey-gooey and oh-so-chocolatey and run by former Theo chocolatier Autumn Martin, Hot Cakes is pure fun, offering warm-from-the-oven cookies and dark, rich molten chocolate cakes ($7–$9), creamy shakes ($8), and the bound-to-make-your-kid-happy grilled chocolate sandwich ($8), a heavenly concoction of dark-chocolate ganache and caramel sauce sandwiched in between buttered and toasted potato bread.

Pie

FREMONT

3515 Fremont Ave. N

206-436-8590

www.sweetandsavorypie.com

$

Accented with bright-blue paint and a walk-up window, this cheery little bakery serves up both sweet and savory mini pies that fit perfectly into pint-size hands. Baked from scratch in individual portions, Pie's sweet options range from classics, like apple, key lime, and berry, to more exotic seasonal choices, like salted caramel apple, eggnog cream, and mango blackberry.

HOT WHEELS

Beep, beep. Food trucks have taken to the city streets, gaining a devoted following for their fun fare. Here are three kid favorites, both for the yummy grub and the inventive sets of wheels; find 'em at any given time by checking their websites.

The Grilled Cheese Experience
206-621-5225
www.grilledcheeseseattle.com

This colorful blue-and-gold truck has diners flipping for its melty sammies; kids will love the oh-so-ooey grilled mac 'n' cheese.

Maximus/Minimus
206-971-4150
www.maximus-minimus.com

This truck, outfitted with a snout, ears, and a tail, resembles a giant steel pig. Fittingly, it offers up awesome pulled-pork sandwiches available with either a spicy or sweet BBQ sauce.

Xplosive Mobile Food Truck
206-612-4739
www.xplosivemobilefoodtruck.com

Offering a unique fusion of Filipino and Vietnamese cuisines (try the lemongrass chicken banh mi, $6), this tricked-out truck—festooned with a stick of dynamite painted on its side—just begs little kids to shout out its distinctive name.

For more recommendations on food trucks, check out the ever-growing list at www.seattlefoodtruck.com.

PART 4:

DAY TRIPS &
WEEKEND GETAWAYS

Let's take this show on the road. Just beyond the city limits lie the **sand-dappled seaside abodes**, **rustic mountain retreats**, **Old West–style towns**, and other **cool urban excursions** of Washington State. Prime for road-tripping, the following getaways are built for your entire brood, with recommendations on what to eat, see, and do in each scenic locale, as well as tips on staying and playing in each.

Take the day to explore the state's many charmers: from picturesque nearby islands, such as **Bainbridge** (page 256) and **Whidbey** (page 266), to mountain escapes, like wooded **Snoqualmie** (page 258) and mighty **Mount Rainier** (page 269). Or double your time frame and explore farther afield, traveling out to the **Olympic Peninsula** (page 270) to see the lush rain forest, or heading for mountainous **Leavenworth** (page 268), a town entirely outfitted in a Bavarian theme.

Both the **done-in-a-day trips** and **weekend-long excursions** are organized by **approximate travel time** (all are under four hours away!) to help simplify planning—and because someone in the backseat is bound to pipe up with the inevitable question "Are we there yet?"

DAY TRIPS

ONE HOUR OR LESS AWAY

BAINBRIDGE ISLAND

Enjoy a slice of island life on Bainbridge, where time is measured more by the ferry schedule than by clock. Take this pacing as your cue, and poke about the charming shops and eateries in as leisurely a way as the tiny tykes will allow.

Get There
Located directly across the Sound from Downtown Seattle, Bainbridge is accessible via **Washington State Ferries** (page 4). Boats depart from Colman Dock on Pier 52 about once an hour. It's much pricier to board with your car, so consider walking on and strollering, or biking on instead. The thirty-five-minute crossing is half the fun; kids can scamper up to the boat's sundeck to watch the city skyline fade into the distance as you jet across the water. Once you've landed, traverse the quick quarter mile up the hill to the downtown area along Winslow Way.

Eat, See & Do
Winslow Way is packed with sweets and treats—from the delectable pastries served at **Blackbird Bakery** (210 Winslow Way E; 206-780-1322; www.blackbirdbakery.com) to the delicious ice cream crafted from seasonal ingredients at **Mora Iced Creamery** (139 Madrona Ln.; 206-855-1122; www.moraicecream.com). Lick away while wandering down to **Waterfront Park** (301 Shannon Dr. SE) to skip some rocks into the Sound, then check out the jewelry-making supplies at **Beads of Bainbridge** (162 Bjune Dr. SE; 206-855-4043) before heading west on Winslow to peruse the shelves at **Eagle Harbor Book Co.** (157 Winslow Way E; 206-842-5332; www.eagleharborbooks.com).

Home to a pirate-themed tree house, a solar-powered water table, an art studio, and an absolutely adorable pretend main street, the **Kids Discovery Museum** (301 Ravine Ln. NE; 206-855-4650; www.kidimu.org) is an excellent spot to spend the afternoon, as is the indoor **Bainbridge Island Aquatic**

Center (8521 Madison Ave. N; 206-482-2302; www.biparks.org).
Hitchcock Deli (129 Winslow Way E; 206-451-4609; www
.hitchcockdeli.com) is a yummy spot to wrap up your visit, as the
deli cures and smokes all its sandwich meats in-house; order
the Cuban B, with smoked ham and porchetta, and either scarf it
down on the ferry ride back or eat it there and then. If you want
a little more "island time," check the schedule for **Bainbridge
Performing Arts** (200 Madison Ave. N; 206-842-8569; www
.bainbridgeperformingarts.com), which frequently offers up such
fare as improv comedy and musicals.

SNOHOMISH
This historic North End town offers a darling antiques district, plus
farms to visit for juicy berries come summer, ginormous pumpkins in
the fall, and u-cut Christmas trees come frosty winter.

Get There
Located northeast of Seattle, Snohomish can be reached in about
forty-five minutes by taking either the I-90 or State Route 520
floating bridge (do note 520 is a toll road; more info at www
.wsdot.wa.gov/tolling/520/520tollrates.htm) then heading up
I-405 North to State Route 522 East. Go north on the country
highway State Route 9. Drive on for 10 miles and over the
Snohomish River Bridge before exiting and following the signs
for downtown.

Eat, See & Do
Start your tour of downtown—which is filled with shops, eateries,
and a historic clock tower, all tucked along the Snohomish River—
by ducking into the stellar **Snohomish Bakery** (101 Union Ave.;
360-568-1682; www.snobake.com) for an almond croissant, best
enjoyed on the patio. Then explore the myriad curiosities of the
antiques shops, but give yourself ample time to poke through the
sweet toys, party supplies, and children's clothes at **Bee Bop &
Lollipops** (1112 1st St.; 360-568-2333; www.beebopsandlollipops
.com). Should another sugar craving hit, give in to it at
Snohomish Pie Company (915 1st St.; 360-568-3589; www
.snohomishpieco.com); a slice of apple berry crumb sure does hit
the spot. Or grab a cone from **Snohomish Scoop & Sweet Shoppe**
(1009 1st Ave.; 360-862-9421).

The afternoon could be spent one of three ways (time to vote!). The first choice, **Snohomish Aquatic Center** (516 Maple Ave.; 360-568-8030; www.snohomishaquatic.com), is wet-and-wild indoor fun for everyone, with a 150-foot waterslide, a zero-immersion area for tiny tots, and a FlowRider simulated surfing ride. Try to visit when the Wibit is up—this floating play structure includes swings, a climbing tower, and a jumping platform. The second option is to take a bike ride on the historic **Snohomish County Centennial Trail** (402 2nd St.; www.centennialtrail.com), which threads north along the old railroad tracks to Arlington. The last option is certainly not the least: exploring one of the beautiful, bucolic farms surrounding Snohomish. Three family favorites are **Stocker Farms** (8705 Marsh Rd.; 360-568-7391; www.stockerfarms.com), a Snohomish institution offering a seasonal produce market (10622 Airport Way), plus an autumn corn maze and u-cut Christmas trees; **Thomas Family Farm** (9010 Marsh Rd.; 360-568-6945; www.thomasfamilyfarm.com), a big hit with teens, thanks to the zombie paintball nights around Halloween; and **the Farm at Swan's Trail** (7301 Rivershore Rd.; 425-334-4124; www.thefarm1.com), which is beloved by younger kiddos, thanks to a 40-foot slide, a hay jump, a petting farm, and live duck races. The last farm also quite famously creates a 12-acre corn maze in the shape of Washington State each fall.

SNOQUALMIE

Nestled at the base of the Cascades among towering evergreens, Snoqualmie offers beginner-friendly mountain hikes and amazing views, which can be spotted from its famous steam train—all aboard!

Get There

About thirty minutes from Seattle, Snoqualmie is located off exit 25 via I-90 East as the freeway begins to wind its way up to **the Summit at Snoqualmie** (page 100), making this and North Bend fun pre- or post-mountain stops. Most of the city highlights are located along or just off Snoqualmie Parkway, so hang a left after exiting the freeway.

Eat, See & Do

Kick-start your day with a visit to **Fisher Creek Park** (7805 Fisher Ave. SE; 425-888-1555; www.ci.snoqualmie.wa.us), a newer park that beckons bigs and littles with a climbing structure, dueling 100-foot zip lines, and a mountain bike park, complete with obstacles. From there, scoot over to the **Northwest Railway Museum** (38625 SE King St.; 425-888-3030; www.trainmuseum.org) to visit the (always free) Victorian-era station, then climb aboard the historic steam train for a wonderful wooded ride to North Bend and back, with a stop at the museum's train shed to peek at the railroad cars from yesteryear. (The train operates April through October, with additional seasonal visits to Santa during the holidays, plus the insanely popular Thomas the Tank Engine–themed rides in the summer.) Next, drive over to the **Snoqualmie Falls** viewpoint (6501 Railroad Ave. SE; 425-326-2563; www.snoqualmiefalls.com) viewpoint at Salish Lodge, where the rushing falls plunge over 270 feet to the rocks below.

Don't forget your hiking boots. A little farther east on I-90 are the lovely **Franklin Falls Trail** (page 91) and the popular **Rattlesnake Lake Recreation Area** (located off Cedar Falls Rd. SE, accessible via exit 32). The picturesque mountain lake acts as the jumping-off point for the (busy) 2-mile trail up to **Rattlesnake Ledge** (www.wta.org/go-hiking/hikes/rattle-snake-ledge), a stunning spot that offers views of Mount Si, Mount Washington, and the lake below; the trail is steep and the viewpoint abrupt, so best to attempt this one with older kiddos only. Little ones will be well entertained along the lakeshore and at the **Cedar River Watershed Education Center** (19901 Cedar Falls Rd. SE; 206-733-9421; www.seattle.gov/util/environmentconservation/ourwatersheds), which often offers crafts activities and educational story times. Celebrate conquering that wicked hike by enjoying a steak dinner at **Woodman Lodge Steakhouse & Saloon** (38601 SE King St.; 425-888-4441; www.woodmanlodge.com) back in town, or by gobbling up a BBQ dinner and an accompanying play at the **Snoqualmie Falls Forest Theater** (36800 David Powell Rd; 425-736-7252; www.foresttheater.org), an outdoor summer performance theater nestled along the banks of the Snoqualmie River.

SIDE TRIP: NORTH BEND
With hearty flapjacks and loaded egg scrambles, **North Bend Bar & Grill** (145 E. North Bend Way; 425-888-1243; www.northbendbarandgrill.com) is a great spot to fuel up before a day of hiking (early birds be warned this homey joint doesn't open until 8 a.m.). Or the kids may just have to humor their *Twin Peaks*-loving parents with a visit to the famous **Twede's Cafe** (137 W. North Bend Way; 425-831-5511; www.twedescafe.com), an old-school diner known for its cherry pie that oft appeared in the TV series.

TACOMA
Thirty miles south of Seattle, this busy port offers attractions for all, from the creature-centric Point Defiance Zoo & Aquarium to a car museum that drives gearheads wild.

Get There
Snag a cuppa joe, then hit the road, traveling down I-5 South. You'll know you're there once you spot the landmark Tacoma Dome off exit 133. The main downtown stops can be accessed via exit 133 and Point Defiance attractions from exit 132B. Do note that parking downtown can be tricky, but the city of Tacoma–run parking garage under the Museum of Glass is a good bet ($5 for three hours), or you can usually find free parking at the Tacoma Dome Sounder station (www.soundtransit.org/rider-guide/tacoma-dome-station).

Eat, See & Do
Like Seattle, the city of Tacoma is also nestled along the Sound, so go to **Point Defiance Park** (5400 N. Pearl St.; 253-305-1088; www.metroparkstacoma.org/point-defiance-park) to start your tour. The picturesque point is home to a rhododendron garden; **Owen Beach** (5605 N. Owen Beach Rd.; www.metroparkstacoma.org/facilities/owen-beach), a sandy spit complete with picnic shelters, kayak rentals, and a paved walking trail; and **Fort Nisqually Living History Museum** (www.metroparkstacoma.org/fort-nisqually-living-history-museum), which contains an original building from the 1850s. Volunteers clad in period

garb demonstrate nineteenth-century activities at this stop, and kids can experience life before electricity (or iPhones!). Grab a sandwich at the whimsical **Antique Sandwich Co.** (5102 N. Pearl St.; 253-752-4069) nearby—don't forget to order a house-baked cinnamon roll topped with honey butter for the drive home). Then it's off to **Point Defiance Zoo & Aquarium** (page 11) to spot creatures from both land and sea. Kids will soon be flocking to Point Defiance to also see the new Pacific Seas Aquarium, expected to open in 2018.

Downtown, car buffs big and small will be salivating over the classic convertibles and hot rods at the **LeMay** car museum (page 86), while train lovers will be obsessed with the model railroad running routes around the **Washington State History Museum** (1911 Pacific Ave.; 253-272-3500; www .washingtonhistory.org). Also nearby, the **Children's Museum of Tacoma** (1501 Pacific Ave.; 253-627-6031; www.playtacoma.org) offers five different themed playscapes to explore. Once inspired there, channel all that creative energy into a zany creation at **Tinkertopia** (1914 Pacific Ave.; 253-778-6539; www.tinkertopia .com); this awesome "creative reuse center" offers cool cogs, buttons, and other recycled supplies for budding artists to craft with during daily "tinker times." Or your kids can sketch their own wannabe glass creature to submit for possible creation at the **Museum of Glass** (page 122). Psst—if you choose the latter, don't miss the opportunity to walk across the 500-foot skybridge known as the **Chihuly Bridge of Glass**, where you'll be surrounded by glass artist Dale Chihuly's colorful creations (they even cover the ceiling!).

If it happens to be a sunny summer evening, there's no better way to wrap up the day than by visiting historic Cheney Stadium to take in a **Tacoma Rainiers** baseball game (page 52). There's hardly a bad seat in the house and there is a fireworks show after every Friday-night home game.

ONE TO TWO HOURS AWAY

BELLINGHAM

Tucked close to Canada, Bellingham is flush with waterfront activities like kite flying and rock skipping, historic streets to explore, and lots of collegiate pride (go, Vikings!).

Get There

A straight shot up I-5 North, Bellingham is about an hour and forty-five minutes from Seattle, but it can also be reached via the more scenic State Route 11/Chuckanut Drive, which passes through the sweet town of Edison (for this route, take exit 231 off I-5; see more on the opposite page). Or let someone else deal with the driving; **Amtrak Cascades** trains (www.amtrakcascades .com) runs daily to and from B'ham.

Eat, See & Do

Downtown Bellingham delights with walkable blocks that nestle up against the waterfront, which includes a marina. It also boasts parks like **Zuanich Point Park** (2600 Harbor Loop; 360-676-2500; www.portofbellingham.com/509/zuanich-point-park), a pretty point often packed with kite flyers on breezy days. Also nearby, the free-admission **Marine Life Center** aquarium (1801 Roeder Ave.; 360-671-2431; www.marinelifecenter.org) allows the kiddies to peer at the many creatures that lurk in Bellingham Bay, from crabs and octopi to sea cucumbers and stars. Snag some lunch at the **Boundary Bay Brewery & Bistro** (1107 Railroad Ave.; 360-647-5593; www.bbaybrewery.com), a family-friendly spot with Duplo blocks in the waiting area; here you can get your fill of pub fare, like burgers, stacked sandwiches, and nachos.

South of downtown, past the campus of **Western Washington University**, the neighborhood of Fairhaven is particularly appealing. Take a stroll through its charming shops, which include children's shops **Fairhaven Toy Garden** (909 Harris Ave.; 360-714-8552; www.fairhaventoygarden .com) and **Wild Blueberries** (1106 Harris Ave.; 360-756-5100; www.wildblueberries-kids.com), the gift and card boutique **Paper Dreams** (1206 11th St.; 360-676-8676; www .paperdreamsfairhaven.com), and the beloved book purveyor

Village Books (1200 11th St.; 360-671-2626; www.villagebooks .com). Should little tummies be rumbling, stop by the red vintage bus that houses **Fairhaven Fish & Chips** (1020 Harris Ave.; 360-733-5021) for crisp fish to enjoy on the **Fairhaven Village Green** (1207 10th St.; 360-778-7000; www.fairhaven.com) across the way. Finish your grand tour by venturing down to **Marine Park** (100 Harris Ave.), about a half mile west, where the pebbles that lie on the beach just beg to be skipped across the water.

SIDE TRIP: EDISON & BOW

Consider the scenic route. Chuckanut Drive runs between Bellingham and the small city of Burlington, offering views of farm country and Samish and Bellingham Bays as it meanders along the coastline. Located 10 miles northwest of Burlington, the town of Edison is famous for its stellar bakery, **Breadfarm** (5766 Cains Ct.; 360-766-4065; www.breadfarm.com), which offers cookies, granola, preserves, and more (it's cash- or check-only here, folks). After exploring town, head east about 2 miles to **Bow Hill Blueberries** (15628 Bow Hill Rd.; 360-399-1006; www.bowhillblueberries.com) for u-pick berries in the summer or fruit products such as pickled blueberries and berry ice cream available year-round in the farm store.

CLE ELUM & ROSLYN

Home to the Suncadia resort and Cle Elum Lake—plus the sun- and snow-filled activities that come along with them—these pioneer towns are delightful throwbacks to days gone by.

Get There

Head for the mountains by taking I-90 East over Snoqualmie Pass. Cle Elum and Roslyn are just thirty minutes past **the Summit at Snoqualmie** (page 100), or about an hour and a half from Seattle.

Eat, See & Do

Gorgeous **Suncadia** (3600 Suncadia Trail; 509-649-6400; www
.suncadiaresort.com), in Cle Elum, calls to both day-trippers and
weekenders. Surrounded by over 6,000 acres of forested mountain
landscape, the resort offers bike rentals and tours, miles and
miles of walking trails, and a mountain golf course, plus myriad
playgrounds, pools, and waterslides for guests. Blissfully warm
and sunny in the summer, the area also boasts fantastic snowfall
in the winter, offering snowshoeing, sledding, and an ice-skating
rink. Twenty minutes beyond the resort, in the town of Ronald,
Cascade Playtime (14181 Salmon La Sac Hwy.; 509-649-2444;
www.cascadeplaytime.com) rents Jet Skis, kayaks, canoes, and
pontoon boats to cruise around sparkling Cle Elum Lake.

Head southeast from the lake and make your way to
Roslyn, an Old West–style outpost that seems to have come
straight out of the movies, with its false-front wooden buildings
downtown. Learn all about the city's journey from mining town
to Hollywood set—the town served as the backdrop for the '90s
television show *Northern Exposure*–at the **Roslyn Museum** (203
W. Pennsylvania Ave.; 509-649-2355; www.roslynmuseum
.com), then take in a flick at the teensy-cute **Roslyn Theatre**
(101 Dakota St.; 509-649-3155; www.roslyntheatre.com). The
eating is good here too. **Village Pizza** (105 W. Pennsylvania Ave.;
509-649-2992) churns out deep-dish pies that satisfy, while the
famous **Roslyn Cafe** (201 W. Pennsylvania Ave.; 509-649-2763;
www.theroslyncafe.com), which also popped up in the TV series,
offers big burgers, hearty sandwiches, and other diner fare.

A farther 3.5 miles southeast in Cle Elum, you can pick up
fishing supplies at **Troutwater Fly Shop** (113 E. 1st St.; 509-674-
2144; www.troutwaterfly.com), where the friendly staffers are
always ready to share tips on where the local fish are biting. If
you need a snack, you can also stop into **Owens Meats** (502 E.
1st St.; 509-674-2530; www.owensmeats.com) for amazing beef
jerky and pepperoni sticks.

OLYMPIA

The capital city of Washington is capital indeed, lending itself
nicely to scenic waterfront strolls and landmark government
tours, not to mention an afternoon spent at the truly terrific
children's museum.

Get There

To get to Olympia, it's about an hour to hour-and-a-half journey straight down I-5 South from Seattle. Take exit 105 to access the main highlights of the city. Street parking is usually no sweat on the capital's sweet downtown blocks.

Eat, See & Do

In addition to its charming downtown, the area of Oly near **Percival Landing** (217 Thurston Ave. NW; 360-753-8380; www .olympiawa.gov/community/parks/percival-landing.aspx) is particularly well suited for strolling, with a 0.9-mile boardwalk that overlooks West Bay. Pose for your own smooch next to the landmark sculpture known as the **Kissing Statue** (located near the intersection of 4th Ave. W and Water St. NW), then pop into the historic **Oyster House** (320 4th Ave. W; 360-753-7000; www.theoysterhouseatolympia.com) to share some warm shrimp-and-artichoke dip, or gallivant a couple of blocks northeast to **the Bread Peddler** (222 Capitol Way N; 360-352-1175; www.breadpeddler.com) for a cheesy croque monsieur. A few blocks up Capitol Way North, you'll find the year-round home of the **Olympia Farmers Market** (700 Capitol Way N; 360-352-9096; www.olympiafarmersmarket.com), conveniently located across the street from pick-me-ups for coffee addicts and cupcake fiends: **Dancing Goats Espresso Bar** (111 Market St. NE; 360-528-8555; www.batdorfcoffee.com) and **Miss Moffett's Mystical Cupcakes** (111 Market St. NE, Suite 107; 360-350-0332; www.mysticalcupcakes.com).

The **Hands On Children's Museum** (414 Jefferson St. NE; 360-956-0818; www.hocm.org) alone is almost worth the drive to Olympia, with over 150 interactive exhibits spread out over two floors and the half-acre Outdoor Discovery Center. The latter will keep li'l explorers entertained for hours, with a gravel dig area, a driftwood construction zone, and a chicken coop. Or give the kids the 411 on how our government works with a free public tour of the **Washington State Legislative Building** (416 Sid Snyder Ave. SW; www.des.wa.gov/services/facilities /capitolcampus/tours/pages/guidedtour.aspx). After the informative hour-long tour, which is offered several times a day, pick up a self-guided tour brochure and then stroll along the capitol campus to see a few of the many memorials.

WHIDBEY ISLAND

Offering a cannon-laden fort, an old-school drive-in movie theater, and sandy beaches, Whidbey Island will really float your kid's boat (er, kayak!).

Get There

About 25 miles north of Seattle, Whidbey can be reached one of two ways, via **Washington State Ferries** (page 4) from the Mukilteo dock (take I-5 North to exit 182, then follow State Route 525 North to the dock), or via the **Deception Pass Bridge**, which is accessible by driving I-5 North to exit 226 near Burlington, then taking State Route 20 West. Depending on the wait, the ferry is usually the quicker of the two routes. In theory—if every traffic light, ferry line, and bathroom break went your way—you could reach the island in about an hour, but best to plan on about an hour and a half.

Eat, See & Do

At 168 square miles, Whidbey offers lots of land to explore, so if you day-trip it, try the geographically grouped schedule recommended here (or, should you care to explore all weekend long, there are lots of sweet spots to stay). From the Clinton ferry dock, drive fifteen minutes north to the town of Langley, where the cute red facade of **Useless Bay Coffee Company** (121 2nd St.; 360-221-4515; www.uselessbaycoffee.com) is sure to draw you in for coffee and hot cocoa. If something heartier is in order, take the crew to the charming **Braeburn Restaurant** (197 2nd St.; 360-221-3211; www.braeburnlangley.com), where locally grown produce reigns and breakfast is served all day long. Now fueled, consider whether to embark on a guided tour by water with **Whidbey Island Kayaking** (Langley Marina, 201 Wharf St.; 360-221-0229; www.whidbeyislandkayaking.com), or to stick to terra firma with a drive about 8 miles southwest across the island to **Double Bluff Beach** in Freeland (6325 Double Bluff Rd.; www.whidbeycamanoislands.com/business /double-bluff-beach). This gorgeous stretch of coastline offers driftwood logs for picnicking and amazing sea creatures to spot in the pools at low tide. From there, it is an absolutely stunning half-hour drive north to **Fort Casey Historical State Park**

(1280 Engle Rd.; 360-902-8844; www.parks.state.wa.us/505 /fort-casey) in Coupeville; the 467-acre marine camping park features the classic Spanish-style **Admiralty Head Lighthouse**, as well as several towering cannon guns and a bluff-side battery that kids can clamber all over.

Should you be returning to Seattle via the ferry, it's probably time to turn around, as you are now about forty minutes from the terminal. However, once the kids catch wind that the beloved **Blue Fox Drive-In Theater** (1403 Monroe Landing Rd.; 360-675-5667; www.bluefoxdrivein.com) is just twenty minutes north of the fort, in Oak Harbor, here's betting you head there instead. Catch a first-run flick from the comfort of your car—you knew that roomy SUV would come in handy—after zipping around the quarter-mile go-cart track that's there too. The kids can then snooze as you traverse the land route home across the aforementioned Deception Pass Bridge, which towers an astounding 177 feet above the glittering water.

WEEKEND TRIPS

TWO TO THREE HOURS AWAY

LEAVENWORTH

This central Washington mountain town is quite impressively committed to its Bavarian theme, with kitschy-quirky shops, bratwurst galore, and, come winter, snowcapped peaks that call for epic sledding.

Get There

Take I-5 North, then State Route 520 East—and across the toll bridge, which you can avoid by instead taking I-5 South from Downtown and using the I-90 East bridge—to I-405 North. Take exit 23 for State Route 522 East before exiting onto US Route 2 East. The pretty drive on this rural highway will take you by the town of Monroe (consider a stop at **the Reptile Zoo**—page 13), as well as up and over **Stevens Pass** (page 99), should you care (or need) to make a pit stop.

Eat, See & Do

You'll know when you've arrived. Leavenworth's many eateries and businesses are bedecked with architectural details straight out of Bavaria, with pitched roofs, petite balconies, and cottage-style accents. Park on one of the sleepier downtown side streets (9th, 10th, and Division Streets are all good bets), then take a tour down the magical Front Street to stop in shops like **A Book for All Seasons** (703 US 2; 509-548-1451; www.abookforallseasons.com); the funny **Hat Shop and Wood Shop** (719 Front St.; 509-548-4442; www.hatshopwoodshop .com), which is filled with toppers for your noggin (time for a few selfies) and handmade wooden toys; and every kid's favorite, the **Kris Kringl** Christmas emporium (907 Front St.; 509-548-6867; www.kkringl .com), filled with ornaments, nutcrackers, and more. Both **Front Street Park** (www.cityofleavenworth.com/city-government/parks/front -street-park) and **Waterfront Park** (www.cityofleavenworth.com/city -government/parks/waterfront-park) nearby offer a lovely repose after all that shopping. The latter park sprawls along the Wenatchee River and is connected to popular **Blackbird Island** (www.wta.org/go-hiking /hikes/blackbird-island-waterfront-park), should you be looking for a longer jaunt.

You can gobble up traditional Bavarian sausages at the **Leavenworth Sausage Garten** (636 Front St.; 509-888-4959; www .leavenworthsausagegarten.com) or **King Ludwig's Restaurant** (921 Front St.; 509-548-6625; www.kingludwigs.com), where similar fare is served with a side of live polka music. In the summer the kids will be entertained by mini golf or the gaming arcade at **Icicle Junction** (565 US 2; 509-548-2400; www.iciclevillage.com); should you be walking in a winter wonderland, trundle them up to the tubing park at **Leavenworth Ski Hill** (page 103) for tubing and snowball fights.

Stay
Sleeping Lady Mountain Resort (7375 Icicle Rd.; 509-548-6344; www .sleepinglady.com), on the outskirts of town, is a great bet for families, offering rooms arranged in clusters, along with two cabins on the property. The former government, youth, and family camp also features a "play barn" filled with board games and billiards, two swimming pools, and a fantastic restaurant. Given its wooded location, the resort is close to hiking, biking, and snowshoeing routes (ski and snowshoe rentals are available at the resort). Stop at the **Wenatchee River Ranger District** office (600 Sherbourne St.; 509-548-2550; www.fs.usda.gov) in town for maps and recommendations.

MOUNT RAINIER
Trekking to Mount Rainier, perhaps the state's most iconic peak, is a true bucket-list trip with whoa-look-up-there views and, if you time it right, waves and waves of wildflowers.

Get There
The journey to the southwest entrance of the national park takes about two and a half hours from Seattle. Take I-5 South to exit 127, then go east on State Route 512 and south on State Route 7. At the town of Elbe, follow State Route 706 east through Ashford to the Nisqually Entrance. It will take you another thirty minutes or so to get to the parking lot at Paradise. As this is a national park, a $25 per vehicle parking fee applies.

Eat, See & Do

The most popular spot within the park is the **Henry M. Jackson Memorial Visitor Center** at Paradise (close by to 98368 Paradise-Longmire Rd.; 360-569-6571; www.nps.gov/mora/planyourvisit /paradise.htm), which acts as a jumping-off point for sledding in winter (more on page 102) and hiking and wildflower gazing during the summer months. The friendly park rangers recommend the **Nisqually Vista Trail** (www.nps.gov/mora/planyourvisit/day -hiking-at-mount-rainier.htm) if you've got little ones in tow, which is stroller-friendly at 1.2 miles and offers beautiful views of the Nisqually glacier. For mightier legs, seek out the 2.5-mile trail past **Bench and Snow Lakes** (same website as the Nisqually Vista Trail), which offers stunning views of the mighty mountain. Work up an appetite? Fill up at the **Paradise Inn Dining Room** (98368 Paradise-Longmire Rd.; 360-569-2275; www.mtrainierguestservices.com/dining/paradise-inn -dining-room), where the hearty breakfast buffet is hard to beat, and dinner features gourmet salads, burgers, and other Northwest fare, such as fish 'n' chips.

Back toward civilization, in the town of Elbe, the **Mount Rainier Railroad and Logging Museum** (54124 Mountain Hwy. E; 360-569-7959; www.mtrainierrailroad.com) offers steam-train rides through the forest and across the Nisqually River, taking visitors to the town of Mineral for a visit to its logging museum. The hour-long stop allows the kiddies to explore the collection of steam trains, plus learn about the area's first pioneers. Train rides run from May through October, with several specialty rides throughout the year.

Stay

Built in 1916, the aforementioned historic **Paradise Inn** (360-569-2275; www.mtrainierguestservices.com/accommodations/paradise-inn) offers comfy lodgings in a truly picturesque setting. (Make sure to swing the kids by the inn's 14-foot-tall grandfather clock.)

OLYMPIC PENINSULA

With lush rain forests, natural hot springs, and a crazy-long sand spit that juts into the ocean, the Olympic Peninsula beckons kiddies way out west.

Get There

The peninsula itself spans over 3,600 square miles, with **Olympic National Park** (www.nps.gov/olym/index.htm) at its center, so a weekend trip does involve picking and choosing (not to mention some driving once you get out there—pack snacks). Consider the following adventure to the towns of **Sequim** and **Port Angeles**, which can be reached by taking the car for a ride on the Bainbridge Island ferry (page 4) and then driving up State Route 305 North for a little over 13 miles. Then, take State Route 3 North for 6.8 miles before taking State Route 104 West to US Route 101 North. Should you be inclined to schedule extra time on the stunning peninsula, visit www.olympicnationalparks.com for more ideas.

Eat, See & Do

Located about two and a half hours from Seattle, Sequim is known as the sunniest spot in the state, and it boasts beautiful beaches that help you take advantage of that claim. Nearby, **Dungeness Spit** (Dungeness, 554 Voice of America Rd. NW; www.fws.gov/refuge /dungeness/map.html)—a 5.5-mile sandy stretch that juts out into the Strait of Juan de Fuca—is home to a bevy of birds and marine life and features a picturesque lighthouse at its point (no worries if little legs can't make it quite that far; any part of the spit you conquer is stunning). On your way back to Sequim for lunch—the down-home fare at the rustic **Old Mill Cafe** (721 Carlsborg Rd.; 360-582-1583; www .old-millcafe.com) should do nicely—be sure to drive though **Olympic Game Farm** (1423 Ward Rd.; 360-683-4295; www.olygamefarm.com) to thrill the kiddies with glimpses of the buffalo, bears, elk, and even tigers that live on the preserve.

Also within easy distance of Sequim are three of the Olympic National Park's natural wonders. The **Boulder Creek Trail** (trailhead located 8 miles southeast of Lake Sutherland off US 101; www.nps.gov /olym/planyourvisit/boulder-creek-trail.htm) blazes through beautiful lush rain forest for 2.5 miles before winding gently uphill to the naturally occurring hot-spring pools. Take a scenic drive to the top of the absolutely spectacular **Hurricane Ridge** (www.nps.gov/olym /planyourvisit/visiting-hurricane-ridge.htm); or rent paddleboards, canoes, or kayaks and paddle about the scenic **Lake Crescent** (www .nps.gov/olym/planyourvisit/visiting-lake-crescent.htm). Wrap things up by heading to the sweet town of Port Angeles, where tasty **Sabai Thai** (903 W. 8th St.; 360-452-4505; www.sabaithaipa.com) awaits noodle and rice lovers.

Stay

If the kids went crazy for those delightfully weird hot springs, consider round two by staying at the **Sol Duc Hot Springs Resort** (Port Angeles, 12076 Sol Duc Hot Springs Rd.; 888-896-3818; www.olympicnationalparks .com/lodging/sol-duc-hot-springs-resort), which offers more mineral pools to soak in. The **Olympic Lodge** (140 Del Guzzi Dr.; 360-205-1193; www.olympiclodge.com) is one cozy base camp, offering plush accomodations in an easy-to-find location near downtown Port Angeles. Or stay at **Dungeness Bay Cottages** in Sequim (140 Marine Dr.; 360-683-3013; www.dungenessbaycottages.com), which sits right next to the spit on its own private beach.

OCEAN SHORES & PACIFIC BEACH

Soak up some surf and sand—probably quite literally when it comes to the kids' ears, eyes, noses, and mouths—with a getaway to Washington's pretty southern stretch of beaches.

Get There

Head for your Pacific Ocean getaway by traveling about three hours southwest, first taking I-5 South to Lacey, where you'll take exit 104 for US Route 101 North. From there head west on State Route 8 and then US Route 12, through the town of Aberdeen, before taking the aptly named Ocean Beach Road out to the coast, where you'll find Copalis Beach at the end of the road. Head about fifteen minutes north to get to Pacific Beach, or about twenty minutes south to get to Ocean Shores.

Eat, See & Do

This stretch of coastline delights with pristine parks like **Pacific Beach State Park** (49 2nd St.; 360-276-4297; www.parks.state.wa.us/557/pacific -beach), a surfside 10-acre campground and recreational spot, fit for digging colossal sand tunnels to China. Nearby is the charming seaside community of **Seabrook** (4275 State Route 109; 360-276-0099; www .seabrookwa.com), a new-ish planned community that offers darling cottages to rent, as well as a town center with restaurants and shopping, bike rentals, and fire pits, plus a playground and pool—all across the street from the beach. In Seabrook snag a bite to eat at **Mill 109** (5 W. Myrtle Ln.; 360-276-4884; www.mill109.com), shop the gifts at **SeaWorthy Home** (202 Meriweather St.; 360-589-1607), or check out the treats at **Red Velvet Bakery by the Sea** (202 Meriweather St.; 360-556-1468).

Eighteen miles to the south, Ocean Shores offers up tons of playtime too, with the **Pacific Paradise Family Fun Center** (767 Minard Ave. NW; 360-289-9537; www.pacificparadisefun.com), which offers mini golf, bumper boats, and an arcade. Other highlights here include renting a boat from the **Ocean Shores Electric Boat Company** (952 Point Brown Ave. SE; 360-289-0487; www.oselectricboat.com) to explore the area's many canals, and knocking down pins at the funky-friendly **Shores Bowl** (125 W. Chance A Le Mer NW; 360-289-9356).

Stay
In addition to the Seabrook rental cottages, **Iron Springs Resort** (3707 State Route 109; 360-276-4230; www.ironspringsresort.com), on the bluffs just above Copalis Beach, is a stellar spot to stay. Having recently reemerged after an extensive remodel, the resort's cute cabins make for ideal family retreats.

PORT TOWNSEND
This Victorian-style seaport boasts not only the crazy-cool Fort Worden State Park (bunker explorations in the dark!), but also a marine science center, a jailhouse tour, and one of the best pizzerias around.

Get There
To reach Port Townsend, which is located about two and a half hours north of Seattle depending on ferry wait times, you can choose to take **Washington State Ferries** (page 4) either to Bainbridge Island from Downtown Seattle or to Kingston from Edmonds. From Bainbridge, take State Route 305 North and State Route 3 North. Then take State Route 104 West to State Route 19 North, which will then wind its way north to State Route 20 East. From Kingston, start at State Route 104. This road will take you into the endearing port town.

Eat, See & Do
Stroller-friendly Water Street is fit for window-shopping, though with such kid-friendly outposts as **Whistle Stop Toys** (1005 Water St.; 360-385-9616), game shop **Completely Puzzled** (1013 Water St.; 360-379-1278), and kiddie clothing boutique **Seams to Last** (940 Water St.; 360-385-5899), you'll probably be pulled inside in just a few steps. Garnering a cultlike following for its fantastic 'za, **Waterfront Pizza** (951 Water St.; 360-385-6629) is a satisfying lunch spot. A frothy-cool treat can be had

at either the **Elevated Ice Cream Co.** (627 and 631 Water St.; 360-385-1156; www.elevatedicecream.com), or at **Nifty Fiftys Soda Fountain** (817 Water St.; 360-385-1931; www.niftyfiftyspt.com), a retro spot complete with 1950s-style swivel stools that, yes, *do* spin all the way around. Take your scoop of homemade ice cream to go and head one block over to **Jackson Tidal Park**—which offers an awesome wave-viewing station—and then move on to the accompanying **Pope Marine Park** (both parks are located near the corner of Water and Madison Street; www.ptguide .com/recreation-activities/city-parks).

Activities abound in this port area of town. Let the kids be the ones to put you in "time-out" in the old jail cells at the **Jefferson Museum of Art & History** (540 Water St.; 360-385-1003; www.jchsmuseum.org). Then head for the high seas with a trip to the **Northwest Maritime Center** (431 Water St.; 360-385-3628; www.nwmaritime.org), where kids can play in the dragon boat out front and peer at the oft-occurring boat-building activities going on inside. The Center also offers free boat tours aboard the majestic 24-foot *Martha J* on weekends. A half mile north, **Chetzemoka Park** (900 Jackson St.; 360-385-7212) is straight out of a fairy tale, with a charming gazebo and cute wooden bridges, in addition to a playground and stellar water views. But whatever you do, be sure to devote a good chunk of time to visiting **Fort Worden State Park** (200 Battery Way; 360-344-4431; www.parks.state.wa.us/511/fort-worden). Resting on a high bluff overlooking Puget Sound, the park was home to a nineteenth-century fort, and many of the quarters and other fort features remain. Play an epic, slightly spooky game of hide-and-seek in the bunkers built into the cliffs—bring a flashlight—then meander down to the seashore to spot the lighthouse. Or learn about the Sound's resident sea creatures at the **Port Townsend Marine Science Center** (532 Battery Way; 360-385-5582; www.ptmsc.org). Be sure to listen in for any orcas (a.k.a. killer whales) in the vicinity, with the museum's set of earphones hooked up to the water.

Stay

If your kids heart the state park, the good news is you can stay there too. There are more than eighty campsites at **Fort Worden** (availability and reservations through www.fortworden.org), including fifty on the beach. In addition, officers' quarters, dormitories, and cottages are available to rent.

THREE TO FOUR HOURS AWAY

LAKE CHELAN

A snowy paradise in winter and a sun-soaked escape come summer, Lake Chelan is fit for water babies, adrenaline junkies, and boating fanatics.

Get There

The journey to Lake Chelan, about four hours northeast of Seattle, starts by heading out I-90 East over the mountain passes and then following a series of rural highways through Wenatchee before hooking up with US Route 97 Alternate North, which will take you to the town of Chelan.

Eat, See & Do

The 50-mile-long lake stretches from Chelan in the south all the way north to the hidden enclave of Stehekin, which is reachable only by boat, seaplane, horse, or your own two feet. Schedule a boat ride on the *Lady of the Lake* (1418 W. Woodin Ave.; 509-682-4584; www.ladyofthelake .com) to check out the remote wooded spot; an all-day tour leaves Chelan in the morning and allows visitors to either spend a few hours in Stehekin, snagging lunch at the **North Cascades Lodge at Stehekin** (1418 W. Woodin Ave.; 509-682-4494; www.lodgeatstehekin.com), or take a bus tour to **Rainbow Falls** (www.lodgeatstehekin.com/stehekin -shuttle-bus.htm) before cruising back to town. In Chelan itself, you'll find several stellar eateries, including the kid-friendly **Apple Cup Cafe** (804 E. Woodin Ave.; 509-682-5997; www.applecupcafe.com), as well as a small downtown shopping district and the stroller-friendly **Chelan Riverwalk Park** (1117 E. Wapato Ave.; 509-661-4551; www.chelanpud .org/parks-and-recreation). Another perfect pairing for kids is to visit the classic **Lakeview Drive In** (323 W. Manson Hwy.; 509-682-5322; www .lakeviewdrivein.com) for shakes and fries, and then waltz over to the expansive **Don Morse Park** (485 W. Manson Hwy.; 509-682-8023; www .cityofchelan.us/parks/donmorse/donmorsepark.htm) to play on the playground, hit up the skatepark, or feed the ducks along the lakeshore.

Another day can easily be whiled away canvasing the north side of the lake and the town of **Manson,** which is home to several shops, restaurants, and wineries (you'll spy the vineyards along the way). A few minutes' drive from downtown Manson, **Blueberry Hills Farm** (1315 Washington St.; 509-687-2379; www.wildaboutberries.com) offers u-pick berries in the summer and a kitschy-cute farm stand

and restaurant. It's a toss-up on whether the loaded breakfast scrambles or chargrilled burgers (topped with homemade blueberry mayo) are the better meal here, so maybe indulge in both and let the kids pick berries in between.

When it comes to keeping the tykes busy, busy, busy, take your pick of several options in Chelan. In the summer, the **Slidewaters** water park (102 Waterslide Dr.; 509-682-5751; www.slidewaterswaterpark .com) delights, with slides that careen down the hillside toward the lake. **Rally Alley** (Don Morse Park, page 275; www.rallyalleychelan.com) offers a different kind of careening, with speedy go-carts that kids can race 'round the track (must 52 inches tall to drive; smaller kids can ride shotgun with a parent). Or rent a cruiser from **Chelan Electric Bikes** (204 E. Wapato Ave.; 509-683-2125; www.chelanelectricbikes.com) to tour about the shores of the lapping lake (youth under age 16 must ride in tandem or as a passenger with an adult; bike trailer rentals available). And everyone will love bowling at **Chelan Lanes** (518 W. Manson Hwy.; 509-682-2251; www.chelanlanes.com). Come winter, get on up to **Echo Valley Ski & Tubing Area** (1700 Cooper Gulch Rd.; 509-687-3167; www .echovalley.org) for snow sports on the slopes.

Stay

Packed with motels, hotels, and vacation rentals, there are lots of lodging options in Chelan. One family favorite is the **Wapato Point** resort in Manson (1 Wapato Point Way; 888-768-9511; www.wapatopoint .com), which sits on its own picturesque peninsula and features condos with kitchens. The kids will also be pleased to hear that the resort can arrange rentals of almost any watercraft you should desire.

SAN JUAN ISLANDS

Welcome to whale country. This beautiful island collection is home to the distinctive black-and-white orcas and many museums, vistas, and parks devoted to spying them.

Get There

Much like on the Olympic Peninsula, there is much to see and do in the islands of the San Juans. For an actually achievable weekend, it's best to pick one island to explore. The following itinerary traverses the beautiful **Friday Harbor** on **San Juan Island**—which is reachable by hopping on the **Washington State Ferry** (page 4) that departs from

Anacortes, about an hour and a half north of Seattle, or via a cool seaplane ride from **Kenmore Air** (www.kenmoreair.com). **Orcas Island** is another fantastic spot to look up (www.orcasisland.org/tourism). The total travel time to drive from Seattle and take the ferry to either San Juan Island or Orcas Island is three and a half to four hours.

Eat, See & Do

Located right off the ferry dock in pretty Friday Harbor, **the Whale Museum** (62 1st St.; 360-378-4710; www.thewhalemuseum.org) is a great spot to kick-start your trip. Kids can learn all about the resident orcas—who are known by individual names in these parts—and check out the recent orca-sightings map. Thus inspired, you could head across the street to **Maya's Legacy Whale Watching** (#14 Cannery Landing; 360-378-7996; www.sanjuanislandwhalewatch.com) to go a-searchin' by boat. Should you prefer to remain on dry land, rent a ScootCoupe from **Susie's Mopeds** (125 Nichols St.; 360-378-5244; www.susiesmopeds.com). Available to families with riders age 5 and up, these cherry-red three-wheeled scooters are the perfect vehicle to spirit you out to **Lime Kiln Point State Park** (1567 Westside Rd.; 360-378-2044; www.parks.state .wa.us/540/lime-kiln-point), a beautiful bluff that is considered one of the best spots to spy whales during the summer months.

Back in town, snag a satisfying sandwich at the **Market Chef** (225 A St.; 360-378-4546), then pop into **A Place to Play** (55 Spring St.; 360-378-0378; www.aplacetoplay.biz), an adorable indoor space outfitted with a life-size boat for playing sea captain, or head into **Paradise Lanes** (355 Spring St.; 360-370-5667; www.paradiselanes.net) to bowl a few games—both are good options in slightly inclement weather. **San Juan Island National Historical Park** (4668 Cattle Point Rd.; 360-378-2240; www.nps.gov/sajh/index.htm), however, is a great sunny-day stop; it's home to the American Camp prairie preserve and the endangered Island Marble butterfly (learn all about both from the friendly rangers), in addition to blissful views of the Strait of Juan de Fuca.

Stay

Earthbox Inn & Spa (410 Spring St.; 360-378-4000; www.earthboxinn .com) is a retro-chic, laid-back spot to hang with the kids, who will especially appreciate the indoor pool.

WINTHROP

This town straight outta the Wild West offers hiking and fishing, riverfront fun, and frontier-style digs.

Get There

Winthrop and the sweet neighboring town of Twisp are about four hours northeast of Seattle. You can reach them by taking I-5 North to exit 208 in Arlington. Follow State Route 530 East and then State Route 20 East into town.

Eat, See & Do

Stop immediately at **Sheri's Sweet Shoppe** (207 Riverside Ave.; 509-996-3834; www.sherissweetshoppe.com) to congratulate yourselves for surviving the drive with a scoop of banana fudge ice cream. Then wander downtown, which could be the set of an old Western with wooden plank sidewalks and buildings with old-timey facades. Explore the **Shafer Museum** (285 Castle Ave.; 509-996-2712; www.shafermuseum.com) for a spell, a collection of late 1800s-era buildings that are a delight to poke around. Next, saunter over to the north end of town, where you'll find the awe-inspiring **Sa Teekh Wa Bridge** (www.sahale.com/sateekhwa.htm); it spans the Chewuch River and connects the town to the 2-mile riverfront **Sa Teekh Wa Trail** (www.wta.org/go-hiking/hikes/sa-teekh-wa-trail). The trail is an excellent spot to watch for spawning salmon in the fall.

Farther afield, the popular **Pearrygin Lake State Park** (561 Bear Creek Rd.; 509-996-2370; www.parks.state.wa.us/563/pearrygin-lake) offers trails for hikers, waterfront for beachgoers, and lots of biting guppies for fisherpeople. In tandem with your lake visit, better also head for the rushing waters of **Falls Creek Falls** (trailhead located across from the Falls Creek Campground off Forest Road 51; www.wta.org/go-hiking/hikes/falls-creek-1), located 13 miles north of the state park. There, you'll find hiking options for little ones too, with the first set of falls just a quarter mile from the trailhead on a paved, stroller-friendly path.

Wintertime means snowcapped trees and mountains in these parts. Head thirty minutes east of town to the **Loup Loup Ski Bowl** (97 FS 4200 100 Rd.; 509-557-3401; www.skitheloup.com), between Twisp and Okanogan, for downhill and Nordic skiing, tubing, and snowshoeing. Or stay in town and go to **Winthrop Ice & Sports Rink** (208 White Ave.; 509-996-4199; www.winthropicerink.com), which offers a rare open-air ice-skating rink. Locals also flock here for the unofficial sledding hill in the adjacent parking lot.

Stay

Fall asleep to the soothing sounds of the lapping river at either **Methow River Lodge & Cabins** (110 White Ave.; 509-996-4348; www .methowriverlodge.com) or **River's Edge Resort** (115 Riverside Ave.; 800-937-6621; www.riversedgewinthrop.com), where many of the cabins and suites feature private patios with river-view hot tubs. About 10 miles northwest of town, you'll also find one of the region's most famous sleeping spots: the **Rolling Huts** and **Methow Tents** (18381 State Route 20; 509-996-4442; www.rollinghuts.com; www.methowtents.com). The epitome of "glamping," the modern and sleek huts designed by Seattle architect Tom Kundig offer such creature comforts as WiFi, fridges, and microwaves in a truly stunning setting surrounded by mountain peaks. The nearby safari tents offer more rustic accommodations with the same can't-be-beat views.

ACKNOWLEDGMENTS

Thanks to Mom, Dad, and Kelsey, who spirited me off on my first Seattle family adventures; and to Casey and Avery, the best research assistants a wife and mama could ever ask for.

ANNUAL EVENTS

Mark your calendars for these annually occurring favorites.

JANUARY

LUNAR NEW YEAR FESTIVAL
Date varies each year, typically late January or early February
International District
www.cidbia.org/events/lunar
-new-year

SEATTLE BOAT SHOW
Dates vary each year, typically mid-January
CenturyLink Field in SoDo
www.seattleboatshow.com

SEATTLE MARINERS FANFEST
Dates vary each year, typically mid- to late-January
Safeco Field in SoDo
seattle.mariners.mlb.com/sea/fan_forum
/mariners_fanfest.jsp

FEBRUARY

SEATTLE MUSEUM MONTH
Occurs all month long in February
Museums in Seattle and across the Eastside
www.seattlemuseummonth.com

MARCH

EMERALD CITY COMICON
Dates vary each year, typically early March
Washington State Convention Center in Downtown Seattle
www.emeraldcitycomicon.com

IRISH FESTIVAL & SAINT PATRICK'S DAY PARADE
Dates vary each year, but always close to the St. Patrick's Day holiday
Festival at Seattle Center, parade in Downtown Seattle
www.irishclub.org/irish-festival-seattle

APRIL

SKAGIT VALLEY TULIP FESTIVAL
April 1–30 every year
Skagit Valley Farms around Mount Vernon
www.tulipfestival.org

MAY

NORTHWEST FOLKLIFE FESTIVAL
Dates vary each year, but always over Memorial Day weekend
Seattle Center
www.nwfolklife.org

UNIVERSITY DISTRICT STREETFAIR
*Dates vary each year, but typically
    late May*
University District
www.udistrictstreetfair.org

JUNE

FREMONT SOLSTICE & PARADE
*Dates vary each year, but always
    around the solstice in mid-June*
Fremont
www.fremontsolstice.com

JULY

BALLARD SEAFOOD FEST
*Dates vary each year, typically
    mid-July*
Ballard
www.seafoodfest.org

**BELLEVUE ARTS MUSEUM
ARTSFAIR**
*Dates vary each year, typically
    mid-July*
Bellevue
www.bellevuearts.org/fair

BITE OF SEATTLE
*Dates vary each year, typically
    mid-July*
Seattle Center
www.biteofseattle.com

DRAGON FEST
*Dates vary each year, typically
    mid-July*
International District
www.cidbia.org/events/dragonfest

**LAKE UNION WOODEN
BOAT FESTIVAL**
*Dates vary each year, but always
    over the Fourth of July holiday*
South Lake Union
www.cwb.org/events/festival

WEST SEATTLE SUMMER FEST
*Dates vary each year, typically
    mid-July*
West Seattle
www.wsjunction.org/summerfest

AUGUST

EVERGREEN STATE FAIR
*Dates vary each year, typically
    begins late August*
Evergreen State Fairgrounds
in Monroe
www.evergreenfair.org

SEAFAIR WEEKEND
*Dates vary each year, with Seafair
    events kicking off in June and
    culminating in August*
Various locations throughout the
Sound
www.seafair.com

VIKING DAYS
*Dates vary each year, typically
    late August*
Ballard
www.nordicmuseum.org/vikingdays

SEPTEMBER

BUMBERSHOOT
*Dates vary each year, but always
    over Labor Day weekend*
Seattle Center
www.bumbershoot.com

WASHINGTON STATE FAIR
*Runs throughout most of the
    month of September*
Washington State Fairgrounds
in Puyallup
www.thefair.com

OCTOBER

FREMONT OKTOBERFEST
*Dates vary each year, typically late
    September to early October*
Fremont
www.fremontoktoberfest.com

ISSAQUAH SALMON DAYS FESTIVAL
*Dates vary each year, but always
    early October*
Issaquah
www.salmondays.org

SEATTLE CHILDREN'S FESTIVAL
*Date varies each year, typically
    early October*
Seattle Center
www.nwfolklife.org/seattlechildrensfestival

NOVEMBER/ DECEMBER

WINTERFEST
*Runs Thanksgiving Weekend to New
    Year's Eve*
Seattle Center
www.seattlecenter.com/winterfest

SNOWFLAKE LANE
*Runs Thanksgiving Weekend to
    Christmas Eve*
Bellevue
www.snowflakelane.com

WINTER FESTIVAL & CRAFTS FAIR
*Dates vary each year, typically
    early December*
Phinney Ridge
www.phinneycenter.org/winterfestival

RESOURCES

Offering up newsy notes and hip happenings, the following publications and websites are worth bookmarking in your browser.

PARENTMAP MAGAZINE
www.parentmap.com

RED TRICYCLE
www.redtri.com/seattle-kids

SEATTLE'S CHILD MAGAZINE
www.seattleschild.com

SEATTLE MAGAZINE
www.seattlemag.com

SEATTLE MET MAGAZINE
www.seattlemet.com

"VISITING SEATTLE"
(CITY OF SEATTLE)
www.seattle.gov/visiting-seattle

VISIT SEATTLE
www.visitseattle.org

"WASHINGTON: THE STATE"
(WASHINGTON STATE
TOURISM ALLIANCE)
www.experiencewa.com

INDEX